Franklin

This book was researched and written with financial support from the Thomas Skelton Harrison Foundation, Philadelphia, Pennsylvania, a nonprofit, nonpartisan foundation. The Harrison Foundation promotes good government and sound municipal finance in the city of Philadelphia and supports work that promotes the general welfare of the inhabitants of that city. The Thomas Skelton Harrison Foundation exercised no editorial control over the contents of this work.

Franklin

THE ESSENTIAL FOUNDING FATHER

JAMES SRODES

Since 1947
REGNERY PUBLISHING, INC.
An Eagle Publishing Company • Washington, DC

Endpaper map provided by the Library of Congress; all other illustrations used in this book provided by the American Philosophical Society, Philadelphia, Pennsylvania

Library of Congress Cataloging-in-Publication Data

Srodes, James.
Franklin : the essential founding father / James Srodes.
p. cm.
Includes index.
ISBN 0-89526-163-4
1. Franklin, Benjamin, 1706–1790. 2. Statesmen—United States—Biography.
3. Scientists—United States—Biography. 4. Inventors—United States—Biography.
5. Printers—United States—Biography. I. Title.
E302.6.F8 S85 2002
973.3'092—dc21
2002000670

Published in the United States by
Regnery Publishing, Inc.
An Eagle Publishing Company
One Massachusetts Avenue, NW
Washington, DC 20001

Visit us at www.regnery.com

Distributed to the trade by
National Book Network
4720-A Boston Way
Lanham, MD 20706

Printed on acid-free paper
Manufactured in the United States of America

10 9 8 7 6 5 4 3 2

Books are available in quantity for promotional or premium use.
Write to Director of Special Sales, Regnery Publishing, Inc.,
One Massachusetts Avenue, NW, Washington, DC 20001,
for information on discounts and terms
or call (202) 216-0600.

To Cecile

The Poet praises his Helen for
"a quarter-century of faultless love."
You have given me so much more than that.

Contents

Preface

orty years at the craft of journalism gives one a taste to tell a certain kind of story. The tale I prefer to tell is how my subject develops as a person as challenges occur. For just as people make history, events certainly shape character.

There is no better tale than the life of Benjamin Franklin and the times in which he lived. The world he was born into had plunged into a total revolution, a revolt against age-old doctrines of knowledge, of morality, and of the way men govern themselves. This is a good time to tell that story as we near the three hundredth anniversary of his birth.

Benjamin Franklin's character was an astonishingly malleable work in progress. Perhaps because he lived so much longer and loomed so much larger than most of his contemporaries, we think of him as marching in a steady line from a humble beginning onto the world stage. The man himself bears some of the blame with the autobiographical rags-to-riches yarns he concocted.

But of all his traits, what catches our eye is his burning ambition fueled by a restless physical energy. In 1748, at a time when few lived past the age of fifty, Franklin, then forty-two, retired from an already active life of accomplishment, prosperity, and public reputation. Instead of spending his likely few remaining years engrossed in the scientific observations he loved so much, he embarked on a series of daring adventures that would consume the last half of his life. He risked everything—his family, his health, his reputation, and, on several occasions, his life. This tale is about that evolution from striving craftsman to daring diplomat, spy, and master builder of a nation. Franklin's life is more dramatic than any yarn the old storyteller could have devised for himself.

At the end of the tale, Franklin emerges as the essential ingredient in a chemical chain reaction of other remarkable characters that produced a great light for the rest of the world. He was the catalyst that made other Founders coalesce and interact with each other; he also was a steady source of the strategies and ideals that fueled the experiment and gave it substance. Without taking a single bit of luster from any of the others who were in at the beginning, it is hard to see how we would be what we are today without the eighty-four-year progress of Benjamin Franklin. He was not typical of the times, nor was he the archetype of our national character—for that, too, is still a work in progress. But Benjamin Franklin was the *essential* American. He became that by sheer hard work and the challenge of an age.

Franklin

Prologue

*I*n the spring of 1755 Benjamin Franklin visited a political ally, Colonel Benjamin Tasker, on his large estate in Maryland. Franklin recounted in a letter how the country squire guided him, his son, and others around the plantation on horseback when

we saw, in the vale below us, a small whirlwind beginning in the road and showing itself by the dust it raised and contained. It appeared in the form of a sugar loaf, spinning on its point, moving up the hill towards us, and enlarging as it came forward. When it passed by us, its smaller part near the ground, appeared no bigger than a common barrel, but, widening upwards, it seemed at forty or fifty feet high to be twenty or thirty feet in diameter. The rest of the company stood looking after it, but, my curiosity being stronger, I followed it, riding close by its side, and observed its licking up in its progress all the dust that was under its smaller part. As it is a common opinion that a shot fired through a water-spout will break it, I tried to break this little whirlwind by striking my whip frequently through it, but without any effect. Soon after, it quitted the road and took into the woods, growing every moment larger and stronger, raising instead of dust the old dry leaves with which the ground was thick covered, and making a great noise with them and the branches of the trees, bending some tall trees round in a circle swiftly and very surprisingly, though the progressive motion of the whirl was not so swift but that a man on foot might have kept pace with it.... I accompanied it about three-quarters of a mile, till some limbs of dead trees, broken off by the whirl, flying about and falling near me, made me more apprehensive of danger; and then I stopped.... Upon my asking Colonel Tasker if such whirlwinds were common in Maryland, he answered pleasantly: "No, not at all common; but we got this on purpose to treat Mr. Franklin."[1]

The essence of Franklin is in this anecdote. Here is Franklin the vigorous and daring, the skilled horseman who could venture close to a frightening funnel cloud while others hung back. All his life he poked into things that gave other men pause, but he did it with a light, self-effacing laugh so as not to appear to take himself too seriously. This light touch wrongly convinced some to consider him a less than serious character. Many came to regret misjudging Franklin, for while he loved to laugh, he was ever serious—and could be ruthless—about the things that mattered most to him. He could poke fun at himself; others did so at their peril.

JUST TWO YEARS AFTER THE INCIDENT at Colonel Tasker's estate, in 1757, the Pennsylvania General Assembly chose Franklin for a special mission to London. He was fifty-one, at the midpoint of his adult life, and had retired from a successful career as a printer and publisher. He had intended, he said, to devote the rest of his life to scientific investigations and experiments. He had a wife, children, a comfortable home in Philadelphia, and wealth enough to content any man to stay put. Yet he itched to be away and to test his skills in another, bigger arena. In the years to come he would return home for brief episodes, but this trip began a twenty-six-year odyssey that would take him to the principal capitals of Europe and make him the point man in America's cause.

The task ahead was a calculated risk both for Franklin and for the seventy-six-year-old colony. Once in London, he was to coax the hardfisted sons and heirs of Pennsylvania's founder, William Penn, into paying a share of the cost of a terrible war that had erupted three years earlier on the province's far western frontier. The conflict we know as the French and Indian War had its origins in 1753, when French troops built a network of forts up the Ohio Valley and north along the shores of the Great Lakes to Canada. This effectively sealed off the English colonies (especially Virginia and Pennsylvania) from any westward expansion beyond the Appalachian Mountains. Frighteningly, the French sent their Indian allies into that far region to drive terrified settlers from their homes. This was the sharp edge of a broad campaign by the French that also crossed the borders of New England and moved down the Mohawk Valley into New York. If King Louis XV could not drive the hated English out of North America altogether, he at least could guarantee that they would spread no farther west.

Franklin understood that getting the Penn heirs to agree to be taxed on their vast landholdings was crucial to the issue of whether Pennsylvania would be able to defend its people and to contribute to the British counterattacks that were being planned. But while King George II had to pay taxes in England, it was not at all clear that colonial assemblies could tax against their will those who held proprietary charters for land in North America. More than money was at stake. The sons of William Penn were bent on rolling back many of the generous guarantees of self-government that their founder father had promised in the 1680s to attract settlers. Pennsylvania had the most liberal colonial charter, and its inhabitants jealously guarded their rights.

Franklin's enemies—and he had plenty—were outraged at his appointment as a special agent to London. Now he would get to swank it up in the fabled metropolis of the British Empire. He would be courted and flattered by the prestigious coterie of scientists who honored his research discoveries from afar. Franklin was not the only Pennsylvanian with a reputation that reached across the sea, but he was by far the best known. Those who remembered his early start as a seventeen-year-old runaway apprentice still considered him a roughneck. Those who worked at the strenuous skilled crafts rightly considered Franklin as one of their own, and they loyally formed a political base for him that could rally the vote or turn out for a brawl. This made him dangerous in the eyes of many of the ruling Quaker grandees who prized order above everything. Others noted with disdain that Franklin appeared to have an unseemly ambition to rise even higher. Like everyone else at that time, Franklin had been adept at placing family members and friends in profitable positions in the burgeoning newspaper and postal system that he oversaw. Now, it was charged, he would seek to advance himself further at Pennsylvania's cost; there were rumors he wanted to be the royal governor and would sell the colony out to the proprietors to get the post.

Most of Pennsylvania's Quaker merchant elite were themselves only a generation or so off the boat as immigrants, but they were suspicious of newcomers. In their eyes Franklin was still a Bostonian, an outsider and a tradesman, a man who worked with his hands at the dirty job of printing. It counted for little that he was the best writer of his day, the publisher of both the most widely read newspaper in America and an internationally famous almanac, and the most important intercolonial public official (as deputy postmaster general for the colonies). He was not a Quaker, and so the ruling community of merchants was not sure he was sound. Although he attended the local Presbyterian church, his public skepticism and jabs in print at most organized religions only added to suspicions.

He long ago had stopped carousing at the dockside taverns with carpenters and brickmasons, but the trappings of middle-class respectability that he assumed seemed too easily come by. He was not humble enough for Quaker tastes; this was especially true for those who remembered him in the streets in a leather apron, with his shirtsleeves rolled up, as he trundled a wheelbarrow of paper back to his print shop. Now he dressed as what he was, a man of affairs, a member of the colony's General Assembly. Yet he was not respectful of the colony's institutions—organized religion, the law courts, and, least of all, the proprietary owners—which bound the province together. He criticized the powerful in print (an unpleasant novelty in this century); worse, he made fun of them with biting satires and parody.

But most damning of all, Franklin had the annoying facility to be absolutely indispensable whenever there was a crisis. He rightly got credit for many of the civic improvements that were pushing Philadelphia to its primacy over Boston as the leading city in North America. In the critical early days of the war he became something of a military hero for leading the local militia in the frontier defenses against the Indians. Overriding it all was his spectacular international reputation for his discoveries of the common identities of lightning and electricity. But not everyone applauded him—many believed that lightning was the visible sign of God's wrath, and to capture it and make it run along wires seemed impious to the extreme.

Still, Franklin had many more friends than enemies. In addition to his fellow craftsmen he also had a firm base in the rising middle class of small businessmen and factory owners. Most important (and rather annoying to those who depended on the favor of the proprietors), he had the admiration and support of many of the most powerful and wealthy men throughout the colonies. These leaders had agreed with an earlier Franklin proposal that the colonies should more closely unite on matters of mutual interest—defense being just one. Many of these men also admired his scientific research because they, too, were experimenting in everything from celestial navigation to the crossbreeding of plants.

So, despite his critics, the majority in the General Assembly voted Franklin's appointment as agent to the Penn family. As a final jab at his opponents, Franklin prompted his son, William, to resign his job as clerk to the Assembly and accompany him to London. William was generally conceded to be illegitimate, and the notion that Franklin would be introducing him into London society galled his critics.

Franklin, with typical self-effacement, assured everyone that he wanted to be out of politics altogether and that this brief mission to London would be his last appearance on the public stage. After all, he had said when he sold his printing and newspaper business in 1748 that he would "in the few years left to me" devote his life to quiet study and his science projects. As with many of his tactical public statements, there was some truth and a little falsehood mixed in.

It is certainly true that most men of that century did not live past age fifty; women had even shorter lives. Yet Franklin was extraordinarily robust even in an age when one had to be hardy just to stay alive. His physical strength and relentless energy had become a byword among his friends. He was hardly going into retirement. The profit-sharing deal he had arranged when he had sold his business would ensure him an ample flow of income for another decade. So whatever he said about the impending end of his days or his desire to escape the bonds of politics, his actions belied him. However frustrating the public arena could be, he could not resist its call. In fact, he never tried.

For Franklin, the trip to London itself was a prize worth almost any price (one price being that he would have to leave behind his wife, Deborah, who refused to accompany him because she feared the long sea voyage). But the normally hard up Assembly had given him the lavish sum of £1,500 to spend during the few months the task should take. This, too, outraged the opposition. Pennsylvania, like the older established colonies, already had two agents in place in London. Many colonial agents were prominent members of Parliament, and most were pleased to receive £200 or so a year for the mundane tasks of obtaining trade permits and pursuing land and debt claims.[2]

But Franklin would have paid his own way for the chance to revisit London, where as a youth he had perfected his printing craft skills and learned so much more. He loved to travel; it was central to the restless curiosity that drove him all his life. Everything grabbed at his attention and claimed his interest. The most common matters demanded explanation, and, in the search for those answers, he sought other answers about his own nature—the greatest mystery he faced.

Franklin believed travel was necessary to his health, and the longer and more arduous the journey, the more good it did him. Although we often think of him as a sedentary man of letters, he was never happier than when he was on the road or on shipboard taking in the wonders before him. He was a large, stocky man with muscles still firm from a life at the printing press and on horse-back. His hair was still brown with only a hint of gray and his hairline had begun only a slight retreat from his broad forehead to mark the passing of time. Although he still clung to some of the Puritan plain habits of his Boston upbringing, he had developed a fondness for the punch bowl, the glass of fine Madeira, and the banquet table. He could just taste the joys awaiting him in London. He was away from Philadelphia before anyone could stop him.

Chapter 1

Traits and Prospects

The Benjamin Franklin who dashed off to London in Pennsylvania's cause was a curious and untypical mixture of eighteenth-century colonial America. He was a town man in an overwhelmingly rural society. He aspired to power and influence but resented and goaded those already at the top. He baffled friend and foe alike with a public face of simple habits and a private taste for more of everything.

He was, first of all, a Franklin. He inherited a range of traits that are one key to the mystery that has puzzled many biographers. The Franklin family's roots were firmly in the English craft classes, and yet they were never as humbly poor as Benjamin later pretended when he talked about his path to eminence. Josiah Franklin, Benjamin's father, was from a landowning Northamptonshire family of strong Calvinist belief. Early generations were farmers and blacksmiths, but later Franklins became skilled dyers of various cloths. Josiah was a silk dyer in the English market town of Banbury.

In 1660, the restoration of Charles II to the English throne rekindled the turmoil between the establishment majority of the Church of England and Roman Catholic families loyal to the Stuarts. Confusing matters was a mix of other Protestant denominations from Presbyterians to Methodists to Quakers. Franklins were pious and fearless Congregationalists who believed that each village church should run its own affairs. Against the law the family kept their own Bible and hid it under a stool. They also held illegal home services with a lookout at the window to watch for establishment church informers.

In 1683, twenty-six-year-old Josiah, wife Anne, and their three children immigrated to Boston with others in their community who looked to the Massachusetts colony for better opportunities and more religious freedom. The move at first seemed a mistake for Josiah: gaily colored clothing was not in line with drab Puritan fashions. As a result, Josiah shifted to the more necessary, but unpleasant, craft of being a tallow chandler—making soap and candles from boiled animal fat.

It was a noxious business, as the boiling cauldrons threw off sickening fumes. Within five years, however, Josiah was able to rent a shop away from his home; he hung his trade sign with its large blue ball on High (now Washington) Street. He also settled his family into a rented house on nearby Milk Street just across from the Old South Church. As soon as he could, he applied to undergo the ten-year probation period for full membership in the church. From contemporary records we know he was an active and ardent participant at Old South, leading the chanting of hymns during services and holding prayer meetings at home during the week.[1]

This was at a time when the religious fervor that underpinned the founding of the Bay Colony was in decline. Only four out of ten Bostonians had formal church affiliation, and the port city (the largest in North America) was a violent stew of taverns and prostitution despite town leaders' regular efforts to keep order. For Josiah, church membership allowed him to practice his faith in the open for the first time.*

An active religious life was a valued passport into acceptance among Boston's influential class, and in the years to come Josiah would be selected to a series of positions of trust, including town constable and clerk of the market. Benjamin absorbed the need for a set of beliefs, but he came to spurn the rigidities of organized worship.

Franklin men were a robust lot. Benjamin could well have been describing himself in this picture of Josiah that he included in his *Autobiography*:

> He had an excellent constitution of body, was of middle stature, but well set, and very strong; he was ingenious, could draw prettily, was skilled a little in music, and had a clear pleasing voice, so that when he played psalm tunes on his violin and sung withal, as he sometimes did in an evening after the business of the day was over, it was extremely agreeable to hear. He had a mechanical genius too, and, on occasion, was very handy in the use of other tradesmen's tools; but his great excellence lay in a sound understanding and solid judgement in prudential matters, both in private and publick affairs. In the latter, indeed, he was never employed, the numerous family he had to educate and the straitness of his circumstances

---

* America's colonies were swelling with new arrivals. By 1700 there were about 262,000 colonists, with 12,000 each in Boston and Philadelphia and 5,000 in New York.

keeping him close to his trade; but I remember well his being frequently visited by leading people, who consulted him for his opinion in affairs of the town, or of the church he belonged to, and showed a good deal of respect for his judgement and advice; he was also much consulted by private persons about their affairs when any difficulty occurred, and frequently chosen an arbitrator between contending parties.[2]

Benjamin apparently also inherited a robust sexuality. Before she died in 1689, in her thirties, Anne Franklin bore her husband seven children in all, though two died as infants—the last little boy outliving his mother by only six days. This left Josiah with five children who needed a mother. He moved quickly to pay court to Abiah Folger, a twenty-one-year-old daughter of an early Nantucket family who had moved to Boston and attended the Old South Church. Abiah married Josiah in Old South in November, five months after Anne's death. She would bear him another ten children, six boys (including Ben) and four girls.

Benjamin inherited another trait from both parents: longevity. Abiah lived to be eighty-five; Josiah, eighty-nine. On the stone he later placed over their graves, Benjamin described his father as "a pious and prudent Man" and his mother as "a discreet and virtuous Woman."[3] Neither had much time to be anything else.

The Franklins were hard workers at an occupation that was sheer drudgery. Abiah, burdened as she was with a teeming household to run, managed to perfect a soap for bathing which became so popular that Benjamin twenty years later stocked a version in his shop in Philadelphia. The children, too, worked at the vats, and at least one set up his own chandlery. Josiah turned his hand to whatever made a profit. He won the contract to sell the candles to the night watch. He also allowed slave traders to schedule inspections and auctions of newly arrived Africans outside his chandlery; newspaper advertisements directed buyers to "the sign of the Blue Ball."*

BENJAMIN WAS THE TENTH, AND LAST, OF JOSIAH'S SONS. He was born in 1706 on January 6, a date he celebrated all his life even though the subsequent calendar revision moved it to January 17, the day we mark now. It was one of the coldest winters on record, but because the day was a Sunday, Josiah bundled Abiah and the baby out of bed and into the Old South Church for an immediate baptism—for a superstition held that a child born on the Sabbath had been conceived in sin on an earlier Sabbath. Yet the haste of the ceremony also could have reflected that Josiah meant for the babe to be his tithe to the church, destined for the clergy.

The little house on Milk Street must have been in constant turmoil. Some friction was inevitable, for Elizabeth, the firstborn, was only eleven years younger than her stepmother; in all, thirty-four years would separate the eldest of Josiah's children from the youngest—Jane, who was born in 1712. Jane and little Benjamin formed a friendship that lasted all their lives. Childhood was a perilous time in those days. Three of Benjamin's older siblings died early, one drowning in an untended vat of soapsuds.

Soon an older brother of Josiah, the namesake uncle of Benjamin, arrived from England in some disarray. This elder Benjamin Franklin also was a cloth dyer but had fallen on hard times; all but one of his ten children had died, and he had come to Boston for a fresh start and to prepare the way for his last son, a maker of cutlery, to join him. Josiah and his brother argued

---

* In 1676, Bacon's Rebellion in Virginia and King Philip's War in New England ended efforts to use local Indians as a source of forced labor, which, in turn, increased the demand for African slaves, who were more tractable because they lacked the option to escape beyond the frontier limits. Slavery remained legal in Massachusetts until the first Revolutionary state constitution, adopted in 1776.

constantly while he lived with the family, but the uncle had a soft spot for his little nephew. He wrote acrostic poems based on his name and urged the boy to better govern his own headstrong, noisy nature.

In later years, Franklin would recall there being thirteen people around the dinner table. Both parents were sober, pious folk, but there must have been some gaiety. Music and fierce conversation were an evening's recreation. Josiah Franklin worked all the hours he could to get ahead, but he also yearned for greater knowledge for himself and his family. Another of Benjamin's early memories was of regular guests invited from the community to eat dinner at the crowded table. The guests were men of business and religious affairs, and for their supper they were expected to discuss with Josiah the issues of the day or some question of church doctrine.

While the men soberly weighed their comments, the children (and Abiah) were supposed to sit silently and absorb useful knowledge that they could not get from books. Benjamin later wrote:

> By this means he turned our attention to what was good, just,
> and prudent in the conduct of life; and little or no notice was
> ever taken of what related to the victuals on the table, whether
> it was … of good or bad flavor … so that I was bro't up in such
> a perfect inattention to those matters as to be quite indifferent
> to what kind of food was set before me, and so unobservant of
> it that to this day if I am asked I can scarcely tell a few hours
> after dinner what I dined upon.[4]

Books were an expensive luxury reserved for only the truly wealthy, but Josiah had a small collection of religious doctrinal tracts that he pored over to prepare himself for his endless debates over virtue. Not surprisingly, then, young Benjamin was an early reader. He recounts that he could not remember a time when he could not read, and his sister Jane said in later years that her brother could read parts of the Bible by the time he was three.

Benjamin apparently was Josiah's chosen child. Although Josiah's seven other surviving sons had been sent off to apprenticeships as soon as possible, Benjamin was enrolled in the Boston Latin School at the age of eight to study religion and the classics. The course was to prepare him for the entrance examinations for Harvard College, the launching pad for any colonial clerical career. He was a quick success. After only eight months, he advanced to the head of his class, then to the one higher, and would have gone into yet a third class of study had his father not removed him. The excuse given was the expense, but Franklin later told his own son, William, that he suspected his father had changed his mind after taking a hard look at the clergyman's penurious life.

Ben was then put into another school, this one specializing in writing and mathematics—more suited for the tradesman he was now to become. He did well for about another year. At that time John Franklin, the oldest son by Abiah, left his father's chandlery and moved to Rhode Island to go into business for himself. Ben was taken out of school and put to work cutting wicks and putting them into the molds for the hot wax; he tended shop, ran errands for his father, and disliked it all very much.

There is a fretful fault line of impatience in the Franklin lineage. Josiah had taken his family to a distant land rather than compromise his religious beliefs. And then his first son born in Boston, also named Josiah, had rebelled against plans to apprentice him and run away to sea, where he was lost. Other sons were quarrelsome, especially James, who had learned the printing trade. Now here was young Ben, grumbling about the shop and threatening to follow brother Josiah to the glamorous life of a sailor.

The father then did something remarkable for those authoritarian times. He walked Benjamin around Boston to visit the workshops and forges so the boy could see firsthand what carpenters, joiners, bricklayers, tinsmiths, cutlery makers, and other craftsmen did. At first Josiah pressed his son into a trial as an apprentice to his cousin Samuel Franklin, who made knives and scissors. But the cousin wanted a fee for taking the child in, and in the end the father decided to apprentice Benjamin to the boy's half brother James, a printer. The boy initially balked but finally agreed.

JAMES FRANKLIN WAS TWENTY-ONE AND THE YEAR before had returned from London, where he had learned his journeyman's skills in the metropolis's thriving print shops. He brought with him cases of type and a new press, and set up as a general printer of business documents and a seller of stationery and printed fabrics. This, by the way, tells us that the Franklin family had been able to acquire quite a bit of capital, or enough at least to obtain substantial credit. A new press and fonts of type could cost as much as £200—five years' earnings for a middling craftsman.

The printing press was a truly revolutionary technology, even more so than the computer and Internet that have so transformed our society. European kings and church hierarchy were wary of the press from the start. Through nearly all of the seventeenth century, English kings forbade presses and type foundries except those licensed in London and at the established universities. Censorship was still a harsh reality well into the next century; jail, confiscation, and ruin were real threats to both writers and publishers. And one could be transported to the primitive colonies for writing what were judged treasonable utterances against those in power.

The experience of the early American colonies stood in contrast. Before presses were licensed in any English provincial city, they were functioning in Boston, Cambridge, Philadelphia, and St. Mary's City, Maryland. In 1693, the year the English restrictions on newspapers outside London were lifted, the first press was set up in New York. Colonial newspapers were a natural by-product of the printer's art. They had to be licensed, to be sure—and were quickly suppressed if they were not—but they made lively reading and often were cautiously critical of the powers that were.[5]

Newspapers not only recorded local events but also reported on the politics, natural disasters, and commercial growth of far-distant colonies. More ambitious publishers developed relationships with printers in other towns and pilfered news from months-old magazines and papers from London. Equally important, the printers began to bind the economies of the colonial communities more closely. Each printer offered a line of commercial documents, bills of sale, contract forms, wills, deeds, and the like. The standardization of business practice came as ordinary citizens were growing more involved in the governing of their colonies.

James Franklin, however, found that the fierce competition among Boston's many presses made it difficult to prosper. In 1719 the Franklin brothers took over the printing of the *Boston Gazette*, one of the city's two weekly newspapers, but after only forty issues they lost the contract.

Life for an apprentice printer was pretty spartan even with a congenial master, which James was not. The two fretted each other from the start. As was the custom, James instructed Benjamin in the two distinct skills of being a compositor and being a pressman, the higher calling. The first required extraordinary hand-eye coordination and immense stamina. A compositor stood at upright cases of many little open drawers. Each drawer held pieces of lead type for every letter of the alphabet, both upper- and lowercase, plus all the punctuation marks and other graphic devices. The typesetter grasped in his left hand a long tray, called a composing stick, that was the length and width of whatever was to be printed, say a column of newspaper type. Looking at the handwritten copy that was to be set up, he used his right hand to flick among the many dozens of drawers, sliding the pieces of type into place on the composing stick—upside down and backwards. When full, the tray was unloaded onto a flat adjustable form, where it made a negative image of what the printed page would show. Once the printing was completed, the entire composing process had to be reversed and be done with even greater speed and total accuracy. Each letter had to be cleaned and put back into its drawer, lest the shop be thrown into an uproar.

The pressman in the meantime had taken the heavy form, trundled it to the press, and laid it carefully onto the bed. He inked the letters, gingerly laid a piece of paper across the surface, and used a ponderous lever to screw a mat down on the paper, pressing it onto the inked surface. It was both drudgery and delicate work, for the pressing had to be done just right or it would smear. Once one side was dried on a line, the process could be repeated on the other side.

The production of a handful of a single two-sided newspaper must have been exhausting. Yet these primitive old wooden presses were wonders. According to a common labor standard, two men serving a single press (one to pull, the other to ink and lay paper) could print a "token" of 240 pages (on one side only) in an hour, or 2,400 sheets in a ten-hour day. Wages of six pennies for 1,000 letters set and printed were the standard during Benjamin Franklin's career, so speed and endurance were essential.[6] As an apprentice, he got only a pittance from his master. But he quickly became proficient at both craft skills, and he began to take pride in his ability. All his life Benjamin considered himself first and foremost a printer. Considering the times, it may well have been the most important skill he mastered.

THE FIVE YEARS UNDER JAMES WERE A TIME of concentrated growth, as Benjamin transformed from a boy into a young man. The work brought constant exercise of the most arduous kind. Yet typesetting usually was restricted to the daylight hours (candlelight led to costly mistakes). So when the light failed, or Boston turned out for one of its many church holidays, there was time to play—plenty, actually, since one of the skills that all apprentices learned was how to make oneself scarce.

Growing up on Boston's waterfront, Benjamin was a fearless swimmer and skilled boatsman. Swimming naked in the harbor was hardy enough, but by his later recollection, Benjamin explored ways to go faster and farther. He made himself what he described as "paddles" for his hands and feet but discovered that while his speed increased greatly, so did his fatigue. One time he convinced a friend to carry his clothes around a lake while he pulled himself through the water using a kite as power.

Because of his large, muscular frame and considerable strength, Ben became the leader of his little group. This was a rowdy time, and scuffles between neighborhood gangs and packs of apprentices were a regular excitement. So Benjamin became adept at fighting and later admitted that even when he had bested an opponent, the rules permitted him to give his foe one more "knock" before letting him rise.

But Benjamin's addiction to books set him apart from the other harum-scarum boys of his class and time. As a younger boy he had read through his father's books on religious doctrine but found they merely made him skeptical. Now, Benjamin plunged into the wonderworld of books in earnest. "The little money that came into my hands was ever laid out in books," he would recall in his *Autobiography*. All his days he remembered as one would a first love the first book he owned, a used copy of John Bunyan's *Pilgrim's Progress*. Once he had devoured that, he sold it in order to buy a collection of all of Bunyan's writing; then he sold that and bought a series of small booklets, forty or fifty in all—a mix of historical biography and digests of classical stories. From there he went headlong into Plutarch's *Lives* of the greats of antiquity and thence to self-guidance books such as Daniel Defoe's *Essay on Projects* and Cotton Mather's *Essays to Do Good*. A local merchant who visited the print shop each day took a liking to the boy and let him borrow freely from his own small library. Benjamin's appetite was ravenous. He begged newly arrived volumes from the counter boys in bookshops so he could read them overnight and get them back first thing in the morning. He borrowed books on arithmetic, read geometry from books on navigation, and pored over volumes on how to think and reason.

All this reading led to his first attempts to write. He wrote two ballad-style poems on current topics—a tragic drowning and the capture of Blackbeard the pirate. James printed them and sent Benjamin out into the street to hawk his creations. Both were instant hits, and the boy's vanity—by his own admission—swelled to the point that his father had to remind him that most poets made a very poor living indeed. Art, the boy was taught, must always serve commerce.

One of the more charming tales in the *Autobiography* is how he tried to perfect his prose writing style in order to become a better arguer. He already was of a disputatious nature, so much so that James had beaten him for insolence on several occasions. Indeed, Ben and another apprentice named John Collins made a friendship out of testing each other in debate on important issues. As he recalled:

A question was once, somehow or other, started between Collins and me, of the propriety of educating the female sex in learning, and their abilities for study. He was of opinion that it was improper, and that they were naturally unequal to it. I took the contrary side, perhaps a little for dispute's sake. He was naturally more eloquent, had a ready plenty of words; and sometimes, as I thought, bore me down more by his fluency than by the strength of his reasons. As we parted without settling the point, and were not to see one another for some time, I sat down to put my arguments in writing.... [He] answered, and I replied. Three or four letters of a side had passed when my father happened to find my papers and read them. Without entering into the discussion, he took occasion to talk to me about the manner of my writing; observed that though I had the advantages of my antagonist in correct spelling and pointing (which I ow'd to the printing-house), I fell far short in elegance of expression, in method and in perspicuity, of which he convinced me by several instances. I saw the justice of his remark, and thence grew more attentive to the manner in writing and determined to endeavor at improvement.[7]

Through intense study, Franklin learned how to better communicate with others. He became adept at Socratic argument, using casually posed questions to undermine his opponent's position. He also came across a volume of back issues of *The Spectator,* a highly literate collection of essays and satire founded by Joseph Addison and Richard Steele in London in 1711. Benjamin outlined the main points of each article, then tried to recreate the article using only the outlines. Sometimes he took some of the stories and turned them into verse and then tried to transpose the poems back into the same narrative style as the magazine's authors. He worked late into the night in his boardinghouse room or came to the printing house early to study; he even took to skipping church. To his delight, his new store of words and the more direct prose styles he studied began to improve his own creations. Over time he learned a personal style that he carried with him all his life—one that son William could have benefited from—whenever he had to argue or convince another. He adopted, he said, a modest diffidence; never using, when I advanced anything that may possibly be disputed, the words certainly, undoubtedly, or any others that give the air of positiveness to an opinion; but rather say, I conceive or apprehend a thing to be so and so; it appears to me, or I should think it so or so, for such and such reasons; or I imagine it to be so; or it is so, if I am not mistaken. This habit, I believe, has been of great advantage to me when I have had occasion to inculcate my opinions and persuade men into measures that I have been from time to time engag'd in promoting.[8]

Or as he later instructed a young Thomas Jefferson, "Never contradict anybody."

In the meantime, his struggle with his half brother continued. One of the books he picked up was an early treatise on the benefits of a vegetarian diet. Since James was a bachelor, he and his apprentices took their meals at a boardinghouse, so Ben's ostentatious spurning of meat was a new cause of friction. Yet when the boy proposed to provide his own meals for half the money James was paying for his board, the printer accepted quickly. Benjamin learned to cook rice and other staples and saved fully half of the money he was given, which he promptly converted into even more books. By avoiding the boardinghouse meals, moreover, he could spend more time alone in the print shop, reading and perfecting the writing skills that would stand him apart from others in that most literate of ages.[9]

James Franklin had ambitions of his own, however. In August 1721, having lost the contract to print the *Boston Gazette*, he launched a competing weekly, the *New England Courant*, which featured essays and poems from his friends, as well as articles attacking the local government for its conflicts of interest. With the first issue, James hit upon a hot controversy that made his newspaper required reading from the start. Earlier that summer a British man-of-war had arrived in Boston Harbor from the West Indies, bringing with it a smallpox epidemic. The *Courant* bitterly fought the radical new preventative of inoculation even after more than 6,000 Bostonians, more than half the town, had been stricken and 844 had died. Most of those inoculated survived.

James wisely pulled back from that topic. But he continued to goad the government and the church powers. In June 1722 he referred sarcastically to the authorities' weak efforts to quell piracy in local waters, and this time he was jailed for a month. In January 1723 he attacked "hypocritical pretenders to religion," and the colony's governing council struck back by forbidding him to publish the *Courant*. He also was threatened with more serious charges to be brought before a grand jury.*

Thus, by a subterfuge, sixteen-year-old Benjamin Franklin became the publisher of his first newspaper. Perhaps he took some secret joy in his master's vexations. He surely must have been pleased when his indenture as an apprentice was publicly canceled and his name put above the masthead, where it would stay until 1726, three years after he had moved on. James remained the master, however; Ben entered into a secret indenture with his brother. The boy grew increasingly restive, and he would later recall that he had been perhaps "too saucy and provoking."

As nominal publisher of the *Courant*, Benjamin felt secure enough to try the literary skills he had been honing in secret. Knowing that any essays he submitted would be turned down automatically, in April he slid his first anonymous offering under the door of the print shop and gloated with "exquisite pleasure" at the effusive praise the satire earned when it was published. James even put a notice in the next issue asking the unknown author to contribute more articles.

* In May, the jury acquitted James, but the ban remained in place.

Benjamin had created the first truly American literary character in Silence Dogood, his essayist.[10] The very name was a clever double pun, first on two of the better known essays by Cotton Mather* on the virtues of silence and on doing good, and also on the custom of fastening virtuous names on women. "Silence" was deliberately American. She had been born on an immigrant ship coming from England, so she was free from any connection to the motherland. Her father had died on the journey and her destitute mother had been forced to put her into the service of a rural clergyman. The cleric had been an unusually kind master and had given Silence free rein through his large library while he patiently educated her in virtue. Then, after marrying her, the minister did her another favor by dying and leaving her a comfortable, secure widow.

Silence made fourteen appearances in the *Courant* between April and October 1723 and was an instant hit. She commented on the pretension to virtue of fictitious neighbors, criticized the clergy and the law, sharply attacked the scholars at Harvard, and bitterly satirized Bostonian poets' embarrassing attempts at colonial verse. Benjamin also printed satirical essays he wrote using comic noms de plume such as Timothy Wagstaff and Abigail Twitterfield in order to poke fun at well-known and ostentatiously pious citizens.

The secret could not last, however, and the prank predictably displeased James. He was being harassed by the Boston authorities, and jailing again could mean the confiscation of his press and banishment. He began to make plans to move to Rhode Island,

---

* Increase Mather and his son Cotton are two of the more notorious characters of early American history. These Puritan clergymen pursued the evil they saw everywhere with a rigid zeal. Increase (1639–1723) urged the execution of the Indian leaders of King Philip's War, rather than their eventual enslavement and exile to the Caribbean. Cotton (1663–1728) presided over the Salem witch trials. Both were undeniably brilliant and had an extraordinary influence on the moral climate of the times. Cotton initiated the campaign for smallpox inoculation. He also recommended books to young Benjamin Franklin and provided him with many of his later ideas for civic improvement in Philadelphia.

where his brother John was prospering and where the climate of tolerance was stronger. Benjamin, of course, would have to accompany him—except that Ben had no intention of staying on with James and had no compunction against trying to blackmail his half brother into setting him free.*

In what he called one of the "first errata" of his life, Ben threatened to expose the secret apprentice bond he had signed and accuse James of committing a fraud over who really was the publisher of the newspaper. Stung, James retaliated the only way he knew how: by telling every other printer in Boston that Benjamin was of bad character, so that the young man could not find a new job anywhere in town.

Even though Boston was by far the largest town in the colonies, it was becoming uncomfortably close for Benjamin as well as James. He was too old to start an apprenticeship in another trade and was stalled in the one he practiced. He had only one choice.

In mid-September, Benjamin ran away to New York. His friend John Collins had convinced a ship captain to smuggle Ben aboard by claiming that the young man was trying to escape a forced marriage to a pregnant girl. When Benjamin arrived in New York, he made his first call on William Bradford, who had the distinction of opening the first printing works in both Philadelphia and New York. As usual, Ben's lively personality made a good first impression (something he benefited from all his life). Bradford told him that he had a full complement of workers but that his son Andrew, at the Philadelphia press, had had a compositor die recently. If he would go there, the prospects of a job were good, this time as a highly paid journeyman.

---

* James Franklin moved to Newport in 1727 and published the *Rhode Island Gazette* from 1732 until his death in 1738. His widow, Ann Franklin, became one of the first women printers in America, and with her son, Jimmy, she began publishing the *Newport Mercury* in 1758. It remains in business today.

AFTER AN ARDUOUS TREK BY FOOT AND SLOW BOAT, Benjamin arrived in Philadelphia, exhausted and with only a Dutch dollar and about twenty pence in his pocket. Even at the distance of nearly fifty years' recollection, Franklin would relish the sight he must have made on that chilly Sunday morning in October. He made his way up from the Walnut Street dock to the center market, where the Quaker meetinghouse was drawing its usual large crowd of worshippers. Soiled and scruffy from travel, he wore his rough work clothes because his trunk was still on its way by ship from New York. His pockets bulged with the spare stockings and shirts he carried, and as he sauntered along, he carried three large rolls of freshly baked bread that he had just bought for three of his scarce pennies.

As he chewed on one of the rolls, he saw a girl standing in the doorway of her home laughing at his "most awkward, ridiculous appearance." It was Deborah Read, later his wife. He would further embarrass himself by going into the Quaker meetinghouse and falling asleep during the silent worship. Finally, he found an affordable inn and slept both the afternoon and the night away.

The next morning, he presented himself at Andrew Bradford's print works, and to his surprise he found William Bradford there; the older man had made the journey ahead of him on horseback. There was no steady job, the younger printer said, but he pointed Franklin to a competitor, Samuel Keimer, who eventually took Benjamin on and found lodgings for him—as luck would have it, with the Read family. John Read, Deborah's father, was a carpenter who would soon leave his family in some distress when he died and his land ventures failed.

As those autumn weeks passed, Benjamin's luck held. A relative of his had recommended the young printer's talents to Pennsylvania's royal governor, Sir William Keith. To Keimer's astonishment, the governor arrived at the shop and asked for Benjamin by name.

He invited Ben, but not his employer, to join him for a drink of Madeira at a nearby tavern, and he proposed sponsoring the young journeyman in a venture that would serve both their interests. The two printers in Philadelphia were not very good, he said, and Ben concurred. Andrew Bradford, Franklin judged, "was very illiterate"; Keimer was a "mere compositor" who had nearly wrecked his press with misuse. The governor offered to give Franklin all the considerable official printing work of the provinces of Pennsylvania and Delaware, journals of the assemblies, official documents, stamps, and currencies. Would Ben's father underwrite such a scheme?

So IT WAS THAT IN APRIL 1724 Benjamin swaggered back to Boston, in a fine new suit and with his pockets jingling with coins, as befitting a prospering journeyman. His old workmates at James's print shop were agog; James himself was surly and barely civil. Josiah, despite his pride in his son's rapid rise and the prestige of a governor's patronage, demurred at backing the venture. His son should work a little longer and build up his own store of capital before going out on his own, he thought. Josiah knew that such ventures often failed. Yet he readily consented to Benjamin's return to Philadelphia. His son still had much to learn, and some distance from home might help.

Benjamin certainly did have much to learn, especially about choosing friends. John Collins, his old debating chum, decided to seek his fortune in Philadelphia, so he went on ahead to New York to wait while Benjamin went to Newport to visit his brother John. John Franklin deputized his younger brother to collect some money owed him in Philadelphia. On Ben's sail to New York to meet Collins, only quick action by a kindly Quaker lady kept the eighteen-year-old from falling in with two thieving prostitutes. And when he got to New York he found his old friend had become a drunkard and was running up considerable debts. Things only got worse when they reached Philadelphia. No one would hire Collins, and he sponged off Benjamin's dwindling store of money held in trust for his brother. Finally their quarreling led to a fight in a boat where Benjamin picked Collins up bodily and threw him into the river. Shortly afterward, Collins left for the West Indies and never repaid his debt. In his *Autobiography*, Franklin pointed out to his son, William, that this misjudgment of a friend and the breaking of a financial trust was another of the "great errata" of his youth.[11]

However disappointed he may have been, Benjamin was comforted by Governor Keith's enthusiasm for his printing project. Keith was ever the cheerful optimist. He urged Benjamin to draw up a list of equipment and supplies to be purchased for the new printing works and then to go to London to oversee the purchases himself. Ben would sail on the annual official mail ship from Philadelphia that carried Keith's documents and reports to the authorities.* The governor promised his protégé he would include letters of introduction to well-placed persons who would help him, as well as letters of credit to finance the trip and purchases.

Since the sailing was still some months away, Benjamin occupied himself as any young bachelor tradesman might. His first attributable job for his new employer was to set the type for a reprint of an essay by William Wollaston, a famous English scientist and moral philosopher.[12] We will hear of him later. In the meantime, Benjamin got along well with Keimer, whom he kept in the dark about the Keith project. The two printers frequented women of the town and spent many nights in taverns, where the younger man baffled his employer with his skillful arguing. In this more congenial climate there were plenty of new friends for debate and for contests over poetry.

---

* Because of the almost constant warfare, England only mustered an annual navy convoy to transport official papers back to London from Philadelphia.

Benjamin also found time to pay court to Deborah Read, and a romance bloomed. But Sarah Read, Deborah's mother, put the match on indefinite hold, the more so once Benjamin's trip to London became firm. Deborah was just eighteen herself, and there would be time enough to consider marriage when Benjamin returned from his journey.

With a kiss and "an understanding," Benjamin sailed in November 1724 aboard the *London Hope* for the adventure that would ensure his fortune. At the last minute, James Ralph, one of his poet friends, decided he could perfect his art by coming along. The young printer made sure the bags with Governor Keith's letters were aboard and settled in to enjoy the voyage. Among the important passengers on the trip was a Quaker merchant, Thomas Denham, who took an immediate liking to the young man.

"The voyage," Franklin recorded, "was otherwise not a pleasant one, as we had a great deal of bad weather."[13]

Chapter 2

Hope and Glory

When young Benjamin Franklin first saw London on Christmas Eve 1724, both he and the city were works very much in progress. Neither would be the same when he returned a second time in 1757. All his life, London would be the city that quickened his pulse. Boston might be his "home country" and Philadelphia might offer great prospects, but London was a Golconda, a diamond city to which all travelers journeyed with rising hopes. His time there shaped the Franklin he would become.

By any measure, London already was a stupendous place, drawing together a population rapidly growing to 600,000 souls—more than 10 percent of the national population. It was a capital greater than Paris and Naples, rivaled for the time being only by Constantinople. The city was in the midst of evolving from the medieval hodgepodge it had been to the modern metropolis it soon would be. Benjamin must have been slack jawed with wonder: the city was fifty times larger than Boston.

There was newness to London in those days. The Great Fire of 1666 had leveled nearly all the buildings within the square mile of walls that marked the official City of London, and had inflicted substantial damage elsewhere. With architect Christopher Wren supervising, streets had been widened and straightened, and new, more substantial buildings constructed. London was spreading out into what had once been open country. Noblemen sought royal permission to construct spectacular squares close to the government complex at Whitehall Palace and the houses of Parliament. There they sited their mansions and sold the land around the squares to others of fashion. Elm-shaded parks were springing up, and at night pleasure seekers of all stations in life thronged the public amusement gardens along the river.

England had officially become Great Britain in 1707, but it was far from a united country, though its dominions stretched around the world. Queen Anne, the last Stuart monarch, had presided over the uniting of Scotland with England, but it took a long time before Scots were treated as equals, much less gentlemen. Those Scots who were not suspected of being Jacobite supporters of a Stuart restoration were believed to harbor heretical religious beliefs, such as Presbyterianism and Unitarianism. These threats seemed real enough. In 1715 there had been a bloody rising to put the son of James II on the throne, and many of the city's leading radicals had, in fact, been trained in Edinburgh. The Scots were disturbers of the English way.

The accession of George Louis, the Elector of Hanover, to Great Britain's throne as George I in 1714 had done little to unite the country. The king spoke no English (German was his native tongue) and put the affairs of government into the hands of his prime ministers. The most notable was the extraordinary Robert Walpole, who devised a system of corruption and power gathering that kept him and the two kings he served safely in power for twenty years.*

It was hard to say whether the king's ministers or the king's court was the more corrupt. George's two mistresses did a lively trade in titles of nobility and land grants, while his two Turkish valets dispensed smaller offices below stairs. Walpole stood out, however, because of the sheer mechanical genius of the political machine he constructed. Since most of the high offices (the more remunerative provided kickbacks of 1 to 10 percent on government contracts) went to members of Parliament, Walpole kept the ministries and his majority in both the House of Commons and the House of Lords firmly in his grip. King George did not interfere.

If British politics was an incendiary mix, the economy had already had one explosion. The city Benjamin entered was still shaking from the collapse in 1720 of the fabled South Sea Bubble. In 1713, one of the terms of settlement of the latest war with France and Spain† gave the British an *asiento,* or permit, to export African slaves into Spain's colonies in the Western Hemisphere for the next thirty years.‡ Breaking into the ravenous market for slaves in Spain's colonies looked like a gold mine, and shares in the South Sea Company, which held the monopoly, began to boom. Merchants and noblemen (and even the king) rushed to invest, and South Sea shares spiked from a price of £100 in April 1720 to an unsustainable £1,000 just before the September crash. The crash caused capital to

---

* Walpole and the king were forced to converse in the Latin they had learned imperfectly as schoolboys.

† With the Treaty of Utrecht, England dropped out of the War of the Spanish Succession, which lasted another year. Queen Anne gained new land in North America from France, Gibraltar, and the slave trade concessions from the Spanish.

‡ This was over and above the North American slave trade established by Parliament in 1698, which created the "triangular trade" of New England rum to Africa, slaves to the West Indies, and Caribbean molasses to New England.

vanish and trade goods to molder in warehouses. The collapse destroyed nearly two hundred other joint stock companies, and the spreading panic nearly brought the Bank of England to bankruptcy and cost George his throne. Only Walpole's canny maneuvering prevented the catastrophe from spreading, but when Benjamin Franklin arrived in the city three years later, bankruptcy sales of foreclosed estates still dominated the newspaper columns.[1]

So London was a dangerous place. The king had escaped one assassination attempt in 1717. The royal coach and those of the nobility were routinely stoned in the streets during the city's episodes of mob rioting. Just living in London could be fatal. It had such a frightening death toll from disease that it offset much of England's general population gains well into the 1800s.

Yet all of England seemed to flow toward London. Thames barges loaded with ship timbers came upriver to the yards, and coal came downriver to fuel the city's factories. Grain arrived to feed its people and be malted into its beer. Beef and mutton arrived on the hoof in herds that churned the muddy streets into a slurry. Also arriving in droves were farm laborers seeking better paying jobs, debtors fleeing from provincial towns, and those of easy virtue of both sexes. Huge merchant ships docked from all over the burgeoning empire, laden with fabrics, spices, and a thousand other valuable cargoes.* The stately river dominated London life. It was a prime source of water, of transport and communications. When London was done with anything material, the waste (including human bodies) found its way downstream. Yet just as the prettiest flowers often grow closest to the dunghill, the city was fast becoming the cultural center of the world.

---

* At this time London was losing its preeminence as a slave trade port to Liverpool. By the time of Franklin's second visit, there were an estimated fifteen thousand Africans living in England; two-thirds of that number were slaves.

To the young Franklin's delight, London was home to nearly two hundred bookshops, most owned by a "conger" of publishers who held a tight grip on their authors' copyrights. There was profit in writing for a general public whose appetite for information and amusement had been set loose from the restraints of the past. Daniel Defoe was proving it was possible to support oneself solely by the pen with such international best-sellers as *Robinson Crusoe* and *Moll Flanders*. The uncertain patronage of the nobility no longer constricted art. These were the early days of a true golden age. Samuel Johnson, who would dominate that age, was just fifteen, three years younger than Benjamin. Alexander Pope had recently made the unheard-of sum of £9,000 for translating *The Iliad* and *The Odyssey*. In the world of London theater, the light Restoration comedies of William Congreve were giving way to the raw scandal of John Gay's *A Beggar's Opera*. This new generation of dramatists did not think much of a play that did not cause a riot on opening night. Discussion, debate, and controversy were the order of the day, and one could find a newspaper for every cause or faction, or start one. Joseph Addison and Richard Steele were producing a profusion of witty magazines such as *The Tatler, The Spectator,* and *The Guardian.* Their stated aim was to bring "philosophy out of closets and libraries, schools and colleges, to dwell in clubs and assemblies, at tea-tables and in coffee-houses."2

WHILE A GOLDEN AGE INDEED WAS DAWNING, things at the moment looked pretty black for Benjamin Franklin, only days away from his nineteenth birthday. He had just discovered that his supposed patron, Governor Keith, had betrayed him.

The disillusion began when the ship's captain allowed Benjamin to search the mailbags for the letters of introduction and credit the governor had promised him. There were none addressed to the friends Keith had promised would help Ben, but there were several to prominent London printers. Straightaway, he took one to a maker of stationery, who saw it was from an attorney who was a crony of Keith's. The stationer denounced the writer as "a compleat Rascal" and tossed the letter back at Benjamin. The boy was stunned—even more so when he discovered that Keith was operating a scheme. The governor was planning to use the young printer to defraud Andrew Hamilton, a powerful Philadelphia lawyer, who was due to arrive soon in London.

Benjamin sought out Thomas Denham and told him everything. As Franklin reported in the *Autobiography*, the kindly Quaker could not help but laugh "at the Notion of the Governor's giving me a Letter of Credit, having, as he said, no Credit to give." No one, Denham remarked, believed anything Keith said, and the author of the letter was indeed a rogue. Moreover, Hamilton was a friend of Denham's and should be informed of the plot as soon as he arrived in London; he would be grateful and Benjamin at least would have two well-placed friends in this strange metropolis. In the meantime, the pragmatic businessman urged the boy to get a job in a print shop quickly and perfect his craft. "And when you return to America, you will set up to greater Advantage," he said.[3]

In his memoirs, Franklin raged at Keith's trick:

> But what shall we think of a Governor's playing such pitiful Tricks, and imposing so grossly on a poor ignorant Boy! It was a Habit he had acquired. He wish'd to please everybody, and having little to give, he gave Expectations.[4]

A "poor ignorant Boy"? Poor, yes, but Benjamin hardly was without resources or prospects. Largely through his own efforts he had acquired a pretty solid education for the day, and he was skilled at one of the most important crafts of modern times. True, he was immature, boastful, and sometimes violent. He was also gullible, but that was due partly to the enormous engine of ambition that churned inside him. He wanted things so badly—advancement, knowledge, approval, wealth—and he wanted them all at once. As with most self-taught people, it was what he did not know that often caught him by the heels, but that just spurred him on to learn even more. So if he overreached and stumbled, as he just had, it would not be fatal. He might be a provincial bumpkin, brash and foolish, but he had youth, strength, and a quick mind, and he was on his way in earnest. And one must not forget his prodigious luck.

Fortune continued to smile. The printers in each printing house of that day were a tight-knit group organized in what they called chapels. Yet the custom was (as it was well into the twentieth century) that a visiting journeyman could claim at least a day's work from a chapel on demand. Benjamin immediately landed a full-time job at Samuel Palmer's works in Bartholomew Close. Because he was quick with the composing stick, he began to earn a decent living.

But his traveling companion from the little Philadelphia poetry club, James Ralph, was a constant drain on his earnings. Ralph was charming enough and ten years older, but his influence on Benjamin was not at all good. He encouraged young Ben to spend his earnings on theater outings and late suppers with women whose virtue was negotiable. Ralph pretended to look for work but was stubbornly determined to become a great poet, even though it was clear to others that he lacked the talent. He finally admitted to Benjamin that he had no intention of returning to America and his family. Instead he moved in with his mistress, a hatmaker. Then he abandoned her when circumstances forced him to accept a lowly schoolmaster's job in the provinces; to lessen the disgrace he adopted the name of Franklin and left his mistress in his friend's care. At this, Benjamin made another of his moral "errata." The lady in question was referred to as "Mrs. T." She, he recalled, having lost her Friends and Business, was often in Distresses, and us'd to send for me, and borrow what I could spare to help her out of them. I grew fond of her Company, and being at this time under no Religious Restraints, and presuming on my Importance to her, I attempted Familiarities...which she repuls'd with a proper Resentment, and acquainted [Ralph] with my Behaviour. This made a Breach between us and when he return'd again to London, he let me know he thought I had cancel'd all the Obligations he had been under to me. So I found I was never to expect his Repaying me what I lent to him or advanc'd for him. This was however not then of much Consequence, as he was totally unable. And in the Loss of his Friendship I found myself reliev'd from a Burden.[5]

THE AFFAIR INVOLVING MRS. T. SHOWS BENJAMIN morally very much adrift. Like many a youth of other times, he had cut himself loose from the "restraints" of his upbringing but had not quite settled on what moral compass heading he would follow. As a young teenager he had been talked into a kind of deism largely because he had been talked out of the orthodoxy that his father clung to so tightly. He tried on notions with enthusiasm and discarded them as easily as he had abandoned his vegetarianism when he left Boston. In early 1725, Palmer, his employer, selected him to set the type for the third printing of a popular treatise by William Wollaston, whose earlier essay Benjamin had helped publish in Philadelphia. This time the scientist-philosopher attacked the deists with geometrical proofs that all the tenets of orthodox religion could be scientifically confirmed. On his own, Benjamin composed and printed his own pamphlet challenging Wollaston. The youth argued that since God was Almighty, everything that happened in the world was by divine intention and, therefore, concepts such as good and evil were irrelevant. Man was free to do what he wanted since God clearly intended it so.[6]

The pamphlet, *A Dissertation on Liberty and Necessity, Pleasure and Pain,* was a puerile effort, and Benjamin was soon talked out of his opinions; he lists it in the *Autobiography* as among his errata. Later he tried to round up many of the one hundred copies he had printed at his own expense.* Yet it was not a fatal error. The essay brought Franklin to the attention of several of the more radical celebrity writers of the day, who questioned him closely at their coffeehouse and generally flattered him beyond measure.† One gentleman even promised him the opportunity to meet Sir Isaac Newton, but that never came to pass. Benjamin did, however, secure a meeting with Sir Hans Sloane, who had succeeded Newton as president of the august Royal Society of scientific leaders. In June 1725, Sloane, who served both Queen Anne and King George I as court physician, invited Benjamin to his home in Bloomsbury to view his extensive collection of natural history specimens and manuscripts. (The artifacts later became the original collection of the British Museum.)[7]

Although Samuel Palmer held no ill feelings toward Benjamin for the pamphlet, Franklin felt the need to move on. He sought a job as a pressman at a far larger house, that of James Watts, near Lincoln's Inn Fields; he was feeling stale, he said, and wanted the more vigorous exercise that pulling on the press bar brought.

Franklin must have been quite a figure now. He was barrel-chested and thick of leg and arm. He had by now reached his full height of five feet, ten inches. He had a large forehead and his long,

---

* The only two known copies of this *Dissertation* are in the Library of Congress and the Yale Franklin collection; it is reprinted in *The Papers of Benjamin Franklin* (Vol. 3, 58–71).
† Most notably, Bernard Mandeville, author of *The Fable of the Bees,* and James Lyon, a surgeon and author.

light brown hair would have been tied in a knot at the back, as was the fashion. Thin-lipped and grey-eyed, he must have been an arresting youth, and one that no other printer dared challenge directly.[8] If Benjamin could toss his friend Collins overboard from the uncertain footing of a small boat, one can imagine what he could do in the fistfights that periodically erupted among the printers in the suffocating shops.

They were a tough bunch, these printers, and rowdy at least in part because they drank so much on the job. Benjamin recalled in his memoirs that one of the dues one paid when joining a chapel was to buy the other fellows roughly one hundred pennies' worth of beer. On becoming a pressman, he promptly did so, although he was not much of a beer drinker himself and instead drank mainly water. Indeed, the printers marveled at the strength of the "Water American," as they called him. Later that summer, Watts decided he needed Benjamin's considerable skills as a compositor and moved him to another floor, whose chapel insisted on its beer money. When he refused, he was treated "as an Excommunicate, and had so many little Pieces of private Mischief done me,...all ascrib'd to the Chapel Ghost, which they said ever haunted those not regularly admitted."* After two weeks, the youth gave in and bought his round. Again, however, his abstemious habits impressed his workmates, who consumed close to a gallon of beer during the workday and who often got so drunk on Sunday that they took Monday off to recover.

He was strong, no doubt of it. He could carry two of the extremely heavy trays of set type up and down the stairs to the printing room floor, whereas the others carried only one with difficulty. Some began to follow his strict regimen of subsisting on bread, cheese, and

---

* The pranks included scrambling the bits of type in the case, shuffling the pages of manuscript he was to set, and destroying type columns he had already set.

water during the day; for the others, he loaned—at high interest—the money he earned so they could continue drinking. Still, it was hard to save the roughly ten pounds needed for a return to Philadelphia, much less to build a stake to set himself up when, and if, he went back. There was just too much to see and do in London. And books to read, scores and scores of books, borrowed from the shop adjoining his cheap lodgings.

And there was celebrity of a kind. Swimming was a skill virtually unknown in the world of the seventeenth century. Most Royal Navy sailors never learned, but the gentry were just beginning to enjoy the sport. Benjamin gave a fellow printer and another friend swimming lessons in the Thames, and they in turn introduced him to some gentlemen who took them all on an outing upriver to Chelsea. When they started back, Benjamin on a dare stripped, plunged into the river, and swam back to Blackfriars Bridge, a distance of three and a half miles. He amazed his cohorts by cavorting and diving under the water for long periods of time, only to surface far downstream. His printer friend even suggested that the two of them tour Europe as swimming instructors, but it was not to be.

It was, instead, time to go back to Philadelphia. And once more, the kindly Quaker merchant Thomas Denham stepped in. Denham had returned in some style to England to pay off debts left from an early bankruptcy. He then began gathering goods for a store he planned to open in Philadelphia. He offered to pay Benjamin's passage back plus £50 a year in Pennsylvania money. This was less than his printer's income, but Denham would teach him how to be the store's clerk and ultimately to run the store. If Benjamin took to storekeeping, Denham would finance a venture for the young man to sell flour in the West Indies and make his own fortune. It was too good an offer to turn down, even though Benjamin was rightly proud of his printing skills. A dependable offer of advancement from craftsman to merchant was not to be refused.

FRANKLIN DID NOT KNOW WHAT HE WOULD FIND when he returned. He had written one terse letter to Deborah Read, telling her only that he would not be returning home soon. She read between the lines and married someone else.* On July 21, 1726, when he and Denham sailed away on the *Berkshire,* Benjamin could not be sure of who he was or what he would become. Ever the orderly Franklin, he systematically set down those virtues he wanted to acquire and perfect upon his return to what he assumed would be his life as a merchant. He soon would be twenty-one, after all. Although he kept a journal of the extremely long voyage home,[9] the exact wording of Benjamin's new rules has been lost, but in a later essay he summarized his thinking at the time. Franklin observed:

> I have never fixed a regular design as to life, by which means it has been a confused variety of different scenes. I am now entering upon a new one; let me therefore make some resolutions, and form some scheme of action, that henceforth I may live in all respects like a rational creature. 1. It is necessary for me to be extremely frugal for some time, till I have paid what I owe. 2. To endeavour to speak truth in every instance, to give nobody expectations that are not likely to be answered, but aim at sincerity in every word and action: the most amiable excellence in a rational being. 3. To apply myself industriously to whatever business I take in hand, and not divert my mind from my business by any foolish project of growing suddenly rich; for industry and patience are the surest means of plenty. 4. I resolve to speak ill of no man whatever, not even in a matter of truth; but rather by some means excuse the

---

* In August 1725, Deborah Read married John Rogers, a potter, who may already have been married. In December 1727, Potter ran away with a stolen slave and never returned.

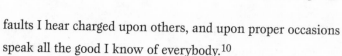

faults I hear charged upon others, and upon proper occasions speak all the good I know of everybody.[10]

These were fairly elementary rules of conduct, but they mark the first of a series of attempts by Franklin to come to grips with a question he would ponder most of his life. Indeed, it was a central question of the Enlightenment: Was it possible to secure a moral, happy life outside the strictures of any organized religion? He was not as sophisticated as he would become and was far from being able to wrestle with notions about God's existence or His purpose for mankind, but he sincerely wanted to become a better person. He would struggle at that forever.

When Benjamin speculated about morality and his place in the scheme of things, his Puritan Boston roots came into play and he imposed a rigorous self-examination. Being a methodical person, he regularly set down his faults and failures (his "errata"), and Franklin critics have used his confessions as ammunition against his reputation. It is true that his soul-searching came in part from his observation that good people seemed to prosper better in this world (witness his father and Mr. Denham), whereas those less good (Collins, Ralph, Governor Keith) always seemed to be in some trouble or other. And we must not forget that the early chapters of the *Autobiography* were aimed at son William's moral improvement. But it is worth remembering that this early diary list and the countless speculations that followed over the next sixty years were prompted mainly by Franklin's deep desire to be a better man than he was already.

Benjamin also had used the long sea journey back to Philadelphia to begin what would be his lifelong examination and recording of scientific phenomena. He set down his observations on a partial eclipse of the sun, the movements of sharks and dolphins, and the tiny marine life sustained on the vast stretches of seaweed moving in the Gulf Stream. As interesting as that was, the voyage was tediously long because of the westerly winds, and so, on October 11, when the *Berkshire* tied up at the dock in Philadelphia, Benjamin closed his journal with a heartfelt "Thank God!"

Chapter 3

The Pursuit of Virtue

Thomas Denham and his young clerk opened their store at what is now 39 Front Street in late 1726; the two shared quarters above. Benjamin had much to learn about merchandise, the skill of selling, and the necessary tasks of bookkeeping and inventory management. In later years, Franklin would draw on this experience when his printing shop sold a wide range of products, including stationery, cloth, his family's soap, and even Indian medicines and tonics. He liked to sell his products because in one sense he was selling himself. He took no real joy in bookkeeping, however, and throughout his life he would have a problem keeping the books in order. As busy as they were, Benjamin had time to look around town to see what changes had occurred in the nearly two years he had been away. One of the first people he ran into was Sir William

Keith. As he recalled in the *Autobiography*, "I met him walking the streets as a common Citizen. He seem'd a little asham'd at seeing me, but pass'd without saying any thing."[1] In the next sentence, he added the telling aside, "I should have been as much asham'd at seeing Miss Read."

Sir William had been ousted as governor in the summer of 1726 but had, a few weeks before Benjamin's arrival, led a local government counterattack that gained him and his followers nine of the ten council seats for Philadelphia and its county. He had hoped from that base to be elected Speaker of the General Assembly, but the Quakers and those loyal to the colony's proprietors suspended their feud long enough to elect someone else.

Politics in the established colonies were always in an uproar. If it was not frontier raids by the French and Indians, it was some peremptory decree from London that would infuriate the provincial legislatures. Royal governors, whose salaries usually came out of locally appropriated funds, often were held hostage by their assemblies, and not a few gave up the job and sailed for England; that had happened in Massachusetts, for example, during Benjamin's apprenticeship.

Several issues were on the boil in Pennsylvania besides the status of the popular, but erratic, Sir William Keith. The South Sea collapse had hit the colony hard, drying up London capital. Parliament had a long-standing policy of restricting the circulation of sterling-based currencies in America, and governors were supposed to discourage local assemblies from issuing money, lest debtors get off easy. Moreover, a dispute had raged since William Penn's death in 1718 over whether heirs from his first or second marriage were to take control of the colony. In addition, a dispute over the boundary with Maryland provided those who leased farmland from the proprietary landlords an excuse not to pay their rents and to protest any attempt to evict them.

On top of all this, the very nature of Pennsylvania was changing. The constant wars in Europe had driven thousands of refugees from the Rhineland and Bavaria to separate communities in Pennsylvania. Often these new immigrants brought their entire families. Their passage could be paid by colonial landowners, and the new arrivals would sign an indenture to work for an owner for a fixed term of years. The contract usually had a provision where they could buy land from their master after their obligations had been fulfilled. Soon enough, the thrift and industry of the German communities brought prosperity—and not a little envy from the Quakers who had sponsored them. Moreover, the first waves of the so-called Scots-Irish had in 1717 begun pushing on to the westernmost frontier. The colony was rapidly becoming three separate communities that the Quaker elite in Philadelphia could no longer rule the way the Puritan elders still influenced life in the Massachusetts Bay Colony.[2]

Yet there was another reason Pennsylvania was becoming more volatile politically than Massachusetts. In the Bay Colony, heirs of the Puritan founders conceived of liberty as their freedom to create an ordered society. In Pennsylvania, although William Penn and his Quaker brethren were just as pious, they let other people find their own way; liberty in that colony became very much an individual thing. Too much so, it seemed, to visitors from abroad. A clergyman from London observed, "The poorest laborer upon the shores of the Delaware thinks himself entitled to deliver his sentiments in matters of religion, or politics with as much freedom as the gentleman or scholar."[3] Another reported, "A saying here: Pennsylvania is heaven for farmers, paradise for artisans, and hell for officials and preachers."[4]

Nevertheless, Philadelphia was thriving—on its way to outstripping Boston as the largest city in the colonies—and it seemed a good time to start a store. The young clerk and the older, wiser

Denham had formed a strong bond. Benjamin loved the kindly Quaker with the same affection he held for his father. In February 1727, however, Benjamin was struck down with pleurisy, a painful infection of the membranes that cover the lungs, and he came close to death. In fact, he recorded in his memoirs that he had given up hope "and was rather disappointed when I found myself recovering, regretting in some degree that I must now sometime or other have all that disagreeable Work to do over again."[5] Then, as he was on the mend, Denham fell seriously ill and eventually died. Before his death he freed Benjamin of his outstanding debts, but when Denham's trustees took over the store, the youth was out of work and without prospects.

By Franklin's account, he was "tempted" back to work for Samuel Keimer, who wanted him to manage his now larger print shop and to train five apprentices. Benjamin suspected that even though he was being offered "large wages," he would be fired as soon as he brought the apprentices up to the skill level of journeymen. Then the five would still be bound to Keimer by their articles of indenture.

His dislike for Keimer grew, and he later described his former friend as "an odd Fish, ignorant of common Life, fond of rudely opposing receiv'd Opinions, slovenly to extreme dirtiness, enthusiastic in some Points of Religion, and a little Knavish withal."[6] Considering that Benjamin had left Keimer in the lurch once already, and soon would do so again, one gets from this rather harsh judgment some insight into how coolly he could cut people adrift when he no longer respected, or had use for, them. Indeed, from the brief descriptions of Keimer, one suspects Franklin saw in him a type of personality that he himself might become if he were not careful. Back in London, Keimer had been a devotee of some of the more outlandish religious sects of the day and had been jailed often for printing seditious articles, as well as for debt. In Philadelphia his taste for annoying the general public continued even when a particular cause (he was an early antislavery writer) was justified. Benjamin was offended at Keimer's grubby personal habits and embarrassed at their public debaucheries in the past.

Keimer for his part resented that Benjamin was clearly a better craftsman and undeniably more intelligent. They quarreled often, and in October 1727 Franklin quit after a shouting match. That night one of the apprentices, a thirty-year-old ex-farmer named Hugh Meredith, visited Franklin in his rooms and urged him to patch things up with Keimer. Their employer was such a poor printer and bad businessman that he must fail, Meredith argued. The way would then be clear for the two of them to move into the vacancy. Meredith's father approved of Benjamin because the young man had curbed Hugh's drinking, so he pledged the money to purchase a new press and an inventory of type from London. By the spring of 1728, when the press arrived and Meredith's indenture to Keimer expired, they could make their move.

In the meantime, Benjamin had to make peace with Keimer. With Meredith as the intermediary, he got his old job back; quite satisfying to Benjamin, Keimer welcomed his return. The printer had just won a profitable contract to print a currency issue for New Jersey, which meant starting a press in Burlington and working closely with the colony's officials. Keimer knew he could not do the job himself and feared losing the contract to Andrew Bradford. Benjamin, however, had the skill to carry it off; indeed, he made one of the earliest copperplate engravings in America for the new money.[7] He also made a host of new friends among the New Jersey officials, much to Keimer's chagrin.

When the two returned to Philadelphia in May 1728, the new partnership's press had arrived, and Franklin and Meredith promptly quit. They rented a house at what is now 139 Market

Street and took in Thomas Godfrey and his wife to help defray the rent. Godfrey was a glazer, an almanac author, and a self-taught mathematician. Not surprisingly, Keimer was furious, and when he learned that the two planned a newspaper to rival Andrew Bradford's *American Mercury,* he quickly introduced a weekly of his own.

AS BUSY AS HE MUST HAVE BEEN, Benjamin's soul-searching continued. In the autumn of 1727, he had organized a self-improvement and conversation club called the Junto. The twelve-member club met every Friday night, and its founding members are interesting not only for who they were but also for what they became. In addition to Hugh Meredith and tenant Thomas Godfrey, charter members included two other printers, a shoemaker, a customs collector, a merchant's clerk, and one gentleman of independent means. All loved literature and poetry, and all were bound by a desire to better themselves in life and to do good in their community. The clerk, William Coleman, became a rich merchant and finally a Supreme Court justice. Two others advanced to become customs officials, and the gentleman, Robert Grace, prospered with an iron furnace he had inherited. Coleman and Grace remained devoted to the Junto's moving spirit, Benjamin Franklin.

Franklin owed the Junto's form and focus to that important figure in his Boston upbringing, Cotton Mather. The cleric had organized neighborhood benevolent societies based around each church there. As with Mather's design, Benjamin devised a list of twenty-four questions that was read to open each meeting. At Junto meetings, however, there were suitable pauses so the members could refresh themselves at the punch bowl. The questions, in effect, brought order to the conversation. Members were asked if they had read anything remarkable lately. Had anyone failed in business or, for that matter, prospered remarkably? Had anyone they knew become a drunkard, taken ill, or had an accident? Was some noteworthy new arrival in town? Was there a deserving young person who needed help? In addition, members were routinely required to create a poem, an essay, or some question of morality or judgment that would improve the participants. Philadelphia, like London, was replete with other clubs—for established merchants, for craftsmen of certain skills, even for the naughty playboys of the town. But the Junto would outlast them all and form the base of Benjamin's friends for the next thirty years until he sailed away for London a second time.

During this time Benjamin wrote two items that provide a window into his search for a personal (and a public) virtue. He wrote and printed his epitaph, perhaps stemming out of his near fatal bout of pleurisy. It is a sweetly written thing and may be the most famous in America.* He also made another attempt to codify a system of personal belief and worship that became his *Articles of Belief and Acts of Religion*.[8] Like William Wollaston, Benjamin acknowledged "one Supreme and most perfect Being, Author and Father of the Gods themselves." To Franklin, the one Supreme Being that overarched mankind's universe was a distant and ultimately unknowable force, but there were lesser gods closer at hand. They could take many forms and be the focus of divine worship for many people scattered all over the world. Importantly, this

---

* The epitaph reads:
  The Body of
  B. Franklin, Printer
  (Like the Cover of an old Book
  Its contents torn out
  And stript of its Lettering & Gilding)
  Lies here, Food for Worms.
  But the Work shall not be lost;
  For it will (as he Believ'd) appear once more,
  In a new and more elegant Edition
  Revised and corrected,
  By the Author.

constellation could intercede with the One God on behalf of the worshiper.

Franklin steadfastly refused to accept most of the doctrinal mysteries of established Christianity, including the divinity of Jesus. Along with Buddha, Mohammed, and other religious figureheads, Jesus was relegated to being an admirable exemplar and teacher, and an intercessor with Divine Providence—but no more.

One must recall that Franklin was a child of the skeptical Enlightenment. He would not believe what he could not prove by reason. Yet he recognized the universal need to believe in something beyond mortal existence. The stark emptiness of atheism and the mechanistic deism attracted only a glance from him. So he built a faith that would bear the weight of an intense double desire. He sought a public and private virtue that was practical and stood the tests of reason while being tolerant of the faith of others. He also had a deep need to believe in a force greater than himself if only to validate (and reward?) his struggles to be a better man. Throughout his life he referred to the great force of Providence and to his multiple gods—sometimes ending his letters to French friends in the plural "A Dieux."

That he should disdain churchly religion is understandable given the turbulent times. Established churches in most countries wielded far more active political power than they do today, and much of that power was seen to be for the clergy's benefit, not for mankind's. Franklin's family's resistance to England's church authority was part of his inheritance. He had witnessed the cruelties of the pious Puritans in Boston, and even in tolerant Philadelphia he found most clergymen interested more in their own positions than in the souls of their parishioners. He would finally stop attending the local Presbyterian church when the minister preached only on the outward signs of public piety, his sermons' "aim seeming to be rather to make us Presbyterians than good Citizens."9

The prayer he directed to his Supreme Being sought all the same virtues and improvements that he sought in his sea journal—he wanted to be more generous, more honest, more helpful, a better citizen and subject, and less a prisoner of his passions, his anger, and his greed. He wanted serenity, but most of all he wanted virtue. Seeing how popular the Junto had become among the young craftsmen of the city, he helped organize others and even dreamed of a worldwide union of virtue. Something of this dream would stay with him always.

Virtue was not an abstract concept to Franklin. Not only was it the surest way to personal advancement, but also it seemed the only way to propitiate his God. This Supreme Being was not so aloof as Benjamin had portrayed Him in his childish pamphlet on free will, but Franklin had grave doubts whether his God could take heartfelt prayers and religious incantations seriously without some proof of a man's good works to back them up.

Franklin was sincerely in awe of his God, in part because of His unknowable distance from man. In his *Articles,* he describes his innermost feelings:

When I stretch my Imagination thro' and beyond our System of Planets, beyond the visible fix'd Stars themselves, into that Space that is every Way infinite, and conceive it fill'd with Suns like ours, each with a Chorus of Worlds for ever moving round him, then this little Ball on which we move, seems, even in my narrow Imagination, to be almost Nothing, and my self less than nothing, and of no sort of Consequence.

When I think thus, I imagine it great Vanity in me to suppose that the *Supremely Perfect* does in the least regard such an inconsiderable Nothing as Man. More especially, since it is impossible for me to have any positive clear idea of that which is infinite and incomprehensible, I cannot conceive otherwise, than that He, *the Infinite Father*, expects or requires no Worship or Praise from us, but that he is even INFINITELY ABOVE IT.[10]

Yet Franklin devised not only his own private liturgy of prayers and praise but also a detailed system of personal perfection that required daily exercise and a weekly accounting of his progress. He came up with a list of thirteen virtues that he would strive to acquire through attention and habit.* In a small notebook he carried with him all his life, Franklin headed his list of virtues with lines from Addison's play *Cato*:

---

* Franklin laid out the virtues as follows:
  1. Temperance.
     Eat not to Dulness. Drink not to Elevation.
  2. Silence.
     Speak not but what may benefit others or your self. Avoid trifling Conversation.
  3. Order.
     Let all your Things have their Places. Let each Part of your Business have its Time.
  4. Resolution.
     Resolve to perform what you ought. Perform without fail what you resolve.
  5. Frugality.
     Make no Expense but to do good to others or yourself; i.e. Waste nothing.
  6. Industry.
     Lose no Time. Be always employ'd in something useful. Cut off all unnecessary Actions.
  7. Sincerity.
     Use no hurtful Deceit. Think innocently and justly; and if you speak, speak accordingly.
  8. Justice.
     Wrong none by doing Injuries or omitting the Benefits that are your Duty.
  9. Moderation.
     Avoid Extremes. Forbear resenting Injuries so much as you think they deserve.
  10. Cleanliness.
     Tolerate no Uncleanness in Body, Clothes or Habitation.
  11. Tranquility.
     Be not disturbed at Trifles, or at Accidents common or unavoidable.
  12. Chastity.
     Rarely use Venery but for Health or Offspring, Never to Dulness, Weakness, or the Injury of your own or another's Peace or Reputation.
  13. Humility.
     Imitate Jesus and Socrates.

Here will I hold: If there is a Pow'r above us,
(And that there is, all Nature cries aloud
Thro' all her Works) he must delight in Virtue.
And that which he delights in must be happy.[11]

The notebook was arranged so Franklin could concentrate on perfecting one of the virtues during a week's strict observance. On a grid, he drew daily lines for each of the thirteen virtues and marked at the end of each day when he had violated any one of them, the aim being to keep that week's targeted virtue spotless. The next week he moved on to another virtue's perfection so that at the end of thirteen weeks he had completed the list, thus committing four quarterly attempts at perfecting himself. He grew so fond of the method he shifted to a book with ivory pages with grid marks in red ink and penciled dots for each imperfection, so the slate could be wiped clean at the end of each exercise. He later had one made for grandson William Temple Franklin.[12]

The virtues he strove for and their order of importance are mainly about Franklin's efforts to control his own appetites. Although not much of a drinker, he found that the ever present punch bowl at the Junto and other night gatherings was becoming too attractive to him. He disliked the way drink clouded his judgment and made him a silly joker and pun maker among his friends. He wanted to work more productively and pay off his debts so that he would have more free time for learning languages and working on a multitude of projects. He also worried about his hot temper and sought a more tranquil life. Interestingly, control over his sexual appetite was one of the less important virtues he sought; indeed, in the original notebook there were but twelve traits listed, and chastity was last. He added the need to become more humble on the advice of an elderly Quaker, and here he looked to both Jesus and Socrates as men to emulate rather than as divinely inspired objects of reverence. His perceived need to be more humble led him to appear in the streets near his shop clad in his shirtsleeves and leather apron as he trundled a wheelbarrow load of newsprint back to the print shop; he could be proud of such humility.

Beyond this struggle to create a better Franklin, however, his life-long search for a religious doctrine was rooted in a dichotomy: all mankind had the need to worship God, but God by his nature was so far away as to be unreachable. So his search basically was an effort to get closer to the Supreme Being he knew was out there in the cosmos. This conviction drove him through a series of experiments as revolutionary as anything he undertook in the natural sciences. It would prove one of his lifelong quests.

FRANKLIN MUST HAVE KEENLY FELT THE NEED to get more control over his life at this time. He and Meredith were struggling to make their print shop a success. Cash was scarce, and they resorted to barter to get jobs—taking venison, sail cloth, and even privately issued currencies of leading merchants (which they had printed). Moreover, to hasten the collapse of Keimer's newspaper into the partners' hands, Benjamin and another Junto member began to write popular satires under the byline of "Busy Body" for Andrew Bradford's *American Mercury*, often lampooning the sloppy printing of their former employer. Also, in his spare hours, Benjamin began studying German with an eye to launching a newspaper for that now prospering readership.

During 1729, Benjamin's friends rallied often to help him along. Andrew Hamilton remained grateful to Benjamin for his help in London five years earlier. The famous lawyer* had become Speaker

---

* Hamilton won lasting fame in 1735 for winning acquittal of printer John Peter Zenger on libel charges. The New York case set a precedent for press freedom in the colonies.

of the General Assembly and had pushed through a series of currency issue bills designed to revive the provincial economy. The first order went to Bradford, but Franklin and Meredith were given a contract to print money for Delaware and then a second issue of Pennsylvania money. Bradford's currency issues and assembly documents had long been criticized for their typographical errors and muddy printing. Soon after he became Speaker, Hamilton made his young protégé the official printer for the Assembly.

In the meantime, Keimer had come to his predicted sad end; before leaving Philadelphia, he sold his newspaper—with the unwieldy title of *The Universal Instructor in All Arts and Sciences: and Pennsylvania Gazette*—to his former underlings. Franklin cut the title down to the *Pennsylvania Gazette*, then dropped the long articles and excerpts from London novels and concentrated on news that was important to his provincial readers. Franklin did almost everything himself. He wrote articles about local events, rewrote news from abroad, penned humorous fillers, faked letters to the editor, and created witty replies. Not only was it the better looking of the two Philadelphia newspapers, but also he was clearly the better writer.

As 1729 became 1730, Benjamin ran a newspaper, a busy contract printing shop, and a small store that sold stationery, business and legal forms, and religious books. The *Gazette* was growing in importance, and Benjamin became cautious about lampooning public officials now that he was one himself. The only controversy he engaged in occurred when smallpox ravaged Philadelphia—this time he favored inoculation.

In July 1730, however, Meredith confessed that he wanted out of the printing business and to return to farming. Worse, his father had been unable to come up with the second half of the money due the merchant who had imported the press. Faced with bankruptcy, Franklin received help from two Junto friends, Coleman and

Grace, who paid off the partnership's debts, and he was able to let Meredith go.

NOW ESTABLISHED IN A BUSINESS HE KNEW would prosper, Benjamin had one final item in his search for serenity and virtue—marriage. His decision to marry was prompted by more than a desire to settle down. As well as can be deduced by traditional Franklin scholars, he fathered an illegitimate son, named William, in early 1730. The mother remains unknown.* When the Godfreys tried to match him up with a relative, he demurred. Upset, they moved out and took their almanac to Andrew Bradford. Franklin recorded one of those candid admissions that many find titillating:

> But this Affair having turn'd my Thoughts to Marriage, I look'd around me, and made Overtures of Acquaintance in other Places, but soon found that the Business of a Printer being generally thought a poor one, I was not to expect Money with a Wife unless with such a one as I should not otherwise think agreeable. In the mean time, that hard-to-be governed Passion of Youth had hurried me frequently into Intrigues with low Women that fell in my Way, which were attended with some Expense and great Inconvenience, besides a continual Risk to my Health by a Distemper which of all Things I dreaded, tho' by great good Luck I escaped it.[13]

---

* Some historians have speculated that Deborah Read Rogers was William's mother, others that the mother was a serving girl in the Franklin home named Barbara. *The Papers of Benjamin Franklin* (Vol. 2, 370–71) records a 1763 letter from a Franklin friend to a Quaker in London that referred to William, then royal governor of New Jersey: "In answer to your hint relative to a certain Gentleman now acting in a public Station, 'tis generally known here his birth is illegitimate and his Mother not in good Circumstances, but the report of her begging Bread in the Streets of this City is without the least foundation in Truth. I understand some small Provision is made by him for her, but her being none of the most agreeable Women prevents particular Notice being shown, or the Father and Son acknowledging any Connection with her."

Indeed it was good luck, for the threat of venereal disease was as frightening as any of the other plagues visited on eighteenth-century society; Samuel Pepys's *Diary* and James Boswell's *London Journal* offer stark proof of that. And on the larger issue of marriage, Benjamin's frank assessment was just as accurate: a marriage into a family that would provide him with a rich dowry was beyond his reach, and those women he could marry, he disdained.

He settled on Deborah Read Rogers, who had sought refuge in her mother's house after her probably bigamous husband had run off. Benjamin felt an awkward guilt about his overlong stay in London, but both mother and daughter welcomed him. Before long, "our mutual Affection was revived," he wrote. Deborah was a buxom girl of middle height with curly red-gold hair. She had a fair complexion and blushed high on her cheeks. Her pale blue eyes could twinkle with laughter or turn hard when she was annoyed. She could be tart but was proud to be Benjamin's wife.

A proper church wedding was out of the question since it was impossible to prove either that Mr. Rogers had already been married or, as was rumored, that he had died in a brawl in the West Indies. The penalties for a bigamous formal marriage were stringent to the extreme; both parties could be publicly whipped and then sentenced to hard labor for life. And even if Deborah was legally a widow, there was a possible legal liability for Rogers's debts that Benjamin could scarcely afford. So on September 1, 1730, they made a public declaration of marriage under common law, and she moved into the Market Street house and print shop.

"Thus I corrected that great Erratum as well as I could," Benjamin declared somewhat complacently.

Deborah Read Franklin, a ready match for her energetic husband.

Chapter 4

Rising Citizen

A common literary device is for the hero to have a nemesis. This opponent not only obstructs the hero's quest but also forces him to change his character if he is to triumph. In Thomas Penn, one of the new proprietors of the Pennsylvania colony, Benjamin Franklin faced a classic nemesis.

In 1731, as Benjamin and Deborah Franklin were settling into married life at 139 Market Street, Penn arrived in Philadelphia from London to get his hands on as much of the province as he possibly could. For the next forty years Penn would haunt Franklin's progress through life, sneering at his accomplishments and trying to checkmate his ambitions for Pennsylvania and himself. In that year of 1731, Thomas was twenty-nine years old to Franklin's twenty-five. Where Franklin had deep pride, Penn was

⌐un. Where Franklin sought ways to make more money, Penn looked for ways to take it.

Thomas was a sour personality, an unhappy mixture of suspicion, insecurity, and pettiness. In an age when eldest sons usually took all of an estate, he labored under a double handicap: he was the second son of the second marriage of William Penn, the colony's founder. Like Franklin, Thomas had known poverty and the ignominy of having to labor in a serving-class position in his youth. A combination of debts and radical political statements kept his father either in prison or on the run from it for much of Thomas's youth, and, as a result, his mother, Hannah, had to set him up as a merchant's clerk in London. Moreover, Hannah was a rigorous Quaker who forced on the boy virtues of meekness and self-sacrifice that went against his nature. Thomas probably had tastes as much in common with his free-spending grandfather, Admiral William Penn (for whom the colony was named), as with his father, who alternated between pious mysticism and luxurious attendance on the court of King Charles II.

Thomas and his brothers, John and Richard, inherited their father's appetites but not his virtues. When in residence at Pennsbury, his huge estate outside Philadelphia, William Penn lived in such opulence (including owning slaves) that others in the Friends community were scandalized. He had vast estates in Ireland and England as well as a tangle of debts and uncertainties over land titles he had purchased from the indigenous Delaware and Seneca tribes. William further complicated matters with a confusing will that left Pennsylvania up for grabs among his heirs. From William's death in 1718 a series of lawsuits dragged through the agonizingly slow English chancery courts until 1731, when the younger sons prevailed over the older heirs from William's first marriage. In the meantime, Thomas and his siblings spent as if the province were already in their hands; they were one step ahead of debtor's prison, with more than £8,000 in overdue loans and thousands more in debts when the matter was finally resolved. In late 1731, Thomas journeyed to Philadelphia to seize control of the proprietary land office and scoop up as much money as he could. It is here that he came under the watchful gaze of Benjamin Franklin, printer to the General Assembly and young man on the make.

FRANKLIN WOULD HAVE BEEN ONE OF THE FIRST Philadelphians to come to the imperious Penn's notice. The *Pennsylvania Gazette* was the best written and most popular of the eight weekly newspapers that regularly circulated in the colonies. In contrast to brother James's paper in Boston (his *Rhode Island Gazette* would begin in 1732), Franklin's weekly carried lots of news and information and was light on political criticism, at least at the start. An important attraction was the stream of satires and humorous sketches that enlivened the paper, but so too were the tables of economic statistics charting shipping, births, deaths, manufacturing, and agriculture from all the colonies. The paper soon became a must-read for anyone with a stake in North America, Thomas Penn included.

Andrew Bradford's rival paper, the *American Mercury*, fell into such disfavor that he was forced to appeal to subscribers in arrears, "especially those who have left off taking this Paper and gone to others."[1] Since Bradford also was the regional postmaster for Philadelphia, he banned his post riders from carrying the *Gazette* to other towns; Franklin merely bribed the riders until he could appeal to Postmaster General Alexander Spotswood in Virginia for a direct order to Bradford to end the embargo.

At the same time, the *Gazette* and his other printing ventures were quickly putting Franklin on the road to prosperity. The newspaper brought sales and advertising income, and from his work as official printer for the General Assembly alone, he could count on as much as £200 a year. In addition, his print shop was publishing a growing inventory of books and pamphlets on religious and historical topics; his shop offered no less than three almanacs, including his own, *Poor Richard's Almanack*, which he would begin publishing in 1733. As Poor Richard Saunders (a fictional persona), Franklin offered readers agricultural advice and a guide to the weather, and he also included humorous burlesques and salty aphorisms.* The booklet became famous throughout the colonies, reaching a circulation of some ten thousand.

All of this meant a rising level of comfort for Benjamin and Deborah Franklin in their new home. It certainly meant the house would have plenty of servants—a good thing, for in 1732 Deborah delivered Francis Folger Franklin, Benjamin's second son. She had grudgingly taken William to raise and, at midyear, had to make room for her mother, who took over the shop vacated by the Godfreys to sell her brand of healing salves. By 1734, business was so good that Franklin was able to combine several lots and build a new house for the family at 318 Market Street.

The only existing portrait of Deborah Franklin shows a woman who would have been a ready match for her energetic husband. She is shown as a sturdy personality with a confident and fearless gaze. One had to be fearless if one was a woman in the eighteenth century. If the threats of ordinary life did not carry a woman away early, childbirth certainly shortened the odds.

A genuine bond existed between the Franklins, although "romance" might not be the word that best describes it. Affection,

---

* Among the many aphorisms he wrote over the course of more than two decades were: "Keep thy Shop, and thy Shop will keep thee" (June 1735); "Wealth is not his that has it, but his that enjoys it" (March 1736); "I never saw an oft transplanted Tree, nor yet an oft removed Family, that throve so well as those settled be" (August 1737); "Experience keeps a dear School, but Fools will learn in no other, and scarce at that" (December 1743); "For want of a Nail the Shoe was lost; for want of a Shoe the Horse was lost; for want of the Horse the Rider was lost" (February 1752); "The Borrower is the Slave to the Lender, and the Debtor to the Creditor" (October 1757).

comfort, perhaps utility—any of these words might more aptly characterize their relationship. He quickly became her "Pappy," and she his "Debby." He doted on baby Franky as devotedly as he spoiled young William. And although he had roamed far and wide as a young bachelor, he stayed close to home at Market Street. There he found he had not only a wife but also a shrewd business partner and adviser. Deborah had an already established status in Philadelphia and her own circle of friends before Benjamin set foot in the town. But she must have seen some promise in that young man she had laughed at so heartily. Throughout her life she was proud to be Franklin's wife.

Some have dismissed or felt sorry for Deborah, but in fact both Franklins gained something valuable by their union. First of all, by marrying her, Benjamin had restored the most precious possession for a woman of that time—her good name. Once John Rogers had run away, Deborah had been left, as one historian has noted, "neither maid, wife nor widow."[2] Marriage under common law did not merely mean the couple was cohabiting. This kind of union was a legal provision as old as England itself and is still recognized in many states today. It meant that Benjamin and Deborah Franklin held themselves publicly to be man and wife, and that declaration not only secured property interests but also brought a measure of respectability. Among other things, the common-law marriage enabled Franklin to purchase pew seats for Deborah at Christ Church, the Anglican house of worship. Franklin himself preferred the more utilitarian preaching of the Presbyterian church when he bothered to go, but Christ Church was where their children were baptized and where he and his family would be buried.

Deborah was more than Franklin's housekeeper, although that would have been a full-time job at a time when a home entailed an endless round of hewing wood, drawing water, preparing meals over an open fire, and cleaning everything from bed linens to chamber pots. She also found herself tending to the printing house shop, where the inventory steadily built from a handful of books and pamphlets to a bewildering variety of inks, paper, silver, buttons, wax, cloth, and patent medicines. She also took over the bookkeeping for the shop, and here one can get a glimpse of a strong character, limited by the poor education most women received in that day, but fiercely proud nonetheless. In one ledger item her temper comes through clearly; it is in her unmistakable hand, but she writes in the person of her husband. She had not recorded a customer's purchase and had forgotten the amount, to Franklin's evident annoyance. She wrote:

> William Saterthwit Dr [debtor] for a Latin Gramer, 3 [shillings] 6 [pence]; a testament, 2.3; a Box of wafers, 0.4; a Quier of paper that my Carles Wife forgot to set down and now the Carles thing donte now [know] the prise sow I must truste to you.[3]

ALTHOUGH THEY CHAFED EACH OTHER as most couples do, Deborah became the anchor of Franklin's domestic life at the Market Street house. If she was never completely happy, it was largely due to the fact that her husband's public life began to take him away where she could not follow. Franklin had a habit of putting parts of his life into separate boxes, which cut Deborah out of much that was important to her husband. They did little entertaining at home in the beginning, and only a few of his most intimate friends ever called on him. As a rising citizen, Franklin often received invitations from the town's wealthier homes, but Deborah herself was excluded. These Philadelphians were punctilious about respectability, the Quaker merchant elite with their ostentatious simplicity even more so. So Deborah stayed home when Franklin went out.

Franklin was a joiner as much as he was an organizer. In that year of 1731, he was the moving force behind (although not the first to propose) a circulating library, the first in the colonies and one that still operates. His Library Company started as a subscription lending club but soon allowed any person of gentility to borrow from its growing stock of improving books and pamphlets. To augment the fledgling library's collection, Franklin sent off to London for books and magazines; Franklin's good friend Peter Collinson, a well-respected naturalist and a fellow of Britain's famed Royal Society, shipped the requested materials off to Philadelphia.

The Library Company is one of the best-known early examples of Franklin's emerging style of getting something done. Rather than leap out in front of an idea as its sponsor, he would prompt others to take the public lead. As the idea gained momentum, he trailed along in its wake, nudging it along here and there. He contributed the essential ingredients of intense energy and skillful organization. Inevitably, Franklin would get the credit and recognition he deserved if the scheme succeeded, as with the library club. But when a scheme foundered, as it did when he tried to get the city to move the pestilential and polluting tannery yards out of town, none of the blamed fixed to him. Thus begins the myth of Franklin the devious. Rather than being disingenuous, however, Franklin early on recognized that communities quickly tired of improving gadflies. The idea, not the sponsor, should be the point—though, it must be said, he was not above using projects like the Library Company for personal advancement.

Franklin's projects also brought him in closer contact with Thomas Penn and his older brother John. Benjamin sought advice on the Library Company's first purchases from James Logan, who had been William Penn's steward and was acting governor of the colony. The older man had a large library of his own and was happy to advise Franklin, whom he recognized as a comer. Wisely, he suggested that the Library Company write a polite request to Thomas Penn asking for his blessing and patronage. Flattered, the proprietor responded, and both John and Thomas were regular guests at Library Company banquets and other social events at which Franklin was chairman. On his return to London in the 1740s, John Penn sent the library a scientific instrument of some interest, an air pump still on display at the Library Company's home in Philadelphia. For his part, although he disdained such public luxuries, Thomas gave the Library Company a lot on which to build a new home for its growing book collection. Thomas even did business directly with Franklin, ordering the design of a rather ornate bookplate for his own growing library. It is not recorded that he paid for it.

Franklin also was quick to join the St. John's Lodge of the Masons, which had been founded two years earlier. Freemasonry had emerged from dormancy in the previous century and was sweeping through Europe and England in the early decades of the 1700s. The movement meant different things in each country, but in the American colonies it was fundamentally a gathering of Protestant (but rarely Quaker) laymen who believed not just in self-advancement but also in promoting the moral uplift of the larger community. To be a Mason was to have a public identity as a member of the establishment; it meant one had friends who would help in time of need. Membership also brought a Mason a more public presence; the order held elaborate public processions and social functions and often appeared in full regalia at such events as the dedication of the new State House (now Independence Hall), which served as the General Assembly meetinghouse.

Now, his nighttime activities were far different from his youthful consorting with "low women." The first Monday of each month was taken up with Masonic affairs, while the Library Company met on the second Monday. From 1736 onward, the last Monday of each month was given to meetings of the Union Fire Company, the first cooperative fire-fighting force in the colonies. Each Friday evening was devoted to his meetings of the Junto. While Junto members changed as their circumstances did, the group remained for more than thirty years a vehicle for Franklin's friends to improve their minds and perfect their morals.

The rest of his weekday nights were taken up with the cut and thrust of provincial politics. As official printer, Franklin had to be on call whenever the Assembly was in session, and he frequently attended the informal meetings in the evenings. After 1736, the same year he organized the fire company, his old patron Andrew Hamilton, now the Assembly Speaker, secured him the post of clerk to the legislative body. This meant that he had to keep meticulous records of each debate and vote and that he was privy to the private arguments and brokered compromises. Even though newspapers of the day could not quote debates verbatim, his new post made the *Gazette* an unofficial journal of record.

As he rose, his radical political views and skepticism became more apparent. Franklin wanted to be part of the province's establishment, but he could not yet control his tongue or his pen when he was provoked. Part of the problem was that he could not resist using the *Gazette* to antagonize rival Andrew Bradford, who regularly sided with both the Quaker political elite and the local Church of England powers. Complaints of impiety were regularly lodged against the *Gazette* for Franklin's satires of some pompous sermon or foolish ruling. Once more he took part in the hot debate over inoculation for smallpox, again urging the preventive measure. Sadly, four-year-old Franky died in one of the recurring plagues of the disease, and Franklin's enemies whispered that the boy had died after being inoculated. Benjamin had to go into print to announce that, in fact, he had failed to inoculate his son but was now about to have his entire household treated against the disease.

Increasingly, Franklin was drawn into the contest between the Assembly, eager to retain its substantial control over provincial affairs, and the Penns, who wanted the colony back in their grip. James Logan, in a fight with the Penn brothers for control of the province's land office, was removed as acting governor and replaced with a more pliant Penn appointee. The brothers required this governor, Thomas Gordon—like all the men who succeeded him—to post a substantial cash bond, which he would forfeit if he did not act as they directed. Moreover, Gordon, and all subsequent governors, had to kick back a substantial portion of the revenue from the various tavern and excise taxes. In truth, however, the governor was a prisoner of two camps: as was the custom in the colonies, the Assembly paid the governor's base salary.

Even after being removed as governor, Logan tried to save his influence over the land office (and his income) by doing what the Penns wanted. He squeezed the arrears due from those who had already bought land; so-called quit-rents, a feudal relic, required property owners to pay a fixed sum to the proprietor each year in lieu of building public works such as roads and bridges. The Penn brothers demanded that all quit-rents be paid in sterling at £10 per one hundred acres instead of £10 Pennsylvania money. This effectively doubled the tax, since sterling was hard to obtain, and it also sharply devalued the province's paper money and thereby threw the economy into turmoil. Worse, the Penns began a campaign in London to have Parliament restrict the Pennsylvania Assembly's power to issue any more money. The Assembly leaders sent a series of agents to lobby for their cause, but unfortunately they did not always choose representatives wisely: during his nine years in the post, lawyer Ferdinand Paris secretly represented the proprietary side.[4]

At the same time, Logan moved to get more land from local Delaware tribal chiefs. In appeasing the Penn brothers, Logan was violating the tradition established by the colony's founder. During his life, William Penn was much revered by the Indians. Although under English law he had no obligation to pay them for the land the British Crown had granted him, he gave the Delawares what seemed to them fair prices for their hunting lands. Further, he promised the tribes that additional land would not be taken unless they willingly sold title. In 1686, the two sides had held talks for a new land purchase, but nothing was final when Penn fell ill in 1712 or when he died six years later.

In order to weaken the power of the Delaware chiefs to resist a land grab, Logan invited leaders of the powerful Iroquois Confederation to come south from New York and impose their rule on the Indians who roamed the heartland of Maryland and Pennsylvania. As part of the deal, the Iroquois chiefs signed off on any future acquisition of property that the Logan-Penn interests wanted.

The local Indians did not quickly grasp what was happening to them. The six tribal nations that had banded together in the Iroquois Confederation formed a sophisticated political unit—and a threatening force of warriors—that made them the most powerful Native American counterweight to the ambitions of both France and Britain.* And, as Penn and Logan knew, when Iroquois tribes had come south in 1720, those Delaware tribes that had not been forced westward had been squeezed into the Wyoming Valley on the Susquehanna River, land so rich that speculators from as far away as Connecticut had made scouting trips. Now the local chiefs were, in effect, trapped, with the settlers to the east, the Iroquois moving down from the north, and the Shawnee tribes in the Ohio Valley to the west. The Delaware tribes could give way and lose land or fight and probably lose even more.

---

* The original five-nation confederacy (c. 1570) included the Mohawk, Oneida, Onondaga, Cayuga, and Seneca tribes. The Tuscaroras joined in 1720, by which time the league numbered about twenty thousand. The Iroquois were adroit at playing one provincial governor off against others, so much so that London early on had appointed a royal commissioner who had overriding power to negotiate treaties, provide gifts, and bargain for scouts and braves to use against the French.

Soon after Thomas Penn arrived in America, the proprietors began negotiating with the Delaware leaders. Rum, bribes, and threats were freely used. In 1735, negotiators dug up the preliminary draft of the 1686 land sale treaty and presented it to the Delawares as an existing contract that their elders had agreed on. The Indians agreed to the terms, which authorized the proprietors to purchase land beyond the present boundary as far as a man could walk in a day and a half. What the tribes did not know was that Penn and Logan had well beforehand surveyed the quickest route, cleared a path, stocked provisions along the way, and hired a skilled team of athletes to do the walking. In the end the Penns staked out a 37,000-acre plot that took them to where the Lehigh River joins the headwaters of the Delaware River. When the Penns offered £2 per acre, just one-fifth of what some settlers were willing to pay, the chiefs balked and were able to get a little more. But the tribal leaders never knew that the Penns had presold huge portions of the land to leading Quaker officials in Philadelphia and London; the brothers were not even spending their own money.[5]

First as official printer to the Assembly, and then also as clerk, Franklin was in a position to learn who was being paid off in these deals and just how rapacious the Penns were. Yet he had little sympathy for the Indians at this time, so he kept silent. In his view, those tribes that were peaceful were welcome to stay and should be treated decently, but basically Indians were a threat to safety and an impediment to the rightful expanding of English needs.

On other matters, however, he was not so reticent about opposing the proprietors. One of Franklin's earliest essays in the *Gazette* called for a regular program of issuing paper currency within the colony so that merchants and farmers had better access to capital for expansion and trade. He also decried plans in England's Parliament for what would become the Molasses Act of 1733, which sharply disadvantaged colonial rum makers for the benefit of the

British West Indian sugar producers. In later life, he pointed to this particular piece of legislation as the seed of the American Revolution, because the bill was the first to contain a blunt assertion of Parliament's power to levy taxes directly on all the colonies.

Most contentiously, Franklin's paper made common cause with Logan for a strong military response to French efforts to extend their territory below the Great Lakes into territory along the Ohio River, up to its headwaters in western Pennsylvania. Logan was a "defense Quaker"—that is, despite the pacifist beliefs of the Friends, he saw France's testing of the western borders as a clear danger. Pennsylvania was the only colony that did not have an established militia, and during Queen Anne's War* the merchants and settlers had been frightened by Indian raids in the west and French privateer attacks up the reaches of the Delaware River basin.

Yet the Quakers refused to countenance an armed force even for their own defense, taking the position that they had no personal quarrel with the Indians and should not be forced to go against their consciences because of wrongs done by others. The Penns, for once, agreed with the Quaker majority in the Assembly. They feared both the expense and the loss of political control over an armed and organized contingent of settlers. So, the episodes of raids and harassment continued at a distance, even through King George's War.†

By 1741, both brothers felt secure enough about the placemen they had installed to return home to London. It seemed they had not much to worry about from Benjamin Franklin; both of the printer's patrons, Andrew Hamilton and James Logan, were out of power. Hamilton died in 1741, and Logan's influence would dwindle until his own death ten years later. The Penns knew that Franklin had

---

* Better known as the War of the Spanish Succession (1702–13).
† The War of the Austrian Succession (1742–48).

steadfastly refused to seek any kind of elective office, and they wrongly deduced that he had no political ambitions.

They misread so much—the character of this quiet, self-effacing man; the raw power of his printing press to advocate ideas; the masterly skill of his pen to present those ideas convincingly. They still saw the rather rough tradesman who pushed his wheelbarrow of newsprint through the street. They did not see what Franklin had become: the well-dressed, confident man of affairs whose reach was beginning to extend beyond the town. He was now the official printer of the New Jersey colony and had a shop in Burlington. Moreover, he had sponsored partners in new printing works and newspapers in New York City and Charleston, South Carolina. The feud with brother James had been patched up, and they began to swap satires and essays between their two newspapers. When James died in 1735, Benjamin helped his widow keep the newspaper in operation and taught their son, Jimmy, the printer's trade.

FRANKLIN ENJOYED ANOTHER IMPORTANT ADVANCE before the Penns left for London that they should have taken note of. In 1737, Andrew Bradford's slipshod accounting practices and general sloth cost him the job of postmaster of the region. Franklin campaigned hard for the position and won. The job increased the reach of the *Gazette*, which was now carrying two full pages of advertisements and had a paid circulation of more than one thousand.

All of this made Franklin more scorned than respected in the eyes of Thomas Penn. The proprietor continued to dole out bits of patronage and recognition to the printer, but Franklin's insistence on challenging the Penns' authority drove them closer to open emnity.

Penn's functionaries in the land office were growing increasingly brutal in driving farmers off the land if their quit-rent payments were in arrears. Farmers and merchants alike viewed these demands as a cruel measure to soak up vital hard capital from the economy. Mobs demonstrated against the proprietors in Philadelphia that summer of 1741, and during one, just before Thomas sailed, he was most upset to see himself burned in effigy outside the State House. He was certain that Franklin had a hand in all this lawless rioting. Penn doubtless decided he would simply have to bribe this jumped-up printer a bit more. Franklin, for his part, likely concluded that things could get back to normal with the proprietors safely back in London. Both were wrong.

This Currier & Ives print has immortalized Franklin's kite experiment, in which he proved that lightning was an electrical charge.

Chapter 5

The Eminent Mr. Franklin

*I*t would be another sixteen years before Benjamin Franklin and Thomas Penn saw one another again in person, though their struggle was far from over. In the intervening years, much would change about the Pennsylvania that Penn left without regret in 1741. Franklin himself would change even more dramatically.

If anything, the pace of his energetic life became more frenetic. During his thirties and forties, Franklin's name became an analogy for busyness. Two of his best intellectual friends were John Bartram, a local botanist and America's first naturalist,* and Cadwallader

---

* John Bartram (1699–1777), a wealthy landowner, pioneered the first botanical garden in America and carried on a wide program of exchanging new plant species with the leading European botanists. He and his son William (1739–1823) predated Lewis and Clark and John James Audubon in their extensive exploration journeys from the Catskills to Florida. Their most celebrated discovery was a flowering shrub in Georgia that William named *Franklinia* in gratitude for Benjamin's fund-raising efforts in their behalf.

Colden, another wealthy devotee of natural science studies.* The two shared the same circle of London friends, but most of all they shared an admiration for Franklin, for his mind and for that engine of ambition that kept him constantly on the move. In a letter Bartram sent to Colden in 1744, he described how absorbed he was with his botanical garden in Darby, outside of Philadelphia: "I am full as much hurried in business as our friend Benjamin for I can hardly get any time to write but by candle light after a very hard days labour."[1]

It is difficult to take in just how busy Franklin could be. In a recent study of Attention Deficit Disorder (ADD), two medical scholars gave this qualified analysis:

> It is dangerous to diagnose the dead, but Benjamin Franklin, for example, seems like a man with a case of ADD. Creative, impulsive, inventive, attending to many projects at a time, drawn to high stimulation through wit, politics, diplomacy, literature, science, and romance, Franklin gives us ample ground to speculate that he may have had ADD and was the happier for it.[2]

Franklin certainly had all these characteristics, but his most important feature was an iron ability to control his burning energy and to focus his omnivorous curiosity on productive work.

By now the outline of the adult Franklin character was fairly clear. He kept his life in a series of compartments, each discrete and separate. We all do this to an extent. But in his case, Franklin had far more compartments than most people and could concentrate his attention precisely on whatever had his attention at the moment.

---

* Cadwallader Colden (1688–1776) was a wealthy colonial administrator, naturalist, and historian of the Iroquois Confederacy. He was the first American botanist to classify plants by the Linnaean system of taxonomy. He became a deputy governor of New York and broke off his friendship with Franklin because of the uproar over the Stamp Act.

He never bothered to become much of a public speaker; contemporaries remarked many times that he often fell silent during public arguments. But when alone with another, or with very close friends, he could, by focusing his full attention on his subject, be remarkably convincing. In politics, and later in diplomacy, he was, and would remain, a creature of the backroom negotiation. By instinct he shunned the limelight of public debate and the ornate oratory of the day. Always he was aware that others would hold his humble birth against him if he pushed himself forward too much.

To be sure, he was far from reticent in print, and through his love of hard study he found himself able to climb through his own merits, unhampered by his background. There was nothing he would not undertake if he could comprehend it. During the 1740s he learned German so he could publish a newspaper for the inland farm communities. German clerics preached against it, fearing the challenge of a Philadelphia newspaper, so Franklin folded it and began to translate French books and pamphlets for the *Gazette*'s readers. He learned enough Italian to later correspond with his widespread network of scientific friends there, and enough Greek and Latin to be able to lift whole passages of ancient wisdom for his use. He bought a farm in New Jersey with an eye to keeping Bartram and Colden company in their botany experiments but was too much of a town creature to stay away from Philadelphia for long.

His publishing business, the foundation of his growing fortune, made increasing demands on him. By the 1740s, he had expanded his publishing network to include a partner, James Parker, who ran print shops and newspapers in New York, Connecticut, and New Jersey. In 1743, his London-based friend William Strahan, one of that city's most prominent printers,* sent him an "obliging,

---

* Strahan won recognition for publishing the first edition of Samuel Johnson's famous dictionary of the English language and later printed the works of such writers as Pope, Swift, and, no surprise, Franklin. He also published an influential newspaper and several magazines.

discreet, industrious, and honest" David Hall, a Scot who had done his apprenticeship at the Watts print shop, Franklin's alma mater. By 1748, Hall was a full partner. In that year, Franklin handed control over to Hall in return for a share of profits that averaged £850 a year for eighteen years; this was separate from his various post office, real estate, and family-partnership ventures.

It was to James Parker that Franklin sent Benjamin Mecom, son of his beloved baby sister, Jane Franklin Mecom, as an apprentice printer. Later he set the young man up with a press in Barbados. After his brother James died, Franklin took in his late brother's son, Jimmy Franklin, as an apprentice. He endured the divine justice of watching Jimmy behave in the same surly and cheeky manner that young Benjamin had shown James years earlier. But having truly reconciled with his brother, he continued to help the widow, Ann Franklin, who was one of America's first female printers. Finally he sent Jimmy back to Newport with his old font of type and equipment enough to put them back into the newspaper business.

Also occupying his attention in these years were the scientific experiments for which he is still celebrated. This was an era, the Enlightenment, when the field was wide open for anyone to examine anything of interest. Merchants became avid botanists, sedate clerics scanned the stars at night, and everyone claimed the right to be a poet. In the forefront of this brawling exchange of ideas was a colonial printer named Benjamin Franklin.

FRANKLIN WAS VERY MUCH A PRODUCT OF the English Enlightenment. Whereas the French Enlightenment of Diderot, Voltaire, Montesquieu, and Rousseau had a philosophical and humanistic flavor and confined discourse within a relatively small elite, the English Enlightenment was a scrimmage in which anyone could play. One can get into a heated argument even today about when the English Enlightenment started—how deep its roots go in the

Protestant Reformation of the 1500s or the scientific revolutions of the 1600s. Yet as good a starting date as any might be January 30, 1649. On that cold, foggy day, King Charles I was hoisted out of a window at the banqueting rooms at Whitehall Palace and onto a roughly assembled scaffold. There he commended his soul to God and had his head chopped off.

Once you kill a king whom God Almighty has selected and installed to rule over a people, then all bets are off. Any question can be asked. One can even address questions directly to God, about God, and what God's purpose is for mankind. John Milton's epic *Paradise Lost* (1667) gave the Devil a plausible complaint against God and had him claim defiantly, "Better to reign in hell than serve in heav'n."

But for ever practical Englishmen, the Enlightenment soon turned to the question of how to create a heaven for mankind on earth. One could still think about anything, but the conclusion had to be of some help, and to the more people, the better. Progress thus became the touchstone for Franklin and other scientist-philosophers of the Enlightenment, and the man who set the rules for them was Isaac Newton.

In 1687, Newton was a Cambridge mathematics professor when he published his universal law of gravitation in his *Principia.** This landmark study explained the motions of heavenly bodies, of falling objects on earth, and even the pull of the tides by reference to gravity. The book was not for everyone, especially not for Franklin, who was poor on theoretical mathematics and who had only a smattering of the classical Latin in which the book was written. But for the creative theorist it opened an important door; it was said, for example, to have been Thomas Jefferson's favorite book.

---

* *Philosophia Naturalis Principia Mathematica*, or "Natural Philosophy of Mathematical Principles." Newton's *Opticks* was published in 1704.

Newton later published his *Opticks*, which introduced an entirely different kind of science. The *Principia* used higher mathematics to demonstrate natural phenomena beyond man's reach. In the *Opticks* he explored a more tangible world, examining fire and heat, magnetic forces, optics and vision, anatomical functions, and, not least, electricity.

Newton influenced Franklin's spiritual development as much as he did his scientific thinking. What *Principia* established was that God, if He existed, lived at the far end of an unknowable universe; *Opticks*, on the other hand, showed man how to build a framework to come closer to Him. In setting out the rules by which scientist-philosophers could approach speculative research, Newton in effect was creating a new language that people all over the world could use to communicate with each other. Thus, the Swedish botanist Linnaeus soon created a procedure by which all plants could be identified by their family, wherever they were found, and astronomy escaped the imprisonment imposed on Galileo.

During his life study of natural science, Benjamin Franklin produced experiments and writing on a staggering array of topics. Early in his adult life he undertook magic squares—a grid of numbers that add up to the same sum whichever way you do the calculation—as a way to become comfortable with mathematics. He studied winds, tides, eclipses, geology, soil conservation, fertilizers, and genetically improving crop strains. He examined how ants communicate with each other and how birds organize their flocks. When his brother John became the first family member of his generation to suffer from urinary tract stones, Benjamin designed, and had crafted, a silver flexible catheter to ease the agony—the first such in America.*

His studies on heat conduction led him to perfect the fireplace that gave him his first international acclaim. In 1740, he installed

---

* The Franklins were prone to gout; Benjamin had his first attack in 1750 at age forty-four.

a set of baffles in the back of a cast-iron fireplace that allowed the smoke to exit freely but also returned heat from the metal stove back into the room. This rendered the room both warmer and less smoky. He declined the offer of a royal patent to earn royalties on the sale of what he called his "Pennsylvania fireplace" but which forever after was known as the Franklin stove. It became an instant best-seller in numerous versions throughout the colonies and quickly became popular in England and Europe.

Electricity was a natural area of interest if only because his early reading of Newton had led him to speculate about the physics of the movement of light and sound. Both the danger and the potential of electricity fascinated many of the Enlightenment experimenters. Lightning was a horrendous threat in those days to people who spent their lives outdoors, to their homes and barns, even to ships at sea. The catastrophe of a lightning strike was enveloped in a mythological horror, as if it were God's judgment on some hapless sinner.

Franklin later recalled being in Boston on family business in the early 1740s when he attended a show of electrical and other wonders performed by a Scottish experimenter. He recalled, "They were imperfectly formed, as he was not very expert; but, being on a subject quite new to me, they equally surprised and pleased me."[3] When the Scot came to Philadelphia at the end of his tour, Franklin bought the man's glass tubes in order to conduct his own electrical experiments. His London friend Peter Collinson sent more tubes, and, in another propitiating gesture later on, Thomas Penn sent the Library Company some condenser jars and other apparatus for generating static electricity.

The mysteries of electricity intrigued Franklin, and he quickly saw an opportunity to harness one of the great forces of nature. Looking at Newton's two philosophies, Franklin had no doubt which he preferred. In a letter to Collinson he stated:

Nor is it of much importance to us to know the manner in which nature executes her laws; 'tis enough if we know the laws themselves. 'Tis of real use to know that china left in the air unsupported will fall and break; but how it comes to fall, and why it breaks are matters of speculation. 'Tis a pleasure indeed to know them, but we can preserve our china without it.[4]

But at the same time, in determining the laws of electrical physics, Franklin would become the first to set the theory behind those laws.

In the winter of 1746 and the spring months of 1747, Franklin began his electrical studies at the point already reached by most European experimenters. The accepted wisdom held that there were two kinds of electrical "fluid," distinguished by whether they were generated by rubbing various substances such as silk or fur against objects made of either glass or resin. Elaborate machines whirled about to produce the friction that generated the electrical fluid, or one could simply rub and rub until there was a spark. It was tiring and dangerous work. In January 1746, Dutch physicist Pieter van Musschenbroek nearly electrocuted himself and an assistant when they accidentally discovered that a jar partly filled with water, with a nail projecting from its cork, can retain charges of static electricity from one of the rotating friction machines. The Leyden jar, as it is known, was for a long time the only condenser—storage battery—that could hold electricity.

This is where Franklin started his research. Peter Collinson had sent an account of the new electrical experiments and included some of the apparatus required to carry them out. Franklin tried to increase the capacity of a Leyden jar by replacing the water with pulverized lead; then he coated a pane of glass with lead and found it was an even more efficient store. Through a Junto friend who was a silversmith, he devised a more efficient friction rotator—in effect, an electric generator. He freely helped a friend, Ebenezer Kinnersley, a Baptist minster without a congregation, begin his own research and conduct public demonstrations that for a time threatened to eclipse Franklin's own fame in America.

In the spring of 1747 he wrote to his friend Collinson:

> I was never before engaged in any study that so totally engrossed my attention and my time as this has lately done. For what with making experiments when I can be alone, and repeating them to my friends and acquaintances who, from the novelty of the thing, come continually in crowds to see them, I have some months past had little leisure for anything else.[5]

So fast was knowledge spreading in those days that Franklin's note to Collinson was written less than fifteen months after Musschenbroek had built the Leyden jar.

Franklin distinguished himself from the other Americans involved in the headlong hunt for electricity's laws by the wide range of his search and the meticulous testing and reporting of his findings. He never guessed at what he could not prove, and once he had proven something, he wrote his findings so explicitly that anyone else could duplicate the exercise and advance on it.

In March 1747, he wrote to Collinson that he had found some electrical phenomena "that we look upon to be new." In a July letter, he outlined two of his basic triumphs in the field—the concept that electricity was a single fluid, and the terms positive and negative, or plus and minus, to describe the forces that create the electrical charge. He also mentioned he was working on "the wonderful effect of pointed bodies, both in drawing off and throwing off the electrical fire"—the first notion of a lightning rod.[6]

Other scientists had speculated that the electrical spark they could rub off a glass tube might be the same thing as a bolt of lightning. Franklin wanted to prove it. Tests had revealed that a Leyden jar had the same amount of electrical fluid in it at all times. The only time one could retrieve a spark was when there was an imbalance between the charge on the coated outside of the jar and the water on the inside. If the outside was positively charged, the inside had an equal negative charge; if the jar was touched, the resulting spark would put everything back into balance. Then one could replace the charge by rubbing a tube or whirling a generator and transferring it into the Leyden jar for storage. From this Franklin concluded that atmospheric changes created their own electrical charges between sky and earth, and that lightning bolts were the same rebalancing of charges that occurred when a spark was drawn off the outside of a Leyden jar.

But how to prove it? And how to store the huge electrical charge that would result if one was able to trigger it from a thunderstorm?

King George's War interrupted these speculations for more than a year, from mid-1747 until the autumn of 1748. Franklin was busy with Assembly affairs and raising the militia. But by 1748, after turning the printing business over to David Hall, he had moved to a new and larger house and returned his attention to his experiments.

In April 1749, he reported to Collinson the making of

> what we called an electrical battery, consisting of eleven panes of large sash-glass, armed with thin leaden plates pasted on each side, placed vertically and supported at two inches' distance on silk cords, with thick hooks of leaden wire, one from each side, standing upright, distant from each other, and convenient communications of wire and chain from the giving side of one pane to the receiving side of the other; that so the whole might be charged together and with the same labour as one single pane.[7]

The "electrical battery" Franklin designed.

In building this battery, Franklin discovered another truth about the atmospheric conditions that lead to lightning. He had been, he wrote Collinson, at first baffled by the observation that one needed an outside contact to discharge a Leyden jar.

> These two states of Electricity, the plus and minus, are combined and balanced in this miraculous bottle in a manner that I can by no means comprehend.... If it were possible that a bottle should in one part contain a quantity of air strongly comprest, and in another part a perfect vacuum, we know the equilibrium would be instantly restored within. But here we have a bottle containing at the same time a plenum of electrical fire, and a vacuum of the same fire; and yet the equilibrium cannot be restored between them but by communication without! though the plenum presses violently to expand, and the hungry vacuum seems to attract as violently in order to be filled.[8]

In short, Franklin wanted to poke into the sky to draw the electrical charge in order to correct the imbalance between heaven and earth. He proposed in 1749 to conduct a lightning rod experiment. On top of the highest building or hill he could find, he would mount a sentry box with a pointed iron rod that extended to a height of twenty or thirty feet. Franklin planned to stand inside on an insulated stool and direct the lightning's electrical charge into a large Leyden jar. He had not yet come to the idea of grounding the rod so the current would continue harmlessly into the earth, but he soon revised his plan. His fellow experimenter Kinnersley began to show a miniature version of the idea in his public shows.

It is uncertain whether Franklin fully appreciated how dangerous his experiment could be. He could still be distracted by the parlor tricks that electricity lent itself to—setting punch bowls alight and making young girls squeal when their hair stood on end. In

July 1750, he sent Collinson a summary of his proposed experiments in a letter titled *Opinions and Conjectures, concerning the Properties and Effects of the Electrical Matter, Arising from Experiments and Observations, Made at Philadelphia, 1749.* Collinson, ever loyal, passed his report onto the Royal Society, where it was read with some interest but then tabled.

On December 23, Franklin learned about the dangers involved. He had invited some of his Junto and other science friends to a pre-Christmas dinner, which he proposed to prepare using electricity. He wrote later:

> Being about to kill a turkey by the shock from two large glass jars, containing as much electrical fire as forty common phials, I inadvertently took the whole through my own arms and body, by receiving the fire from the united top wires with one hand while the other held a chain connected with the outsides of both jars. The company present (whose talking to me, and to one another, I suppose, occasioned my inattention to what I was about) say that the flash was very great and the crack as loud as a pistol; yet, my sense being instantly gone, I neither saw the one nor heard the other; nor did I feel the stroke on my hand.... I then felt what I know not well how to describe: a universal blow throughout my whole body from head to foot, which seemed within as well as without; after which the first thing I took notice of was a violent quick shaking of my body, which gradually remitting my sense as gradually returned.... That part of my hand and fingers which held the chain was left white, as though the blood had been driven out, and remained so eight or ten minutes after, feeling like dead flesh; and I had a numbness in my arms and the back of my neck that continued till the next morning but wore off.... I am ashamed to have been guilty of so notorious a blunder.[9]

Politics intruded on his experiments again in 1751. That spring, he was elected a city alderman and later a General Assembly member in his own right (he would be reelected each year until 1764). Meanwhile, in London, his electrical observations were receiving a wider audience. Collinson arranged for the publication of Franklin's letters and the *Experiments and Observations* with a foreword written by Dr. John Fothergill, the celebrity doctor-scientist who served as apothecary and physician to London's most prominent citizens. A separate version appeared in the popular *Gentleman's Magazine*. The English electrical researcher William Watson, sensing a rival, took the precaution of reading an abstract of the Franklin pamphlet to the Royal Society in July, noting only those discoveries that coincided with his own and leaving out any mention of lightning rods.

But in France a translation of the pamphlet energized experimenters there. King Louis XV saw some of the Franklin experiments performed in early 1752, and in May, in a garden eighteen miles from Paris, scientist Thomas-François D'Alibard built a sentry box on Franklin's description, complete with a forty-foot-long iron rod through the roof. On May 10, a thunderstorm generated such a flow of electrical discharge down the rod that the observers were easily able to charge a number of condensing tubes. The experiment was repeated in Paris eight days later, and King Louis ordered the proofs sent to the Royal Society in London with a special mention of both Franklin and Collinson. In London, just ten days after Watson's sly presentation to the Royal Society, the experiments were performed again to widespread acclaim. Soon thereafter, tests were repeated in Belgium, Italy, and as far away as Russia.

None of this instant fame had reached Franklin himself. He had thought to wait to perform his experiment until the new steeple could be erected on Philadelphia's Christ Church so it could serve as an elevated platform. Then another idea came to him. Although his sentry boxes had proven one did not have to actually be inside a cloud to tap into lightning charges, Franklin figured the closer one could get to the sky, the more fruitful the test would be.

What happened next has become the great Franklin myth as immortalized in the Currier & Ives print (and countless others) showing the portly doctor flying his kite in a country thunderstorm. The myth has become the focus of a century-old conflict over whether the story was a complete fabrication or perhaps a highly edited accounting of an event that took place long after Franklin had received the news from France.[10] Franklin himself confused the issue by not immediately publishing his version of the event.

But the best account of the famous kite experiment is one written fifteen years after the event by Joseph Priestley, the great English scientist (and theologian), presumably from detailed conversations with his friend Franklin. According to Priestley's account,[11] Franklin in June (after the French tests but before he had received word) constructed a kite out of a large silk handkerchief and light wood crossbars. Taking his twenty-one-year-old son, William, he went into the countryside and launched the kite into an oncoming thunderstorm. Then they prudently sought shelter in a shed with an insulated floor. They waited for some time and doubted whether anything would happen when Franklin suddenly noticed that the loose strands of the hemp kite string were standing erect, as if they had been suspended from a Leyden jar. Franklin had suspended an iron key from the string (taking care to grip the string below the key), and he gingerly poked a finger at it. To his intense pleasure, a visible spark arced between his knuckle and the key. As the rain began to soak the string, the flow of electrical charge poured down the string, and he quickly filled the condensing tubes he had brought along. He had proven his own sentry box hypothesis himself. Lightning was indeed an electrical charge that passed between clouds or between clouds and the earth—his conjecture from his 1749 proposal.

Part of the controversy centers on what Franklin did next. Again, he kept his discovery secret, the best evidence indicating that it was partly out of fear of ridicule but mostly because his sense of drama told him he had a scoop of considerable importance. That summer, as he installed the first grounded lightning rods on public buildings (including, most likely, Christ Church and the State House), he began preparing a full report of both the kite experiment and the lightning rod proposal, which would appear in the *Gazette* as well as the 1753 edition of the popular *Poor Richard's Almanack*, due out October 1. He also ran a wire from the lightning rod on his own house into his study, adding two bells and a clapper that would ring whenever the wire was charged. In October, he wrote Collinson of his kite trial.

Even today there is a lot of speculation about what Franklin knew and when he knew it. It is enough, however, that his European contemporaries—including rivals in England—were generous in according his proofs first place in these two important discoveries. Ever after, the experiments were called the Franklin, or Philadelphia, experiments. The final seal on his triumph came in 1753, when the Royal Society awarded him its coveted Copley Medal—equivalent to today's Nobel Prize. There were challenges to be sure, but no one took them seriously, and Franklin never bothered to respond. His writings were quickly reprinted—five editions in English, three in French, and one each in German and Italian.

The fulsome acknowledgment by ambitious colleagues has a ready explanation. They saw two things that have been lost in the passage of time. First, Franklin transformed a parlor trick into a new branch of science that is of crucial importance to this day. (It is not a coincidence that social scientists have long recognized that growth in a nation's economic wealth is accompanied—perhaps preceded—by the increased use of electricity for transforming human labor into things of value.) He may have told Collinson that it was not important "to know the manner in which nature executes her laws," but here he provided the theory and supplied the proofs. Moreover, he supplied the vocabulary for this new branch of science with such new terms as plus and minus, electric battery, and electric motor. He perfected the prototype generator that still lights our cities, and he pointed the way to how we might put this enormous new power to mankind's use.

Second, and perhaps more important, Franklin confirmed a methodical system of hypothesis, experiment, and proof that became the standard procedure for generations of scientists in a host of other areas of inquiry. That chain links today's astrophysicists back through Edison, Bell, and Morse to Franklin. When we turn on a light switch in our homes, we join him in his library in Philadelphia. If Newton dominated the scientific landscape of the seventeenth century, Franklin surely dominated that of the eighteenth century.

EVER CIVIC-MINDED, BENJAMIN FRANKLIN DID NOT let his scientific experiments remove him from the public arena. More people were coming to acknowledge his probity and superior good sense. Whether he marched out front or let someone else lead the way, Franklin's civic schemes began to recommend themselves more easily. He won backing for a Pennsylvania Academy that is the ancestor of today's University of Pennsylvania; he advanced the first plan for a joint private-public matching fund-raising for a free hospital; and he brought together the proliferating fire-fighting companies to pool resources for the first fire insurance policies. All these institutions still flourish today. In response, the Penn brothers put him on various commissions. He was put on the advisory common council and, as noted, became a town alderman. Once he had been selected for one of Philadelphia's seats in the Assembly, William seamlessly moved into the job of the Assembly's chief clerk. Franklin moved up the ranks of freemasonry, becoming grand master of the St. John's Lodge and later for the Atlantic region.

In 1753, as recognition for his public contributions—and perhaps, as some suspect, because the Penns wanted to seduce him—Franklin was made joint deputy postmaster general for all the American colonies. There he earned praise throughout the colonies and renown for posterity. He created the first truly modern postal delivery system, with relays of riders from Charleston, South Carolina, to Portland, Maine. Mail was now promptly delivered and secure from prying eyes. Notices of arriving mail were printed in local newspapers, and for the more isolated, he created the penny post to deliver letters to rural farms.* For the first time in history, in 1761 the postmaster general in London would begin receiving net revenues from America, which in some years would run to £500 or more. Franklin and William Hunter of Williamsburg, his fellow deputy postmaster general, would recoup their initial investments in the post and earn a healthy return. (An ailing Hunter would ultimately leave most of the business to Franklin.)

More than any other single accomplishment, Franklin's postal reforms truly drew the colonies together. Between 1754 and 1756, Franklin traveled hundreds of miles to visit every post office in the colonies, tirelessly mapping routes and making schedules. He dramatically reduced mail delivery times: Philadelphians could now expect to receive a response to a letter sent to Boston within three weeks, where it had often taken two months. He also required all newspaper publishers to pay postage for issues mailed to subscribers and made the mail service open to all colonial periodicals.

---

* Franklin assigned relatives and printing partners to postmaster jobs throughout the colonies, most notably his son, William, who became the first postmaster of Philadelphia and later comptroller of the whole network. This was not simply nepotism, however: Franklin wanted to ensure he had control over the system.

Long before he instituted his postal reforms, however, Franklin had realized the benefits of bringing the colonies closer together. The first attempt was modest enough and involved, as usual, early efforts of wealthier and more prominent friends. It was his botanist friend John Bartram who first argued that colonies were no longer separate plantations designed to serve only the interests of the absentee owners. Rather, the colonies had common interests—in science, commerce, defense, and politics—that bound them closer each day. Franklin agreed that there should be a formal network of the best minds of the colonies, some organization in which those leaders could share their thinking on a thousand topics and advance the common cause.

But Bartram was absorbed by his botanical gardens in Darby, so it fell to Franklin to organize what became the American Philosophical Society—to this day the hemisphere's most distinguished institution of the mind. In 1743, he published *A Proposal for Promoting Useful Knowledge among the British Plantations in America.* Carl Van Doren described what Franklin had in mind as "an intercolonial Junto."[12] Indeed, five of the first ten Philadelphia members also attended Junto meetings. But Franklin also drew inspiration from the various societies in London that not only shared discoveries among members but also published them so every inquiring mind could benefit, such as the august Royal Society and the more utilitarian Society for the Promotion of the Arts, Manufacturing, and Commerce.

The Philosophical Society helped link American achievers back to their English colleagues in the Enlightenment, which was indeed part of Franklin's plan. In fact, many Americans were already getting recognition from London for their accomplishments. A year earlier the Royal Society had recognized Franklin's old tenant Thomas Godfrey for inventing the quadrant, an instrument for calculating the altitude of celestial beings. Bartram, meanwhile, was botanist for King George II; he shipped hundreds of seeds and plants through Peter Collinson each year. and others in London fed new information and materials back to Franklin and others in America, networking on a wide range of subjects and issues.

Despite their early quarrel over Godfrey's matchmaking, Franklin invited his former tenant to become his society's resident mathematician; Bartram, Colden, and other colonial luminaries also were recruited in 1744. The problem was that, while many were happy to join his new society, few were actually willing to send Franklin proofs of experiments for him to broadcast to the rest of the world. He also found that many early members were "idle gentlemen." Others clearly preferred the recognition that could come from the various, more prestigious London institutions. Franklin had tried to set the tone with his improvements on the "Pennsylvania fireplace" he had invented in 1740, but tinkering with the Franklin stove was not his priority. A war was on, and he knew that the colonies needed more than his learned society to band them together. Defense became a priority.

WAR AND ITS RUMORS WERE A CONSTANT of Philadelphia life from 1739 onward. King George II declared war on Spain for the effrontery of attacking English privateers who raided commerce among Madrid's South American colonies. The next year, the war spread due to conflicting claims to Austria's throne. France joined forces with Spain against Prussia, and that was enough for King George. France was suddenly facing British troops in Europe and in North America. By the summer of 1747, there was convincing evidence that French raiders based in the Caribbean were planning a substantial operation up the Delaware with the intention of sacking Philadelphia and burning the plantations along the river. In addition, the French prodded Shawnees and those Delawares who had been forced into the Ohio Valley to come back over the Allegheny Mountains and attack the isolated farms of Scots-Irish pioneers. The Delawares closer to home, still stung by the so-called Walking Purchase fraud, openly supported the raids.

As usual, the Quakers were divided about what to do, but there was little doubt as to where Franklin stood. Almost from the beginning, he had campaigned hard for a standing militia. Using the *Gazette*, he advocated establishing such a group of trained citizens to guard the province from the twin threats of Indian raids on the western frontier and French and Spanish privateer attacks up the Delaware River. He jeered at the peace Quakers for their pious pacifism, hinting that their purses were of more concern to them than their convictions. His newspaper regularly headlined any Indian atrocity anywhere in the colonies and played up French moves to tighten their grip on the Great Lakes region.

So, as threats mounted in 1747, Franklin forced the issue. First, he conferred privately with influential pro-defense supporters, including James Logan, several members of the newly formed American Philosophical Society, friends from the Junto, and some pro-Penn officeholders. They agreed that Franklin would publish in the *Gazette*, and later in pamphlet form, a series of articles to rally public opinion behind a militia. Out of this came one of Franklin's early important documents, *Plain Truth; or, Serious Considerations on the Present State of the City of Philadelphia and Province of Pennsylvania. By a Tradesman of Philadelphia.*[13] Franklin, of course, was the "Tradesman," and everyone knew it.

Adopting the guise of a tough-minded, plain man of business, Franklin scorned Philadelphians for being concerned about the coastal raids but aloof to the Indian threat, and he criticized farmers in the hinterlands for being oblivious to the privateers. But he reserved his hardest knocks for the peace Quakers and for his fellow merchants who balked at contributing anything until the

Quakers came around. "Till late I could scarce believe the story of him who refused to pump in a sinking ship because one on board whom he hated would be saved by it as well as himself," he wrote. Pennsylvania had at least sixty thousand men "acquainted with firearms, many of them hunters and marksmen, hardy and bold," who could defend the province well. If their leaders would not lead them, they could lead themselves. He proposed a mass meeting; first, however, being Franklin, he held a series of smaller meetings. Once the merchants were behind him, he put his plan to the gentry, and only then did he call the open public meeting, which drew an encouraging twelve hundred signatures of volunteers to join a locally raised militia. Franklin was offered a colonel's rank but wisely judged himself unschooled for the task and so joined as an ordinary soldier. As an earlier gesture of commitment, Franklin had secured for sixteen-year-old William a commission as an ensign and saw him spend the winter of 1746–47 in a colonial militia camp at Albany, New York, in support of a campaign against Canada.

Franklin threw himself into military matters with his customary zeal. The militia was an association of volunteers, not an adjunct of the government, and funds had to be found right away. He organized a lottery to raise money to buy guns immediately from Boston and, on longer delivery, from London. He even rode to New York and plied Governor George Clinton with enough Madeira wine to overcome his initial refusal to lend Pennsylvania eighteen new 18-pounder brass cannons. They were mounted at the fort that had been constructed at the mouth of the Delaware, and Franklin took his turn at night on guard duty to show he was no better than anyone else.

Peace came again after 1748, but Franklin knew it was only an interlude. The days of an innocent English paradise in America, if it had ever really existed, were surely over now. On the one hand, the colonies faced an exciting future if they could just learn to manage their own affairs in a spirit of cooperation. On the other, both common enemies and former friends were holding them back from that future. The French and Indians wanted them driven into the sea, or at least barred by the Appalachians. Parliament and the proprietors were edgy rivals who demanded more control over those local choices that had once been nobody's business but the colonies'.

The American colonies could not stay where they were. It was not enough for Pennsylvania to arm to defend its distant borders. For Franklin, it became clear that the colonies had to band together in a united force to protect each other. British troops were thinly spread and British commanders considered it more glorious to fight French troops in Canada or the Ohio Valley than to protect mere farmers from Indian raids.

To Franklin's mind, a more united set of colonies would surely bring America greater standing in England. A common front would also ensure that the colonies could expand farther west once the French were driven away. But could such a union be achieved in time?

Chapter 6

Join or Die

*I*n the six-year time-out between the end of King George's War (1748) and the opening of the French and Indian War (1754), Benjamin Franklin began to form his plan for an American defense union. This would be the foundation for a more ambitious plan both to unite the colonies and to extend the colonial reach west beyond the Appalachians, thereby bringing America a higher visibility back in England. In this, Franklin merits credit for raising the ideas of American union and, as a consequence, independence.

Again, Franklin took a cue from someone else. A New York government official in 1751 wrote a plan to placate the Indian tribes and use them as a weapon to secure the frontiers from the French. The Iroquois Confederacy, after all, resented the French incursions into the land the tribes claimed in the Ohio Valley. Whereas most

...onial charters for the mid-Atlantic provinces (Virginia ...ed) recognized the Appalachian Mountains as the limit of ...ir boundaries, the French pushed into this disputed Ohio region, building forts and forming alliances with rival tribes in the area. The French would not be the only target of this plan, however; at the same time the powerful Iroquois tribes could push the renegade Delaware and Shawnee tribes out of Pennsylvania.

Franklin approved of the notion and suggested forming a special council representing the colonies to deal with both Indian and defense matters. A royal governor appointed by the Crown would preside over the council, while the amount of a colony's tax contributions would determine its representation on the council. Thus, Americans would raise their own money for their own common purposes—gaining representation through taxation.

The French and the Indians were the most immediate problems on Franklin's mind. But the proprietors, too, were an issue, and in this case he was concerned not just with the Penns but with all absentee owners of the colonies who were demanding increasing flows of income while trying to roll back long-established local control over public decisions. Then there was Parliament, which restricted America's ability to grow beyond its early role as a supply warehouse for the empire.

Franklin began to put the broader view about his cause on paper and to circulate it privately for comment among Bartram, Colden, and other colonial advisers. What was eventually published in 1755—*Observations Concerning the Increase of Mankind, Peopling of Countries, etc.*[1]—was a compound of extraordinary vision about what America could be and what it must be. It was, historians would later agree, substantial parts optimism, Malthusian population economics, and manifest destiny, with a dash of unalloyed racism thrown in.

ONE MUST RECALL THAT AT THIS TIME IN HIS LIFE, and indeed for many years to follow, Franklin would have thought of himself as an Englishman and as a loyal subject of the king. He might be Boston-born and Philadelphia-bred, but his ties to the Mother Country were an important part of the mix. Nevertheless, *Observations* offers the first hints that Franklin could consider other options for America beyond being a home for English settlers and an outlet for English merchants.

The spark was another of the so-called Navigation Acts, a series of measures that Parliament had begun enacting in the seventeenth century. The Molasses Act of 1733 had already raised Franklin's ire, for he knew that such acts were meant to preserve America as a depot for the empire. According to the mercantilist tradition of rigidly controlled trade, the colonies would furnish the raw materials of the Industrial Revolution and then become the consumers and importers of Britain's finished goods.

This time, in 1750, Parliament sharply curtailed iron production in the colonies, particularly Pennsylvania, which had rich coal and iron ore deposits and plenty of German iron masters. Pennsylvania and some other colonies had seen their shipments of pig iron back to England exceed the total domestic output of British iron producers. Parliamentary members from Birmingham, Sheffield, and elsewhere had protested fiercely. What they feared most was that the Americans would begin to make steel, something prohibited at the moment, and the quickest way to head off that threat was to curtail iron output.

Franklin scoffed at the notion that England had anything to fear from a country "so vast ... that it will require many ages to settle it fully." No new arrival had to work for another for long before setting up on his own; therefore, he maintained, American labor would never be cheap and the colonies would never be an import threat to English producers. To the contrary, he argued, with 1.6 million inhabitants and population booming,* America in a couple of generations would have more people than would England, and thus the colonies would represent a vast market for British goods.

In *Observations*, Franklin also spoke out against what he viewed as disturbing trends in the colonies—and here he gets into trouble with the modern reader. To his dismay, he now found himself in an ethnic minority. English migration to North America had dwindled to a trickle since the 1730s, as the early days of the British Industrial Revolution offered prospects to many at home who might have emigrated in earlier times. Since the seventeenth century there had been enclaves of Swedes and Dutch in Delaware and New York, but whole communities of German speakers from the Palatinate had come to dominate the interiors of colonies from New York to Maryland, and to make political demands. Consider also that the succession of wars and Stuart-led revolts inflamed life in Ireland and Scotland and led to a rush of new arrivals—battered, sullen, and in no mood to drink the health of good King George. Indeed, it takes an effort to realize just how foreign the Irish, Scots-Irish, and Scottish immigrants appeared to "Englishmen" like Franklin when they began to arrive in America from the 1720s onward. Finally, of course, the rising volume of African slaves in the colonies was disturbing to someone like Franklin, not least because of the violence that resulted.†

The change had been dramatically swift. In 1700, there were an estimated 262,000 inhabitants scattered throughout the colonies, nearly all white and overwhelmingly English; now most of the English colonies, with six times as many people as at the start of the century, had ceased to be exclusively English in any real sense. By

---

* Between 1750 and 1770, colonial population nearly doubled from 1.2 million to 2.2 million.
† Slave revolts were an ever present threat throughout the colonies; two rebellions in New York City, in 1711 and 1720, were suppressed only after the most grisly executions.

the end of the decade, Massachusetts would have more Africans (5,000) than Scots-Irish (4,000); non-English residents throughout the rest of New England made up as much as 30 percent of the population. And the further south one went, the less English the colonies became. By 1760, the percentage of settlers of English descent would drop to 45 percent in New York, 40 percent in New Jersey. Franklin's own Pennsylvania would have, by decade's end, as many German and Dutch (about 63,000) as those identified as English, each group comprising about 30 percent of the population. Scots, Scots-Irish, and Irish settlers further inland would number 42,000, and there would be roughly 4,500 Africans. In the southern colonies, the slave population often was larger than that of the various European settlers, and in some of the more rural regions of colonies such as South Carolina, blacks outnumbered their owners ten-to-one.[2]

Observations contains Franklin's first remarks about slavery in the colonies. His utilitarian nature soured him toward captive labor, but not for moral reasons—at least not yet in his development. With cold explicitness, he counted

> the interest on the first purchase of a slave, the insurance or risk on his life, his clothing and diet, expenses in his sickness and loss of time, loss by his neglect of business (neglect is natural to the man who is not to be benefited by his own care or diligence), expense of a driver to keep him at work, and his pilfering from time to time (almost every slave being by nature a thief).

In the first version of the pamphlet, but removed from later ones, Franklin also let fly with a screed that caused an immediate backlash from the German community and that has haunted his reputation ever since.

Why should the Palatine boors be suffered to swarm into our settlements and, by herding together, establish their language and manners to the exclusion of ours? Why should Pennsylvania, founded by the English, become a colony of aliens, who will shortly be so numerous as to Germanize us, instead of our Anglifying them? ... The number of purely white people in the world is proportionably very small. All Africa is black or tawny; Asia chiefly tawny; America (exclusive of the newcomers) wholly so. And in Europe the Spaniards, Italians, French, Russians, and Swedes are generally of what we call a swarthy complexion; as are the Germans also, the Saxons only excepted, who with the English make the principal body of white people on the face of the earth. I could wish their numbers were increased. And while we are, as I may call it, scouring our planet by clearing America of woods and so making this side of our globe reflect a brighter light to the eyes of inhabitants in Mars or Venus, why should we in the sight of superior beings darken its people? Why increase the sons of Africa by planting them in America, where we have so fair an opportunity, by excluding all blacks and tawnys, of increasing the lovely red and white? But I am partial to the complexion of my country, for such kind of partiality is natural to mankind.[3]

Franklin a racist? Yes. Like nearly every other Anglo-American at that moment, Franklin could hardly yet see the spark of humanity behind the traumatized, dehumanized exteriors of the Africans within his view. His earliest childhood memories were of slaves being auctioned underneath the Blue Ball sign of his father's chandlery. The *Gazette* regularly carried advertisements for the sale of white indentured servants. There also were numerous notices offering Africans for permanent bondage, either singly or in fragments of families.[4]

Franklin's evolution into America's most prominent antislavery activist was still decades away. We know from his accounts and records that Franklin may have bought his first household servant, named Joseph, as early as 1742, and that he bought and sold others in the decade that followed. There is no evidence as to what work these captives did, but one can hazard that they were not trained in printing skills and that they probably did the arduous work needed to keep up the crowded Franklin household.

And crowded the house must have been. Deborah had given birth to a second child, a daughter, Sarah (forever known as Sally), and the boys, William and Jimmy Franklin, shared space with a changing cast of apprentices and clerks who lodged there. There is evidence that the Franklins mostly used white servants inside the house as cooks and maids, although in later years Deborah kept a young African boy as a kind of adopted child. We do know that Franklin complained elsewhere, as he did above, that captive labor usually did not pay back its expense.[5] This was a conclusion slowly being reached throughout the northern colonies, where the crops that required the labor of gangs of slaves—such as tobacco, cotton, and jute—did not prosper as they did in the colonies farther south.

In later years, Franklin tried to embellish his later, sincere conversion to the cause of abolition by noting that in 1729 he had published one of the earliest pamphlets against slavery. But his early doubts about the practice were utilitarian. Distracted by more immediate public issues—immigration, Indian raids, colonial defense—he did not yet pay much mind to the plight of African slaves, even those in his midst. In the event, on his 1757 journey to London he took two African slaves with him.

If he thought about civil liberties at all in our terms, Franklin drew a sharp line between labor by compulsion, whether by voluntary indenture or bondage, and such protections as freedom of speech and freedom of religious worship. His newspaper had long since grown out of its early hesitancy and now challenged the actions and plans of the powerful of whatever faction. In his own life he by instinct preferred the original (even the eccentric) question to the doctrinal certainty. And he welcomed difference in others. He led a fund drive to rebuild Philadelphia's synagogue, the only house of worship for the town's growing Jewish community. More controversial, he joined cause with Quakers who resisted efforts by the proprietors and local Church of England officials to shut down a small Roman Catholic chapel.

FOR A TIME, IN 1754–55, IT LOOKED AS IF Franklin's plan to combine the questions of defense and uniting the colonies might be an idea whose time had come. While he traveled throughout the colonies on postal business, he lobbied for support for his notion. One of his early targets was the powerful Massachusetts governor, William Shirley. Cautious Virginia governor Robert Dinwiddie voiced some sympathy for the plan and later went so far as to allow Iroquois braves into his province as a military counterweight against the Shawnees. Another important ally was a young colonial administrator named Thomas Pownall, who had come to New York from London as secretary to the royal governor there.*

One thing the colonists had going for them was Indian resentment against the French incursions into the Ohio Valley. If the tribes of the Iroquois Confederacy could be conciliated, and if enough of the colonies could act in concert, then London might be prompted to send enough military aid to tip the balance against the French. It was worth discussing.

---

* Pownall (1722–1805) later became governor of Massachusetts (1757–60). He returned home to become a member of Parliament (1767–80), where he defended America's cause during the Revolution.

So in May 1754, even as the Pennsylvania Assembly was dithering over whether to send militia to help Virginia fight the French on the frontier and to appropriate a mere £10,000 for defense, the Assembly agreed to send Franklin and other commissioners to Albany for a formal congress of the colonies on the matter. Acting governor John Penn, the son of proprietor Richard Penn, went as one of the commissioners. His main mission was to get more land from the Indians.

Two interesting points about the Albany Congress, as it is known: one, it was called not by the colonial governors but by the Board of Trade in London (which oversaw England's interests in its colonies), explicitly to bring the Iroquois back into the fold and to do little else; two, not all the colonies were invited, and some that were asked did not bother to come. New Hampshire, Massachusetts, Pennsylvania, Maryland, New Jersey, and Virginia had been asked to participate. The last two did not bother, but Rhode Island and Connecticut sent delegations on their own.

Before he left on the journey, Franklin published in the *Gazette* the first political cartoon in America, the famous "Join or Die" picture of a rattlesnake in eight pieces marked with the initials of New England, New York, New Jersey, Pennsylvania, Virginia, Maryland, North Carolina, and South Carolina.[6]

Unity was not the first thing on the minds of the delegates when they finally assembled on June 14. The Six Nations of the Iroquois were in a truculent mood. Chief Hendrick (Tiyanoga) of the Mohawks gave the most repeated of the complaints against the British colonies and their lack of support for Indian interests beyond the Ohio. "Look at the French; they are men; they are fortifying everywhere. But, we are ashamed to say it, you are all like women, bare and open, without any fortifications."[7]

While the royal official for Indian affairs made the obligatory conciliatory speeches, handed out ceremonial wampum belts, and witnessed the burial of the hatchet, other colonial representatives confused the issue by working their own private deals with the Six Nations leaders. In particular, John Penn was out to bribe Iroquois leaders; he bought enough Indian land west of the Alleghenies to extend Pennsylvania to the Ohio River and Lake Erie, all for the price of two thousand Spanish pieces of eight (one thousand down and another thousand on settlement).

Somehow a discussion of colonial union managed to make it onto the delegates' agenda. Franklin's plan to appoint a council representing the colonies was the best known, and his idea would mean that the various colonial assemblies would not have to reach any sort of consensus immediately. Instead, as Franklin outlined in his plan, the Albany commissioners would appeal directly to the Board of Trade, and through it to Parliament, which would appoint a governor-general over all the colonies for the purpose of joining the Indians and the settlers into a cohesive military alliance to drive the French away. This governor would be a military man and his salary would be paid directly by the Crown, thus freeing him from the assemblies. As a lure to the various colonial assemblies, the governor-general would also begin planting new settlements west of the mountains to extend the boundaries of the provinces.

Although it would be many months before Franklin acknowledged it, his famous Albany Plan of Union was dead on arrival. British officials were not about to help finance a standing army of American colonials with only one political appointee over it. Nor were the various legislatures willing to accept his plan; they were not about to have yet another royal governor bossing them around and demanding money. Even the Pennsylvania Assembly voted the plan down, waiting for a day when Franklin was absent.

But several other points are worth noting. To begin, the Albany Plan for the first time got Americans thinking about what could happen if they united. Second, the plan introduced the idea of opening new lands to shield the old provinces and unleash an economic and population boom. As for the Indians already there—too bad.

And third, with the Albany Plan, Franklin returned to the question of whether Parliament could tax the colonists without their consent. One of the most cherished freedoms granted at the accession of King William III in 1689 was that Englishmen could be taxed only by their own representatives in the Commons. Where were America's delegates to that body? Governor Shirley of Massachusetts, while favoring military coordination, had suggested that the Board of Trade might find union more acceptable if taxes laid on the provinces by Parliament could finance colonial defense. Franklin vetoed the idea.

At this point, union still had two meanings. It of course meant uniting the colonies in common causes, but such a union would also bring America into closer union with Mother England. For Franklin, this was a benefit. He still saw the relationship—and he used the analogy constantly—as one in which a wise mother did not limit the growth of her good children but rather gloried in their prosperity.[8]

NO ONE WOULD KNOW IT FOR SEVERAL WEEKS, but while the Albany negotiations were ongoing, a twenty-two-year-old Virginia militia officer named George Washington had surrendered to an overwhelming French force near Fort Duquesne (where Pittsburgh is now) and was marching his troops back home. Fort Duquesne was one of a network of forts the French had built along the Great Lakes and into the Ohio Valley that threatened to seal the English settlers off from lands beyond the Appalachians. Washington had ambushed a patrol of French regulars and Indian levees, but the superior French force turned on Washington and his Virginians and overwhelmed them at their entrenched camp, Fort Necessity.

Thus, while the debate about union rumbled along in the press and assembly halls, Washington's defeat focused British and colonial attention on the frontier struggle. War was on.

In December 1754, as part of troop shipments for a campaign against Canada, the British sent two regiments to Virginia to drive the French from the Ohio Valley. General Edward Braddock of the Coldstream Guards was to lead regiments of fierce Scots highlanders into the wilds of Pennsylvania to capture Fort Duquesne, then wheel north and reduce the French forts along Lake Erie. The Scots, who were controlled by their British officers only by the lash and the threat of hanging, were not about to be schooled in frontier-style warfare. Braddock had soldiered with success in Europe, where lines of supplies stretched securely back to England, but the situation was far different in America. When he arrived at his assembly headquarters in Frederick, Maryland, he was outraged to find that the governors of Virginia, Maryland, and Pennsylvania had not followed up on their formal promises to round up hundreds of wagons of forage and provisions for his troops; there were but twenty-five there when he arrived.

Braddock was ambitious. He wanted to expand on his explicit orders and clear the French out all the way to Niagara, then launch an attack on the fortress at Frontenac, which guarded the mouth of the St. Lawrence River at Lake Ontario—all before winter set in, around October. Yet Thomas Penn and his agents in Philadelphia had deceived Braddock, convincing him that the Pennsylvania Assembly was laggard in raising money for military support because the Quakers were illegally trading with the French at the western forts. In fact, adequate supplies had already been gathered and were just awaiting transport. But the farmers who owned the huge Conestoga wagons wanted to know how they were to be paid.

That Braddock also stubbornly refused advice about how to conduct the campaign is now part of our American legend. For the moment, all Franklin knew was that as the postmaster of the colonies he had to arrange a system of high-speed communications between the general, who was commander in chief in North America, and all the governors. For that purpose alone, he and his son, William, journeyed to Frederick. Learning of the supply disaster facing the British regiments, Franklin volunteered to round up the wagons and forage and get them to Cumberland, Maryland, where Washington was waiting with his militia and Indian scouts. Braddock gave him £800 and Franklin advanced another £200 of his own. With these bounties on offer, Franklin printed and circulated posters throughout Lancaster, York, and Cumberland counties, and within two weeks he had assembled 150 Conestoga wagons with four horses each and another 259 packhorses.[9]

Braddock was so pleased that he commissioned Franklin to provide regular supplies to troops on the march, which required the Philadelphian to advance another £1,000 of his own money. So this ill-conceived army of Scots clansmen and raw militia set out toward its destiny in June 1755. On July 9, more than two-thirds of the officers (Braddock included) and one-half of the soldiers were killed in a panic-stricken melee in the woods near Fort Duquesne. The battle was short of a massacre only because of George Washington's tactical skill in rescuing what he could, getting the remnants of the force back over the mountains to safety. Although his military track record so far was pretty awful, Washington was learning the craft of soldiering. He also learned a valuable political lesson. Because of the public disillusionment over the annihilation of the seemingly invincible British army, this taciturn Virginian suddenly found himself a hero.

Franklin himself faced total ruin throughout that summer of 1755 because he had stood as guarantor for all the wagons and horses he had recruited for the march. Nearly everything portable (including Braddock's war chest of gold coins) had been lost, for the wagoneers had abandoned their property and fled the battle. The liability he faced was nearly £20,000, far more than he possessed. Although the British paid off the bulk of it in late autumn, Franklin would still be haggling with a new commander in chief, General John Campbell, the Earl of Loudoun, right until his ship sailed for London in the summer of 1757.

But things got even worse. With the British and militia troops in disarray, the Indians rose up in earnest. Some Iroquois bands moved to the French side, and normally placid—although resentful—Delawares began to sack farmhouses east of the Alleghenies and isolated German communities closer to the center of the province. War was nearing Philadelphia.

This, then, is when the contest with the Penns began in earnest. Finally galvanized, the Assembly voted a £60,000 appropriation and to tax the proprietors. It also adopted Franklin's bill for Pennsylvania's first lawfully created militia, with elected officers under the approval of the governor and the commander in chief. Franklin was put in charge of a special committee to manage the defense money. In the midst of this, fresh impetus was added when a Shawnee band murdered all the people in the Moravian village of Gnaddenhuetten, seventy-five miles from Philadelphia. Leaders of the German community came to the Assembly and threatened to move en masse into the city for refuge unless forts were built for their defense.

Even though he was approaching fifty and had become somewhat plumper because of an acquired taste for Madeira wine and rum punches, Franklin did not hesitate to take command of fifty cavalrymen and three wagons of tools and supplies to build a line of defensive forts. In the meantime, a force of militia rangers was being formed and trained to man the forts. So, just a week before Christmas, Franklin, with son William as his aide, set out on horseback in the freezing Pennsylvania winter for the Moravian settlement of Bethlehem.

The mission was to build stockades on a line from Easton on the Delaware River through Bethlehem on the Lehigh to Reading on the Schuylkill. He also was to recruit locally based militia volunteers to supplement the rangers. Because of the spreading panic, Franklin had trouble enlisting men to guard their own communities. Some of the German communities under attack had already sent runners to the French outposts to seek terms. To stiffen their sinews, the Assembly offered a bounty to any settler who killed an Indian and brought the scalp as proof. Franklin for his part had clearly been studying military practices and advocated a Spanish strategy of using packs of fierce dogs for both scouting and attack.

The crisis got still worse. In the first week of January, the troops he had stationed to guard a key mountain pass at Gnaddenhuetten had been overrun, and a hole in the line exposed the frontier again. Franklin, who had been back in Bethlehem organizing refugee relief, set out with a band of axmen and carpenters and a militia guard, and in just one week they had constructed a substantial fort with firing steps and two mounted cannon to secure the territory. In the next week, Franklin's small band built two more forts, fifteen miles in either direction from the Gnaddenhuetten enclosure, while he placed five hundred militiamen along the line and set up regular provisioning and relief.

It was Franklin at his best, always on the move. He consoled refugees and arranged for supplies. He led scouting parties against the Indians. Unschooled in military engineering, he studied on the go and constructed his primitive stockades so impressively that the Indians moved their raids elsewhere for a time. Along the way he took copious notes on the communal living habits of the Moravians. The Moravians, for their part, reflected their admiration by calling him "General Franklin." News of this greatly irritated the governor and pro-Penn forces back home.

This irritation increased even more (and extended back to Thomas Penn) when Franklin returned to Philadelphia in February and was unanimously elected colonel of one of the newly formed militia regiments. Much as the governor would have liked to, there was no way to stop it. But how the proprietors must have seethed at this title of respectability. Their outrage grew when the exuberant regimental officers made a huge fuss over Franklin. Troops escorted him to the town limits on horseback with their swords drawn when he left a few weeks later to visit his fellow postmaster general in Williamsburg. One must remember that in this time, whose hat was taken off first and who bowed more deeply to whom were vital (and could be fatal) points of etiquette. To show a public homage to Franklin that should be reserved only for a royal governor, well, it was just too much.

Franklin aside, Thomas Penn simply could not understand what these people in *his* province thought they were doing. What they should be doing was making money for themselves and for him. But instead they involved themselves in matters that were none of their business, spending money on civic luxuries and then demanding that he reach in his own pocket to help them out. He had a hundred reasons "why they should not have the appropriations to themselves. I think their Hospital, Steeple [on Christ Church], Bells [also for Christ Church], unnecessary Library, with several other things are reasons," he wrote to one of his partisans.[10] It was no coincidence that Franklin had led or supported all of these projects.

Still, Penn believed that any man could be bribed. It was just a matter of finding the right reward. That is why some have suspected that Penn pushed to have the Royal Society award Franklin the Copley Medal in 1753 for his truly innovative observations on lightning and electricity. The most likely scenario is that Penn did not use his influence to block the award and perhaps even pushed it along a bit. Of course, it was no coincidence that William Denny, the latest in the parade of governors sent by the fretful Thomas Penn, carried over the medal from London and presented it to Franklin with great public fanfare.

UNDOUBTEDLY, FRANKLIN DESERVED HIS MEDAL, just as he deserved the other honors bestowed on him in these years. Because of his scientific advances and his founding of the American Philosophical Society, in 1756 he was elected to both the Royal Society and the Society for the Encouragement of the Arts, Manufactures, and Commerce. At the same time he received an honorary degree from the College of William & Mary, so, together with the honorary degrees Harvard and Yale had awarded him in 1753, he now had recognition from all three of America's leading institutions of learning.

But Franklin was not content. While in Williamsburg for his fête, he conferred with young George Washington about the prospects of building a toll road between Philadelphia and Winchester for both commercial and military reasons. Back in Philadelphia he organized municipal efforts to clean the streets, to light them at night, and to provide watchmen, the first such effort in the colonies.

None of this satisfied him. He was clearly restless, as his letters to friends attest. He began an indiscreet flirtation by mail with a young girl in Rhode Island and probably irritated Deborah no end. Though he had retired from the active business of printing and storekeeping in 1748, he never found the complete ease he sought to devote his time to the science studies that absorbed him. Politics, which alternately bored and enraged him, continued to demand his presence. His military duties similarly occupied him, and although he had entered the military arena completely untutored, he became the province's foremost military strategist.

WHILE THE ASSEMBLY AND THE GOVERNOR WRESTLED each other over money for defense, the sums needed got larger every day. Substantial numbers of the Quakers within the Assembly began to relent and back a stronger military posture. Finally, in December 1756, the Indians attacked Franklin's fort at Gnaddenhuetten, burning it and the village to the ground. At the time of the attack, Franklin was in Easton, Pennsylvania, attending a meeting with Tedyuskung, the lead chief in the Delaware Indian delegation; Franklin was trying to bribe the Delawares into peace while the Penns tried to pry more land from them.

In early 1757, the situation was no better. Governor Denny had trumped the Assembly by reversing field and urging them to appropriate the unheard-of sum of £120,000, again without taxing the proprietors. The Assembly countered with a bill to raise £100,000, with Penn taxes included. Denny vetoed the bill and threatened to denounce them to the king. Finally, Lord Loudoun arrived to broker a settlement, with Franklin representing the Assembly in the meeting with Denny and the commander. Franklin gave way and agreed to talk the Assembly leaders into complying with the governor's plan, but they still clung to the previous year's bill and to the demand that the Penns pay up. If they did not comply, Loudoun threatened, he would not divert British troops from his Canadian campaign south to protect Pennsylvania. The Assembly grudgingly passed a bill that Denny would sign but then passed a petition to the Board of Trade and the Privy Council (the king's most senior cabinet ministers) to plead its case against the Penns. Special delegates would be sent to argue the case. Speaker Isaac Norris, the Quaker leader, begged off because of age and health. Franklin said he would go at once.

Franklin made William resign his clerkship, and by April 4 the party of four (Franklin, William, and two African slaves, Peter and King) was off to New York to board a packet ship to London. There should be no surprise at his haste. He was aching to be gone from the place, even for a little while. On the voyage, he would write his last issue of *Poor Richard's Almanack*. In recent years, Richard Saunders, the fictional author, had become less patient with his readers and his essays had taken on a more censorious tone. In this final issue, Franklin featured his essay "The Way to Wealth," which urged his fellow Americans to greater prudence and less selfishness. It was his valedictory warning to the country he loved.

Clearly, Franklin had come to believe that he knew better than his fellow colonials what Pennsylvania needed. The Assembly had given narrow and explicit orders. He was to persuade the Penn brothers to allow their lands to be taxed so the province could adequately fund a defense. But Franklin had grander ambitions for his homeland, and for himself.

Chapter 7

First Blood

Although Franklin had been eager to set off for London, the trip had not had an auspicious beginning. While in New York he had tried to settle accounts with Lord Loudoun, but the commander in chief airily dismissed his request for the final, albeit nominal, payment with the acid comment that the American had probably stolen enough from government funds to make a profit. This was not Franklin's first taste of English arrogance toward colonials, but it stung him deeply, all the more because he could do nothing but bow and accept the insult. Worse, Franklin's ship sailed without him, taking his boxes and provisions. He booked passage on an official packet ship that was to take important war plans from Loudoun back to the government, but the ship rode at anchor well into the summer, and Franklin and all the other passengers were confined on board. It seems Lord Loudoun could never finish a memorandum without beginning a new one, and for Franklin the enforced tedium was painful. More provisions had to be rowed out from New York before the ship was finally, in June, released to sail across the Atlantic.

Even in the best of conditions such a trip was fraught with danger. The sea voyage was peril enough, but this was wartime and capture by a hostile French warship meant delay and possible imprisonment. When the month-long voyage at last neared its end, Franklin and the rest were nearly shipwrecked near the British port of Falmouth when the crew lost sight of a crucial lighthouse beacon. This was not a propitious start for the mission.

Yet Franklin's spirits rose on the morning of July 17, as the thick fog that had enshrouded the packet boat rose "like the curtain at a playhouse," revealing "the town of Falmouth, the vessels in its harbor, and the fields that surrounded it." It was "a most pleasing spectacle."[1]

Having dodged capture by French warships and endured the normal hardships of a sea voyage (not to mention the final close call), Franklin understandably made a quick devotional call at a local church.[2] Then he bundled his party into a private coach bound for London. On the nine-day journey they stopped for some sightseeing at the prehistoric ruins of Stonehenge. By July 27, they were safely billeted at the Bear Inn on the Southwark side of old London Bridge.

THE FIRST TO CALL WAS HIS LONGTIME FRIEND and correspondent Peter Collinson. Collinson was valuable for his contacts within London's various communities of influence. The naturalist had brought Franklin to the attention of the Royal Society, and through that group Franklin had widened his circle of correspondents, with whom he exchanged a voluminous correspondence on topics from botany to religious speculation. Yet Collinson, a Quaker, also was an active partner in his family's prosperous trade in luxury fabrics. Thus his network extended deep into the merchant community from London to North America.

Collinson scooped up Franklin and his entourage and took them to his home while a search began for fit lodgings for his friend.[3] At the same time, Franklin and son William set out to transform their appearances from the rude provincials that their clothes proclaimed them. William, now twenty-seven, had casually read law back in Philadelphia and was now to be entered as a clerk-pupil at the prestigious Middle Temple guild of lawyers.

According to Franklin's account books (now held by the American Philosophical Society in Philadelphia), they patronized such modish tailors as Regniers and Christopher of Jermyn Street for new suits. There were new wigs to be purchased—the full, shoulder-length style—as well as new shoes and silver buckles, new linen for shirts and handkerchiefs. They bought the luxurious accoutrements that marked the true gentleman of the day—dress swords and walking sticks, a watch, new eyeglasses, stationery, and a leased carriage. With thoughtful generosity (and a little guilt) for the wife and daughter left behind, Franklin shipped the first of many boxes of the latest fabrics, rugs, china, and silver. It is quite an inventory for a man who did not plan to be in London more than a few months.

Finally, lodgings were found for the new representative and his party at Number 7 Craven Street (now Number 36). Today Craven Street is a narrow one-block lane that starts behind the Charing Cross railroad station and ends at the Embankment along the Thames River. In those days the street went down to the waterside and housed numerous shops for wine merchants and metal crafters, whose products could be transferred among other warehouses along the busy river. Except for two years he spent back in Pennsylvania,

Franklin would until the eve of the American Revolution make his permanent home on Craven Street and put himself in the solicitous care of his landlady, the widow Margaret Stevenson.

Just as the arrivals had settled in, another friend visited Franklin. William Strahan, a reticent Scot who had made his way in the cutthroat London publishing arena, had become acquainted with Franklin twenty years before when the American began placing orders for type, paper, and other supplies for his press. The business relationship had become a friendship, as their correspondence grew more affectionate and intimate. At one point, Franklin had dreamed aloud of marrying William to the Londoner's daughter.

Despite their extensive correspondence, Franklin and Strahan were in fact meeting for the first time. Sometimes long-distance friendships do not stand the test of face-to-face meetings, but this was not the case with the two printers. A few weeks after Franklin's arrival, Strahan wrote a reassuring letter to Franklin's wife, Deborah, in which he said, "I never saw a man who was, in every respect so perfectly agreeable to me. Some are amiable in one view, some in another, he in all."[4]

A third friend to call on Franklin was John Fothergill, the busiest doctor in London. Fothergill was especially interested in the diseases that regularly swept through London and in finding new uses for the host of new herbs and plants being discovered in the New World. Fothergill's real importance to Franklin lay in the fact that he was the undisputed leader of the English Quaker community and had immense influence among the Friends in Philadelphia. He thus had wide experience in the political ins-and-outs that absorbed both the merchant class and the power brokers in the ministries.

The two men warmed to each other at once. The doctor gave Franklin good advice: He should not open up too public a campaign against the Penn brothers right away. The best tactic would be to avoid making direct appeals to the ministries or to leading parliamentarians. Rather, Franklin should open informal contacts with the proprietors themselves, starting with a polite courtesy call to assure the Penns that he had their interests in mind. This was good tactical advice, and Franklin would much later realize the wisdom—never begin a negotiation with your final offer.

A DAY OR SO LATER, HOWEVER, Franklin chose to do otherwise. Scarcely had his party settled in when Collinson sent exciting news. As Franklin recorded in his *Autobiography*:

I then waited on my old friend and correspondent, Mr. Peter Collinson, who told me that John Hanbury, the great Virginia merchant, had requested to be informed when I should arrive, that he might carry me to Lord Granville's, who was then President of the [Privy] Council and wished to see me as soon as possible. I agreed to go with him the next morning. Accordingly Mr. Hanbury called for me and took me in his carriage to that nobleman's, who receiv'd me with great civility; and after some questions respecting the present state of affairs in America and discourse thereupon, he said to me: "You Americans have wrong ideas of the nature of your constitution; you contend that the king's instructions to his governors are not laws, and think yourselves at liberty to regard or disregard them at your own discretion. But those instructions are not like the pocket instructions given to a minister going abroad, for regulating his conduct in some trifling point of ceremony. They are first drawn up by judges learned in the laws; they are then considered, debated, and perhaps amended in Council, after which they are signed by the king. They are then, so far as they relate to you, the law of the land for the king is the legislator of the colonies."

I told his lordship this was new doctrine to me. I had always understood from our charters that our laws were to be made by our Assemblies, to be presented indeed to the king for his royal assent, but that being once given the king could not repeal or alter them. And as the Assemblies could not make permanent laws without his assent, so neither could he make a law for them without theirs. He assur'd me I was totally mistaken. I did not think so, however, and his lordship's conversation having a little alarm'd me as to what might be the sentiments of the court concerning us, I wrote it down as soon as I returned to my lodgings.[5]

Franklin reported this event while he was working on the last installment of the *Autobiography* in 1788, three decades after it took place, but the recollection of Granville's hostility has a jolting freshness to it that shows it clearly rankled long afterward. Yet Granville's callous attitude toward colonial powers of self-government should not have shocked Franklin. The secretary would share the Penn sense of absolute ownership because he himself was a proprietor of the North Carolina colony; also, Granville was Penn's brother-in-law.

Underlying Granville's belief in the king's supremacy was another well-known, and increasingly irksome, English attitude. The American colonies were to be suppliers for the factories of the Mother Country—they never were to become self-sufficient, economically or politically. Of course, as early as 1733, Franklin had earned himself and the *Pennsylvania Gazette* a reputation throughout the colonies for his essays complaining about the stifling Navigation Acts.

Though somewhat daunted by the exchange with Lord Granville, Franklin prepared for a frontal assault on the Penns, asking Fothergill to arrange for a meeting with the proprietors.

Thomas and Richard Penn now held between them clear title to forty-five million acres of Pennsylvania, a tract that stretched from the Delaware River boundary with New Jersey on the east all the way west to the foothills of the Appalachian chain. Elder brother John had died in 1746, and Thomas, as next in line, therefore controlled three-fourths of the holdings. One thing he would not allow was for others to control his lands, much less to tax them.

In mid-August, the Penns received Franklin at Thomas's home in nearby Spring Garden. After the elaborate courtesies and expressions of mutual goodwill, the adversaries got down to the first exchange, which was recorded in the *Autobiography*:

> We then went into consideration of our several points of complaint, which I enumerated. The proprietaries justify'd their conduct as well as they could and I the Assembly's. We now appeared very wide, and so far from each other in our opinions as to discourage all hope of agreement. However, it was concluded that I should give them the heads of our complaints in writing, and they promis'd then to consider them. I did so soon after, but they put the paper into the hands of their solicitor, Ferdinand John Paris, who managed for them all their law business in their great suit with the neighboring proprietary of Maryland, Lord Baltimore, which had subsisted 70 years, and wrote for them all their papers and messages in their dispute with the Assembly. He was a proud, angry man, and as I had occasionally in the answers of the Assembly treated his papers with some severity, they being really weak in point of argument and haughty in expression, he had conceived a mortal enmity to me, which discovering itself whenever we met, I declin'd the proprietary's proposal that he and I should discuss the heads of complaint between our two selves, and refus'd treating with any one but them.[6]

Within five days Franklin had prepared this informal outline and submitted it to the proprietors. The Penns and Paris promptly passed the complaints along to the king's senior legal advisers for an opinion on the nature of proprietary authority. It was not until early November 1758 that the legal experts predictably upheld the powers of the Penns to order their governors to overrule actions of the Assembly. They kept Franklin uninformed of this initial victory until nearly the end of that year.

Franklin was scarcely in a position to hound the proprietors during the winter of 1757. A few days after he had drafted the complaints for the Penns, he fell ill with what he described in a letter to Deborah as "a violent cold and something of a fever." From the symptoms of raging fever, excruciating headaches, and delirium that he later recorded, it appears he may have contracted malaria during the weeks he languished on shipboard. In most other circumstances an attack of this severity would have proven fatal and Franklin's story would have ended there.

But Dr. Fothergill's fascination with the medical discoveries of the New World had led him to import large quantities of cinchona bark, whose medicinal properties had been discovered by Spanish missionaries in Peru a few years earlier. Cinchona was the basic source of quinine, and the physician made Franklin swallow strong herbal teas and even chew the bark itself in what would appear to be near toxic levels until the fevers subsided two months later. But it took a full year for Franklin to regain his former robust good health, and even then he continued to consume, under protest, the herbal teas his friend forced on him as a preventative. He nevertheless had similar, albeit less serious, episodes of "colds" for some time thereafter.

In the meantime, he fretted at the roadblocks the Penns kept throwing in his way, particularly after they began to complain about his conduct to their allies in Philadelphia. His friend Fothergill was moved to reassure fellow Quaker Israel Pemberton, another Franklin ally in the Assembly:

Benjamin Franklin has not yet been able to make much progress in his affairs. Reason is heard with fear: the fairest representations are considered as the effects of superior art: and his reputation as a man, a philosopher, and a statesman, only seem to render his station more difficult and perplexing.... You must allow him time, and without repining. He is equally able and solicitous to serve the province, but his obstructions are next to insurmountable: Great pains have been taken, and very successfully, to render him odious and his integrity suspected, to those very persons to whom he must first apply. These suspicions can only be worn off by time, and prudence.[7]

How the Penns and their lawyer Paris must have gloated at the first favorable ruling about their powers. Thomas Penn boasted to one of Franklin's foes back home that his "popularity is nothing here, and that he will be looked very coldly upon by grate People, there are very few of any consequence that have heard of his Electrical experiments, those matters being attended to by a particular Sett of People, many of whom of the greatest consequence I know well, but it is quite another sort of People who are to determine the Dispute between us."[8]

Penn got it wrong. But then, this story is as much about people who were mistaken about things as it is about those who got it right.

WHEN THOMAS PENN HAD RETURNED HOME to London in 1741, he had left in place a group of local allies who depended on his grace and favor for their own positions in the Pennsylvania hierarchy.

Those who remained loyal could count on offices and, more important, inside land deals that would enrich them far beyond their own abilities. In reasserting proprietorial power, however, Thomas solidified an opposition against himself among the Quaker merchant grandees who were appalled at his corruption and among the rising citizens (Franklin chief among them) who saw the proprietors as a destructive threat to the province's future.

While Franklin was in the midst of his voyage to London in the summer of 1757, Penn unwittingly gave the opposition based in the General Assembly a weapon to use against his rule—another outrage against the Delaware Indians. Pennsylvania was now in the third year of its fierce frontier war, and in July 1757, Penn's agents called the Delawares to a long conference at Easton, Pennsylvania. The agents announced they had discovered new titles to land that would extend the proprietary domain west to the Susquehanna and the rich Wyoming Valley, where the tribes were concentrated. Tedyuskung, the Delaware chief, demanded to see the title deeds, which were fraudulent. This time he brought along his own English clerk, Charles Thomson, who kept detailed minutes of the confrontation. Tedyuskung turned the minutes and other supporting documents over to the Assembly leaders, who sent them on to Franklin. The last thing the Assembly wanted was an outbreak of Indian violence so close to Philadelphia.

Even while Franklin recovered from his grave illness, the struggle with the Penns continued. The brothers pretended that they had to study Franklin's informally prepared draft of the Assembly's nineteen acts, which raised the taxes, put Franklin in charge of any money taken from the Penns (a real insult), and protested the Indian land swindle. The proprietors then asked Franklin to prepare them a bill showing specifically how much money the Assembly was requesting, for they knew the agent lacked that authority. When he conceded he could not do that, they tried to bypass him and deal directly with Speaker Isaac Norris and the Assembly. Any such exchange, of course, would take months, and the Assembly wisely rallied behind Franklin. At every step, the Penns tried to fob the Pennsylvanian off onto their attorney, Ferdinand Paris, but Franklin would deal only with them directly.

The proprietors launched a campaign in the press to portray the province and its legislature as recalcitrant shirkers during wartime and Franklin personally as a bumptious grifter. Through loyal placemen back in Philadelphia, Thomas Penn even circulated the rumor that Franklin was betraying the colony in order to receive a knighthood in London.

Still in his sickbed, Franklin responded in kind. Under son William's name, he refuted attacks on the province by publishing letters in the *London Chronicle*, his friend Strahan's newspaper, and in the *Monthly Review*, a pro-Whig magazine (also printed by Strahan). He then set to work, again with William's help, on a book, *An Historical Review of the Constitution and Government of Pennsylvania,*[9] which laid out the Assembly's case. He was delighted to patch up his old friendship with James Ralph, who had failed at poetry during his time in London but succeeded so well as a writer of political hatchet work that the government paid him £300 a year not to write. Ralph helped in the editing and Strahan printed the pamphlet at Franklin's expense. Franklin, however, did not have the energy to write it. Recent scholarship into the secret authorship has credited Richard Jackson, a barrister so respected for his encyclopedic knowledge of the law that he was called "Omniscient Jackson." Jackson was an instant recruit to Franklin's side and used his knowledge of legal precedent to bolster Pennsylvania's case. Although the booklet was ready in the summer of 1758, it was held back until June 1759. It would have a telling effect on public opinion and on the government ministers as the time approached for deciding the case.

Jackson was soon to become a member of Parliament and later to become one of Pennsylvania's regular agents. He would remain always one of Franklin's closest friends. One trait the older man admired in Jackson was his skill with invective. Particularly bitter to the Penns was Jackson's characterization of them in the *Historical Review*:

> And who or what are these proprietaries? In the province, unsizable subjects and unsufficient lords. At home, gentlemen it is true, but gentlemen so very private that in the herd of gentry they are hardly to be found; not in court, not in office, not in Parliament.[10]

This 1759 cut was only one of many that Franklin aimed at the brothers beginning as early as January 1758. He had published the report by Tedyuskung's secretary, Charles Thomson, on the causes of the tribal anger at the proprietors. In addition to the steady stream of letters and unsigned articles he addressed to the London newspapers, Franklin wrote about the Penns often to his Assembly supporters in Philadelphia. In one to Speaker Isaac Norris, his scorn of Thomas Penn outgrew his control. He wrote of one conversation with Thomas in which he had argued to the proprietor that the original William Penn charter of the province gave the Assembly

> all the powers and privileges of an assembly according to the rights of free-born subjects of England, and as is usual in any of the British plantations in America. "Yes," says he, "but if my father granted privileges he was not by the royal charter empowered to grant, nothing can be claimed by such a grant." I said: "Then if your father had not right to grant the privileges he pretended to grant, and published all over Europe as

granted, those who came to settle in the province on the faith of that grant, and in expectation of enjoying the privileges contained in it, were deceived, cheated, and betrayed." He answered that they should have themselves looked to that; that the royal charter was no secret; they who came into the province on his father's offer of privileges, if they were deceived, it was their own fault. And that he said with a kind of triumphing laughing insolence, such as a low jockey might do when a purchaser complained that he had cheated him on a horse. I was astonished to see him thus meanly give up his father's character, and conceived at that moment a more cordial and thorough contempt for him than I ever felt for any man living, a contempt that I cannot express in words, but I believe my countenance expressed it strongly, and that his brother, who was looking at me, must have observed it. However, finding myself grow warm, I made no other answer to this than that the poor people were no lawyers themselves and, confiding in his father, did not think it necessary to consult any.[11]

Norris showed the letter around, as was intended. And, as might be expected, Penn loyalists made a copy and sent it speeding back to London. Thomas was outraged at the "low jockey" jab; in common usage it meant a shabby trader who sold horses of doubtful condition to the gullible—the used car salesman of the day. His rage at Franklin grew each time the two crossed paths. Franklin wrote to Norris again in June 1759, "When I meet him anywhere, there appears in his wretched countenance a strange mixture of hatred, anger, fear, and vexation."[12]

FRANKLIN'S TASK AT THE OUTSET HAD BEEN to persuade the proprietors to allow their lands to be taxed so the province could adequately fund a defense, but other issues intruded. The Assembly had arrested two Penn loyalists for libeling the Quakers, and Franklin had to fight that too before King George II's Privy Council. In addition, the Penns had instructed their governor to forbid the Assembly from issuing any new currency to finance a militia or to pay for Pennsylvania's share of the British expeditions against the French in Canada.

There was a host of little vexations, too. One of the counter-charges laid by the two men the Assembly had jailed in 1758 was that the Quakers were punishing Thomas Penn for abandoning their faith and joining the Anglican Church. In fact, Penn had never concealed his impatience with having to appoint royal governors who too often became captives of the Assembly, which disbursed their salaries. As a Quaker, Penn was prohibited from swearing an oath of fealty to the Crown and so could not be governor himself; by switching denominations, he could position himself for total control over his land. This was all the more imperative for Penn since the current governor, Sir William Denny (who had posted a £500 bond to carry out the proprietor's orders), was coming too much under the Assembly's sway on the matter of appropriations for defense.

Indeed, Governor Denny was the first break in the Penn's bulwark. In April 1759, he assented to an Assembly bill that issued £100,000 for defense, the currency to be redeemed later by tax revenues that for the first time included proprietary land. Denny had an important ally in this personally risky act, General Lord Loudoun. The military commander of Britain's North American forces had pressed all the colonial governors to raise militias and provide supplies for the ambitious campaign to take the war to the French strongholds in Canada. Governor Denny resigned—the Penns were afraid to foreclose on his bond—and his grateful protector Lord Loudoun allowed him to resume his colonel's commission in the army.

The battle would seesaw between the two contending sides. Even though the Assembly had freed the two pro-Penn provocateurs in the spring of 1758, there still was the matter of whether the lawmakers had acted legally. In January 1759, William Smith, one of these henchmen, arrived in London to plead before the Privy Council that he had been illegally charged.

Franklin had befriended Smith when he first came to America and had secured for him the position of provost for the Pennsylvania Academy, which Franklin had organized in 1753. Smith repaid that kindness by gravitating quickly to the proprietors' side and being a bitter critic of his early patron. He bitterly slandered Franklin wherever he could; he charged that the electrical experiments had been stolen from Franklin's clergyman friend Ebenezer Kinnersley, even though that scientist had publicly acknowledged the truth. Franklin angrily rebutted the slanders, but in the end he offered this wry retort:

> I made that man my enemy by doing him too much kindness. 'Tis the honestest way of acquiring an enemy. And, since 'tis convenient to have at least one enemy, who by his readiness to revile one on all occasions may make one careful of one's conduct, I shall keep him an enemy for that purpose.[13]

In May 1759, Franklin and the Assembly scored first in the battle with the Penns when the Board of Trade heard lawyers for both sides argue the Indian fraud claims. Thomas Penn had tried to influence Lord Granville and Lord Halifax, the senior colonial ministers, before the hearing, but his visit would not be successful. Franklin demanded before the Privy Council that the proprietors produce the title deeds they claimed gave them the new land rights. When the lawyer Paris refused, Franklin produced copies of the obvious forgeries and gave them to Lord Halifax. The normally slow-moving board quickly turned the matter over to the royal superintendent for Indian affairs, who told the Delawares to stay where they were.

Paris died in December 1759, which meant more delay. The Penns, as was their right, hired another private lawyer, Henry Wilmot, but at the same time they secured the services of the king's chief legal ministers, the attorney general and the solicitor general. These officials represented them before the Board of Trade and the Privy Council as the wrangling dragged on.

The Penns had scored some early points of their own in June 1759 when the Privy Council's committee on plantation matters ruled that the Assembly lacked the power to arrest Smith and the other agitator for libels against it, even though Parliament had, and frequently used, such authority in England. The real test was to come over the Penn family's demand that the Privy Council revoke the Assembly's £100,000 money issue, money that already was in circulation. Such a veto would rescue the Penns from being taxed but would throw the colony's economy into upheaval.

Here the brothers ran up against the king's overriding need for more money from the colonies to pay for his war. The Calvert family, the proprietors of Maryland, and other colonial owners also were resisting local taxation of their lands, so if the Privy Council ruled in favor of the Penns, it could throw into grave doubt the plan to shift part of the war burden onto the colonies being protected by the king's soldiers.

On the other hand, the Penns had growing influence among their class and within the government as their fortunes grew apace. And many ministers disliked these Americans, who seemed much less docile than they had been in the past. England was having its own troubles with democracy at the moment. Parliamentary power, though still supreme, was under siege by the king's faction on the one hand and the mobs in the London streets on the other. Having wrested power from kings, the ministers jealously guarded their authority. The politicians were not about to share with a bunch of farmers in the faraway colonies.

As Pennsylvania's petition was before the Committee on Plantation Affairs of the Board of Trade, Franklin reminded Norris, "You may conjecture what a reception a petition concerning privileges from the colonies may meet with from those who think that even the people of England have too many."[14] One of the officials Franklin sought advice from was Charles Pratt, the king's attorney general, who, though he represented the Penns, still was sympathetic to Franklin personally. He counseled the agent privately on whom to see and what to say within the ministerial circles.

During one such session Pratt made an eerie prophecy. He warned that the Americans someday were likely to demand independence, despite their current oaths of loyalty to England. Franklin countered that "no such idea was ever entertained by the Americans, nor will any such ever enter their heads, unless you grossly abuse them." That was just what worried him, Pratt replied, that the English capacity for making a bad situation worse might bring his vision to life. He was closer to the truth than he knew.

Franklin, however, saw the struggle within England's government elite as an opportunity for greater togetherness between the colonies and the Mother Country. What had begun as the French and Indian War was now the Seven Years War, and England under George II was fighting another global struggle with Spain as well as France. Suddenly governments, colonial and royal, needed money as badly as the Penns wanted land. The task, to Franklin's mind, was to make Pennsylvania a more important partner in the eyes of the king and his ministers.

As 1759 BECAME 1760, FRANKLIN TRIED to take the province's case directly to William Pitt, the de facto prime minister. This was a risky move on a number of counts. Pitt held the power but not the top position in a shaky coalition of parliamentary forces. King George II disliked him intensely. Pitt's hold on power was directly related to his single-minded, and so far highly successful, conduct of the war. He was not about to get personally involved in what was a provincial dispute with a proprietor, especially since the wrangle involved the interests of other proprietary colonies.

William Pitt, later first Earl of Chatham and forever after called Pitt the Elder, was one of those meteors that light up the English political sky from time to time. He was just in his early fifties (he was born in 1708), but for nearly twenty-five years he had dominated the House of Commons with his unparalleled genius in the brawling floor debates. His criticism of King George's War helped bring down the unassailable Robert Walpole in 1742. Though crippled by gout and plagued by depressions to the point of collapse, Pitt was the most able man of his time and singularly scrupulous with both the public purse and the perquisites of power. It was a fair complaint about him that he treated his supporters worse than his enemies and that his only real interest was in concentrating power in himself. Yet he spoke fearlessly for the common people of England (although he was never comfortable with them in person) and would be one of the major voices in support of the American cause as the Revolution drew close.

Pitt conducted the war brilliantly, to the dismay of the French. From 1757 onward, Britain captured Bengal from the French and began to solidify a hold on India. Both Fort Duquesne and Louisbourg, which guarded the mouth of the St. Lawrence, fell in 1758; Quebec was taken in 1759. By 1759, all of Canada was British, as was the French sugar island of Guadeloupe in the Caribbean, which was forty times wealthier. A lively debate began as to which possession—if either—was to be offered back to the French to secure a prompt peace.

Franklin had never been able to secure a direct meeting with Pitt during his time in London, and it was clear that the minister would refuse any direct appeal for aid. Yet it was possible to brief Pitt about Pennsylvania's plight and trust the minister to act behind the scenes on the plantations committee that he headed. In one letter, Franklin outlined the Assembly's complaints against some of the officials the Penns had suborned. He added a personal postscript at the bottom of the letter: "Between you and I, it is said that we may look upon them all to be a pack of d——d r——ls, and that unless we bribe them all higher than our adversaries can do, and condescend to every piece of dirty work they require, we shall never be able to attain common justice at their hands." He ran his pen through this last sentence but left it readable.[15]

In June 1760, the Board of Trade committee held a series of hearings, initially rejecting seven of the nineteen acts the Assembly had sent, including the currency issue and taxation of the Penn lands. But when Franklin appealed, the committee held further hearings. At one, Franklin recorded much later, Lord Mansfield (the chief justice and a Privy Council member) called him into a side room and asked if he would guarantee that issuing the money would not injure the Penns. Franklin assured him that no injury was intended and agreed to sign a compromise that the unsurveyed Penn land would not be taxed and their surveyed land would be taxed at a rate no higher than that of other property owners.

Wilmot, the Penn lawyer, agreed to the compromise, but he specified that the tax money the Penns owed must come out of arrears owed to the land office and not out of the proprietors' pockets. The deal was struck. With unusual haste, the full Privy Council in August ratified the arrangement, and King George II gave his royal assent in September.

As a result, the Assembly's issue of £100,000 stood (and presumably the legislature could issue money in the future) and Penn lands would be taxed, so the Pennsylvanians felt triumphant. It was an important victory for self-government. It also put Franklin in charge of Pennsylvania's share of a parliamentary war appropriation to aid the colonies. In all, with some of the Penn money included, he was able to set up an investment fund of more than £30,000 to pay for colonial military purchases.

But given how much land the Penns held, their contribution to the province's revenues was minuscule.* If anything, Thomas Penn's grip on power would increase. With William Denny gone, he could name a new and more pliant governor (this one offered a £500 per annum kickback), and increasing numbers of judges and law officers were his nominees. He even for a time blocked efforts to conciliate those Delaware tribes that had returned to the English side in the war with the French.

Most of all, Penn was now free of any restraints in his campaign to get rid of Benjamin Franklin as Pennsylvania's agent, indeed to destroy him totally if he could. Only then would his hold on Pennsylvania be unchallenged, or so he thought.

* Carl Van Doren estimates that the Penns paid only one-fiftieth of the funds raised that year.

Chapter 8

A New Nemesis

enjamin Franklin had come to London three years earlier to persuade Thomas Penn if he could, and to maneuver around him if he must. By any reasonable judgment he had achieved what he came for: the Assembly had won the power to tax the proprietors and the king's most senior ministers had repudiated Penn for his shady dealings with the Indians. Franklin should have sailed home victorious in that winter of 1760, back to Philadelphia to resume the quiet life he said he yearned for.

But he stayed. Why?

For one thing, though he had achieved his specific mandate, much still had to be done in London. To begin, there was the matter of £15,000 that had to be dragged out of Thomas Penn's pockets. The money had to be invested and managed in London to pay merchants there for the arms and supplies the militia needed at home. Everything, gunpowder especially, had to be imported from England. Even Franklin's opponents would concede that he had the business and technological know-how to do the job. In fact, those who were ambivalent about, or opposed to, having Franklin as Pennsylvania's point man did not have enough power to replace him because of all the rival political factions in Pennsylvania—the peace Quakers and the defense Quakers, the rising antiproprietary classes and the pro-Penn forces. Many believed tales that Franklin was living the high life in London, but they could do nothing about it.

Another, often overlooked reason for his prolonged stay is that Franklin was visibly weary of Pennsylvania. He still wanted to work for the province's betterment but was no longer sure he wanted to go back and live there. He had grown tired of being constantly hammered upon by a political community back home that was more bitterly divided with each passing day. As early as the summer of 1755, he had written to his London friend Peter Collinson:

> I like neither the governor's conduct nor the Assembly's, and, having some share in the confidence of both I have endeavoured to reconcile 'em, but in vain; and between 'em they make me very uneasy.... If my being able now and then to influence a good measure did not keep up my spirits, I should be ready to swear never to serve again as assemblyman, since both sides expect more from me than they ought, and blame me sometimes for not doing what I am not able to do, as well for not preventing what was not in my power to prevent.[1]

Later he had written, "I abhor these altercations, and if I did not love the country and the people would remove immediately into a more quiet government, Connecticut, where I am also happy to have many friends."[2]

In truth, there was little likelihood of his moving away, at least to another colony. But internal political strife was not the only reason for his discontent. A deeper difference was emerging between the North American colonies and the sister British plantations in the Caribbean and India. Put most simply, America was becoming less like England every day. This went even beyond the demographic changes he had decried in *Observations*. America's very reason for being now differed sharply from that of the other British colonies. By tradition an Englishman went off to India or the West Indies to get as rich as possible and then come back home. The nature of the economic activities there was strictly exploitive: to get as much of the materials of the place—sugar, fabrics, produce, and the like—and sell it at home at the highest price to Englishmen, who then turned those products into goods for European markets. This was the heart of the mercantilist age, and few colonial adventurers planned to stay where they sought fortune.

But while the early North American colonies were founded to provide the same kinds of raw materials and unfinished goods, a strange thing began to happen almost from the start in the 1600s. Many of the first arrivals were refugees from the cycles of political or religious persecution. They stayed and set down roots. Newer arrivals pushed past the burgeoning seacoast towns to buy land. They worked themselves to a state of economic independence that made a demand for a political voice inevitable.

True enough, Franklin welcomed all this, as he himself was proof that a humbly born person could acquire land, wealth, and civic prominence from his own energies. He sincerely believed that others could duplicate his own good fortune—indeed, that his own security lay in others' having the same success. Yet this belief was at the root of his present unhappiness. Frankly, he despaired of the way Pennsylvania was turning out. After thirty years of expending his tireless energies for his adopted home, Franklin concluded that things were getting worse, not better. People were striving to better themselves but not their community. Among Franklin's more radical views was that anything a man owned more than the bare necessities to keep him clothed, fed, sheltered, and occupied could be considered the property of society, since it was the community of effort that produced the surplus. As he summed up in a letter to his friend Strahan, "I imagine that what we have above what we can use, is not properly ours, tho' we posses it; and that the rich Man who must die, was no more worth what he leaves, than the debtor who must pay."[3]

Even more disturbing, Franklin was being forced to reevaluate what it meant to be an American colonist. At this point in time, many in the colonies saw no conflict in considering themselves both Americans and Englishmen. As Americans they thought of themselves as superior to newer arrivals from other parts of Europe, more self-reliant and adventurous. But it also was important that they had, by charter, all the rights of freeborn Englishmen. That was a significant safety line for a people dangling at the outer limits of civilization.

As Lord Granville had pointed out, however, so much of what his countrymen believed about themselves was mistaken. Only two colonies—Connecticut and Rhode Island—were free of the restricting hands of proprietors. Elsewhere the provincial assemblies, which had grown used to making local laws and raising local funds, clashed with the colony owners, who wanted more say and more profit. Now the national government in the form of Parliament was poking its nose—and taxing power—into the struggle. No good could come of it, and the provinces seemed ill suited to the struggle of resistance.

Franklin had written two pamphlets—his *Observations* and *Plan for Settling Two Western Colonies in North America*—that argued the case for America as a prosperous part of a far larger English community. He reasoned that an expansion of the colonies to the west would bring both prosperity to England and greater political strength to the colonies. He wrote:

> Now I look on the colonies as so many counties gained to Great Britain, and more advantageous to it than if they had been gained out of the seas around its coasts and joined to its land. For, being in different climates, they afford greater variety of produce; and, being separated by the ocean, they increase much more its shipping and seamen. And since they are all included in the British Empire, which has only extended itself by their means; and the strength and wealth of the parts that are the strength and wealth of the whole; what imports it to the general state whether a merchant, a smith, or a hatter grow rich in Old or New England?[4]

Franklin also foresaw that as population and wealth expanded by geometric numbers in America, the balance of English interests would shift out of the confines of its tight little island and expand across the vast, empty (of all save Indians) continent to the shores of the Pacific. Now there was an empire Britain should aspire to.

Thus, both because he chafed at the Penns' proprietorship and because he wanted his colony (and all the others) to be an important part of the British Empire, Franklin had one last motive for staying on in London. Without any mandate from the Assembly, he began a new campaign: to wrest Pennsylvania from the proprietors and return it to Crown control. Kings had taken provinces back from bad proprietors before, and it was time, he felt, to save Pennsylvania from Thomas Penn's misrule.

Because of his anger at Penn's behavior, this likely was Franklin's strongest motivation to stay. Thomas Penn had targeted Franklin and was looking for even more control over his colony, not less. It would be a bruising struggle, Franklin knew, but his blood was up. He would look to the king to solve the colony's problems.

ON THE MORNING OF OCTOBER 25, 1760, George Augustus, King George II, thought he would go for a turn around the Kensington Palace gardens before he began work on the boxes of official documents that awaited him. Suddenly the right ventricle of his heart ruptured, and soon he was dead.[5]

It was little more than a month after Franklin had won the king's assent to tax Pennsylvania's proprietors. Like most Englishmen, Franklin rejoiced in the advent of King George III, who was twenty-two and was believed to hold such liberal and reformist principles that he was dubbed the "Patriot King" even before his coronation eleven months hence. Franklin believed firmly in fortune, and he saw this as his opportunity to take Pennsylvania away from the proprietors.

As a boy, George William Frederick had been a sluggard who liked to sleep all day and who turned sullen and obstinate when he did not get his way. He adored his father, Frederick, the Prince of Wales, and was heartbroken when in 1751 the prince died suddenly from an abscess caused by the blow of a tennis ball. From the age of thirteen onward, George was completely under the domination of his mother, the Princess Augusta, who brought from the small German court of Saxe-Gotha a punctilious insistence on royal prerogatives. She constantly nagged at him, "George, be king." And now he was to be one.

As is common with princes-in-waiting, George had no preparation or training to succeed his grandfather on the throne. George II and the boy's father had loathed each other, at least partly because Frederick sneered at his father's corrupt court. Ultimately Frederick and Augusta set up a rival court and drew around them supporters who were ambitious to vault to the front of the line then dominated by Robert Walpole and his ministers. King George at one point actively considered having the Prince of Wales kidnapped and exiled to the wilds of America. George II made some efforts to reconcile with his grandson, but the boy clung to his mother's prejudices.

Franklin had reason to welcome the reign of George III. He had numerous friends and contacts in the circle that had paid court to the Princess Augusta and the young prince. The various learned societies also rejoiced at the prospect of having a kindred spirit on the throne. George, while not well educated, was intelligent and fascinated by the visible and mechanical side of science. He particularly loved advances in agriculture and shipbuilding. He would be an enthusiastic patron of the same societies that Franklin belonged to. From time to time he even mentioned Franklin's name in conversations with others, and he considered using Franklin's design for lightning rods to protect some government buildings. Royal patronage, perhaps a title and English estate, might follow.

Franklin had implicit faith in the new king's sense of self-interest and justice. Surely the king would see that his American colonies were being badly run by greedy proprietors; if he would just unburden his loyal colonists from the constraints of both proprietor and Parliament, a glorious empire would be his.

Quite wrongly, however, Franklin and others believed that the young king was of a reformist mind. This was largely because his principal tutor, a Scot named John Stuart, and others with influence over George were among the freethinkers of the day. Backing the reform movement was a swelling public outcry against the blatantly corrupt operations of both the old king's court and the parliamentary majority held by the ministers. Commoners and merchants alike looked forward to a king who would root out contract scandals that hampered government efficiency. They also dreamed of a peacemaker who would halt the disastrous run of wars that had drained the country. They wanted a benevolent intellect that would preside over an explosion in thought and achievement in a true golden age for Britain.

But what George III wanted was power; he wanted to be an absolute monarch of the kind not seen since the English Civil War a hundred years before. If he could achieve that, he did not want much more in the way of reform. "I will have no innovations in my time," he declared.

Feeling the lack of broad public support, the previous Hanoverian kings had been forced to rely on their ministers almost totally; in so doing they gave away much of their power to reward and punish and were left to wheedle what money they could from Parliament. George III planned to claw back as many of these royal prerogatives to appoint and grant as he could. He also wanted to surround himself with ministers who could command majorities in the House of Commons and the House of Lords and at the same time do his bidding. It also was clear to George (because John Stuart had convinced him) that it was time to call an end to the latest war with France, even if it meant giving back some of the possessions won by force of arms. Insofar as he had given any thought to the American colonies, he considered them his by right and thought that the colonists had a duty to be loyal subjects and to make him still richer so he could become more powerful.

Thus the sluggardly George turned into an energetic monarch set on a determined course. He moved deliberately, however. He did not at first disturb his grandfather's government, which was headed by the Duke of Newcastle but was really the creature of William Pitt, who was masterfully conducting the war with France. The king would move only after victory was assured and the French had been swept from their holdings in America and India.

George III was bent on challenging the status quo; he would test the common wisdom that held that only Whig parliamentary government could make a nation great and just. England was ripe for yet another bloody revolt. If George III did not seize power from these corrupters, the mob would and anarchy would follow. This was not a case of restoring the Tory landed nobility to power; there were too few of them to matter, and they would back the Crown anyway. So would the Church of England bishops seated in the House of Lords. But the Whigs, the untitled squires who ruled the shires and the merchants of the bigger cities, held a monopoly on power. Once the great force for British democracy, the Whig revolution had dragged a constitution of civil liberties out of King William III in 1689. Now the ruling class had given themselves newly created titles and had scrambled for place and profit. A large minority of reformers on the Whig side of the House of Commons might be coaxed into a king's party if the rewards of power were credible.

Franklin could not know this, but a new nemesis was moving onto the stage. Thomas Penn would continue to taunt, vex, and block Franklin whenever he could right up until his death in 1775. In George III, however, Franklin would have a lifelong adversary who was a shrewd judge of character and an adroit manipulator of political alliances, and who had a bulldog tenacity. The king had huge empty holes in his education, especially about history; he was arrogant, obstinate, and bent on a course that he could never win. But, as we shall see, while many of his ministers often underestimated Benjamin Franklin, King George III never did.

FRANKLIN WAS WORKING HARD ON BEHALF of Pennsylvania, but of course he continued to divide his life into discrete compartments. Even while fighting his bitter battle with the Penns, Franklin had launched himself into the debate over peace with France. Since the death of George II, that debate had built up considerably, for it was known that the young king and John Stuart (soon to be the Earl of Bute) strongly favored ending the war at once. In contrast, Franklin had since as early as 1759 opposed concluding a quick peace with the French. He also had been outspoken on the question of whether either Canada or Guadeloupe, or both, should be returned in order to secure peace.

Franklin's articles on this subject appeared in Strahan's *Chronicle*, and in the spring of 1760 he published them as a pamphlet. He argued that even though the French sugar island offered immense short-term profits, it should be given back, if anything, rather than giving up Canada. Using population estimates, trade figures, and droll satire, he pointed out that the American colonies could fill the area between the St. Lawrence River and the Mississippi in less than a century and that British trade and influence would "spread around the Whole Globe, and awe the World."[6] His most telling point, however, was the obvious one to English minds. As long as the French bordered British colonies in America, the threat of incursions by them and their Indian allies would require more redcoats and pounds sterling ad infinitum. Remove the French from the region and even the Indians would be brought under control.

Starting with these articles and the pamphlet, Franklin began to give the concept of American union a double meaning that suited his double purpose. Canada, he argued, should be brought closer to the other American colonies to give the whole region wider room to grow and be populated. An expanding union of North American colonies could not help but be drawn closer to England, if only because the colonists would be too self-absorbed in their own interests to ever consider independence or nationhood.

His argument was neither a contradiction of his Albany Congress plan for union nor simple disingenuous political rhetoric. By arguing that the colonies could be both united and more loyal to England, Franklin was trying to ease parliamentary Whigs' growing fears that America could not be trusted unless it was subservient. He often used a metaphor of the mother who is honored all the more for letting her children thrive. There was little prospect that the colonies would break away on their own. He went further in the pamphlet:

> If they could not agree to unite for their defence against the French and Indians, who were perpetually harassing their settlements, burning their buildings, and murdering their people; can it reasonably be supposed there is any danger of their uniting against their own nation, which protects and encourages them, with which they have so many connexions and ties of blood, interest, and affection, and which 'tis well known they all love much more than they love one another?...I will venture to say a union amongst them for such a purpose is not merely improbable, it is impossible; and if the union of the whole is impossible, the attempt of a part must be madness; as those colonies that did not join the rebellion would join the Mother Country in suppressing it.

Then Franklin issued a caveat similar to the warning he had made to Charles Pratt, the king's attorney general, two years before:

> When I say such a union is impossible, I mean without the most grievous tyranny and oppression. People who have property in a country which they may lose, and privileges which they may endanger, are generally disposed to be quiet, and even to bear much rather than hazard all. While the government is mild and just, while important civil and religious rights are secure, such subjects will be dutiful and obedient. The waves do not rise but when the winds blow.[7]

His aphorism about the waves and winds would be repeated a number of times in the years to come as the storm of revolution drew nearer.

Chapter 9

Degrees and Separation

$\mathcal{B}$enjamin Franklin was repeatedly insisting that he would soon return to Philadelphia, and yet something always kept him. As we have seen, his resentment toward Thomas Penn certainly motivated him to keep working on behalf of the colony, and his growing distress over what Pennsylvania was becoming did not make him want to return home any sooner. But beyond all of that, Franklin was simply thrilled to be in London. His ability to compartmentalize allowed him to enjoy all that the great metropolis had to offer even while he advanced the cause of the colony.

As he had in Philadelphia, Franklin constructed a home base of operations in London where he was the focus of all attention and every comfort. At Craven Street, he could seek refuge in his library with his experiments, then sally forth refreshed into the public arena. This almost exact replica of his Philadelphia environment was near Charing Cross, the epicenter of teeming London.

Samuel Johnson made an acute judgment when he said, "Fleet Street has a very animated appearance, but I think the full tide of human existence is at Charing Cross." And so it was. Fed by the wide Strand, which ran above the banks of the Thames westward from Fleet Street, this mammoth crossroads was populated at all hours of the day. Covent Garden was to the north, the Exchange and the Law Courts to the east, and the government complex at Westminster and Whitehall to the west. Coffeehouses nudged next to such great mansions. At night, revelers of both sexes made their way from theaters in Haymarket to pleasure gardens across the river Thames. Craven Street, one of the many small lanes that jutted off the thoroughfare, ran down to the riverbank. From there nearly all the places important to Franklin were within easy walking distance.

Margaret Addinell Stevenson was that most fortunate of English women, a widow of property. Her domain was the house at Craven Street, which had a basement kitchen, three floors above, and an attic garret.* Her merchant husband, now conveniently deceased, had left her another house across the street. She also had three sisters who were similarly situated, owning real estate in their own right without any man to control it or them. Mrs. Stevenson was delighted to have Franklin, William, and the two slaves as boarders; it was a foolish woman who did not welcome the protection of some respectable and powerful man, if only to ensure her independence. There are a few letters and some household accounts but not much of a personal record of Margaret Stevenson. She was, by the recollection of others, a forthright and prickly personality with

---

* Number 36 is being restored as the Benjamin Franklin House museum and education center.

everyone save Franklin—think of an English version of Deborah—which must have suited him very well indeed.

Franklin's quarters were all he could have wanted. Mrs. Stevenson kept the ground-floor front room for receiving the growing number of callers who wanted to see the American agent. A smaller room behind was for dining, tea, or cards, and a pantry was behind that. On the floor above, Franklin occupied a four-room suite dominated by a fourteen-by-twelve-foot front room; it boasted three floor-to-ceiling windows, which Franklin frequently threw open for his daily "air baths"—deep-breathing exercises in the nude—which must have made a spectacle for the Craven Street neighbors. To the rear was another large room where Franklin built his library and laboratory. Behind that was a smaller room where Peter slept and where his master's clothes were stored. At the very rear of the floor plan was Franklin's tiny bedroom. Mrs. Stevenson and her teenage daughter, Mary (called Polly), lived on the floor above. Other transient tenants, many of them Americans, had rooms on the third floor. William and King occupied the garret until the young man went off to pursue his law studies at the Middle Temple.*

From Craven Street Franklin marched forth each day to advance both his colony's cause and himself. He rose early and took pride in shaving himself instead of indulging in the customary luxury of having a barber call at the house. Then he breakfasted lightly on tea and porridge. After that he might receive callers or spend several hours answering correspondence from home and from his science colleagues in Europe. If time allowed, he worked on one of his many research projects. He built a clock with a simpler mechanism; perfected a damper for the house's smoky, inefficient fireplaces; and worked on pumps and steam engines, on the differences between

---

* King ran off and was taken in by a woman who taught him music. Franklin made no effort to recover him.

rainwater and seawater, and on the absorption of heat by different colored cloths.

Late in the morning, Franklin would begin his round of calls at the Board of Trade offices at Whitehall. From there he might attempt to see a changing cast of ministers who were responsible for colonial affairs. Some of the king's ministers would see him at once, others only privately at their homes; some allied themselves with the Penn brothers and refused his calls altogether. He had also made some friends within the permanent bureaucracy, including John Pownall, secretary to the Board of Trade and brother of Thomas Pownall, Franklin's ally at the Albany Conference in 1754. This meant he could at least get his arguments considered even if they were not officially presented.

If Parliament was in session at Westminster, he might be seen listening to the debates from the visitors gallery. The rest of the day, he would drop by the coffeehouses that catered to merchants who traded with a specific colony. The Pennsylvania Coffee House was where he collected his mail and newspapers from home, but he also was a regular at the cafés devoted to Maryland, Virginia, and New England merchants. While he often returned home to receive callers in the afternoon, and for tea, Franklin spent most nights going to club dinners or learned society meetings. On Monday nights he dined at the George and Vulture Tavern with a group of scientists and explorers that included Captain James Cook. He also dined with a literary club at the Prince of Wales Tavern in Conduit Street, and at the Philosophers' Dining Club at the Mitre in Fleet Street. On Thursdays, he was faithful to his London Junto—known as the Club of Honest Whigs—which dined at St. Paul's Coffee House.

This was the group of friends closest to his heart. It included Bishop Jonathan Shipley, a wealthy cleric and member of the House of Lords who would become an outspoken supporter for the American cause during the Revolution. Other Honest Whigs were the scientist Joseph Priestley; Andrew Kippis, the editor of the *Biographia Britannica;* William Watson, his erstwhile rival in electricity; several scholar-officials of the British Museum; and his friends Dr. Fothergill and John Pringle, another eminent physician. James Boswell, the biographer of Samuel Johnson, and historian-philosopher David Hume attended when they were in town. The Honest Whigs were mostly dissenters by conviction, libertarian by ideal, anti-Parliament by politics; they were fascinated by questions where science, philosophy, and religion intersected.

Dr. Pringle would surpass William Strahan the publisher as Franklin's closest personal friend in London. While the two printers always remained fond of each other, Strahan disapproved of the Pennsylvanian's radical challenges to authority, and they finally agreed to disagree. Pringle, on the other hand, had both the eminence and questing mind that Franklin aspired to.* As the British army's chief physician during King George's War, he had won fame for ordering improvements in the quality of medicine and sanitation provided the soldiers. He, too, held the Copley Medal from the Royal Society and would replace Linnaeus as one of eight foreign members of the French Academy of Science. Small wonder that Franklin dined at Pringle's home nearly every Sunday night. Pringle was a dour character, but he was a skeptic and could engage Franklin on any topic that caught their interest. They soon discovered a mutual addiction to chess and to travel. James Boswell, a patient of Pringle's, wondered at the closeness of the friendship between the physician, with his "peculiar sour manner," and Franklin, who was "all jollity and pleasantry." Boswell remarked, "I said to myself, 'Here's a prime contrast: acid and alkali.' "

---

* Sir John Pringle (1707–1782) is considered the father of modern military medicine. He also wrote widely on scientific research, from Priestley's research on gases, to gravity, to Captain Cook's methods of preventing scurvy. A Scot, he also shared Franklin's religious skepticism. He became a physician to the queen and later to George III, who knighted him.

Franklin also devoted many hours to the two learned societies that were his joy and pride. The Royal Society of London for the Improving of Natural Knowledge was nearly a century old at this point and had boasted Sir Isaac Newton as its first president. Franklin's status as a fellow of the Royal Society and as a winner of its most prestigious prize, the Copley Medal, was the honor he prized most. The eminent botanist Sir Joseph Banks now presided over the supreme collection of England's greatest scientific minds, of both the academic and lay variety. (Even today, the Royal Society remains the leading force in the advancement of pure science in scores of disciplines.)

But while Franklin regularly attended the Royal Society's formal functions, his heart and mind was most engaged by the more prosaic Society for the Encouragement of Arts, Manufactures, and Commerce.* Founded in 1754, at about the time Franklin had been circulating his *Proposal for Promoting Useful Knowledge among the British Plantations in America*, the society offered prizes and development grants for a host of mechanical devices and agricultural staples. Franklin had freely adapted this grant system for his American Philosophical Society.

As in Philadelphia, he worked behind the scenes and let others stand in front; to be sure, pushing himself forward would have offended his English colleagues. Soon enough, however, they learned, as so many others had, how useful he was. When they found they could not do well without him, his prominence increased and his friendships grew. The society drew merchants, clergymen, and political figures to its projects, as well as established scientists. A typical meeting might draw the owner of the Vauxhall Gardens amusement park, the chaplain to the royal family, and

* Since 1908, it too has been a *Royal* society.

other fellows from the Royal Society; Thomas Penn often attended as an interested patron.[1] William Pitt also became a sponsor.

Franklin joined many of the committees that the Society for the Arts established to promote improvements in all aspects of human life—on cobalt, corn grinders, rattraps, and timothy grass. In December 1760, the society named him and friend John Pownall as cochairmen on the Committee on Colonies and Trade. For the next two years this panel dispensed grants to American inventors and botanists working on a vast array of projects—improving carrots and corn, producing cheaper potash, breeding sturgeon, producing isinglass, hemp, silk grass, and opium, and much more. Franklin also recruited scores of new members for the society on both sides of the Atlantic. This was the life he had dreamed of back in Philadelphia, and he savored it with delight. He was accepted—no, admired—by men who were above him in station, equals in ability, and comrades in the great debates of the day.

But even this would not be enough. Franklin became involved in the Reverend Thomas Bray's plan to build orphanages in London, New York, Rhode Island, and Williamsburg to shelter and educate young Indians and black slaves who had been abandoned during the turmoil of the colonial wars. Here we see the first substantive shift in Franklin's attitude toward the African. Bray was turning the black waif castoffs of London into educated and useful individuals, and this resonated with Franklin, who attributed his own success to education. He soon became chairman of the fund-raising arm of the organization, known as the Associates of Dr. Bray, which included many of the notables from his other learned societies. At one such meeting he was introduced to the illustrious Dr. Samuel Johnson, who disliked Franklin's politics and refused thereafter to meet him again.

The famous dictionary creator was not the only Londoner who spurned Franklin. One of the more obvious places to seek contacts would have been one of the many Masonic lodges of the city. But there is no record of Franklin's ever being invited to join, even though he had been a provincial grand master at home. Of course, the Freemasonry movement was far different in the colonies from what it was in England. In America, Masons were very much of the rising classes, whereas the nobility and establishment church controlled the lodges in England. Prince Frederick, the late father of George III, had begun a tradition in which Princes of Wales became active Freemasons. Such men never would have admitted a provincial tradesman who espoused radical political notions and sought the company of dissenters and freethinkers. Nor, for that matter, was Franklin ever admitted to the private London clubs of the aristocracy such as Whites, Almacks, and Brooks; this eminently social creature would always be kept at arm's length by the English power elite.

REMARKABLY, DESPITE HIS HECTIC LIFE IN LONDON, Franklin still had time to travel throughout England on journeys that took weeks, sometimes months, and that would have exhausted lesser men.

Since Parliament usually adjourned during the summer, most of official London sought refuge until early autumn at their country estates, coming back for short stays when official business demanded. Franklin had toured Northamptonshire in search of relatives in 1758 and paused at Cambridge to conduct some electrical experiments with a colleague there. In 1759 he had journeyed to Scotland and back. It was a grueling trek, since Scottish roads were almost nonexistent and the inns along the way more dangerous than the roads. Yet Franklin remained convinced of the benefits of travel; he often lamented that he fell ill when not on the move.

The 1759 trip is an instructive one in that it shows Franklin's capacity to immerse himself in a multitude of tasks. First, this long trek was to express his gratitude to the University at St. Andrews,

which earlier in the year had awarded him an honorary doctorate—
he would evermore be, to friend and foe alike, Dr. Franklin. But he
also intended to put his case, his province's case, to the leaders of the
Scottish Enlightenment. So it was important that he make a good
impression. His account ledger shows that he paid £8 to his wig-
maker, Howard of Jermyn Street, to have his and William's wigs
refurbished. New suits were ordered for both men and a post chaise*
was leased from the man who provided Franklin's town carriage.
There were other outlays: £11, four shillings, to Mrs. Stevenson for
a month's room and board, and a small disbursement to one of the
many women who importuned the agent for help, a Mrs. Henry
Flower, who got £3, twelve shillings. The ledger provided no explanation for this latter expense.

The payout to Mrs. Flower has raised eyebrows, and perhaps for
good reason. Young William, who had just been admitted to the bar
a year earlier, had gotten an unnamed woman pregnant, but he
was of no mind to take the child as his own when his own
prospects were still on the rise. Some arrangement had to be made
to care for the mother and the child, and Benjamin almost certainly
made it.

William, or Billy as he was called at home, was often seen at the
Duke of Northumberland's house and other mansions, where he
pursued the twin goals of political office and a good marriage to a
wealthy woman. He was a bit taller than his father and had the
same thin-lipped, high-browed good looks. Billy quickly became
more of a polished Londoner than his father and was far more vol-
uble and entertaining at a large dinner table. Eminent men who
admired the elder Franklin confessed to liking the son as well.
Father and son were particularly close during these years. Together

---

* A two-wheeled, one-horse carriage with a folding canopy.

they had campaigned on the Pennsylvania frontier, weathered an ocean voyage, and struggled for the Pennsylvania cause. They were good companions for what would be an arduous journey.

On arriving in Edinburgh, Franklin was fêted and made a Guild Brother of the City. The most influential and warmest of Franklin's new Scots friends was Henry Home, Lord Kames. Here was a man to the American's taste. Kames was at the beginning of a thirty-year career of distinction on the Scottish high court benches, but he also was active in promoting fisheries, arts, and manufacturing throughout Scotland. He was, in addition, something of a philosopher, battling with another Edinburgh celebrity who welcomed Franklin, David Hume.

The American then went up to St. Andrews for the formal investiture of his doctorate.* On the way through Glasgow he met and discussed the mercantilist economic constraints on the colonies with Adam Smith, who was just outlining his theories of free markets. Heading back to Edinburgh, he visited with new friends who ranged from the great city's booksellers and printers to the most senior physicians of the day. Here he promoted his views against the proprietors (which were more acceptable up north) and sounded out the still resentful Scots about what a proper relationship with the Crown should be. Franklin was pleased to find that many Scots approved of him and his politics—though not all, to be sure. Hume, for one, disputed his views at every turn; nevertheless, they remained cordial to one another, and the philosopher later wrote Franklin one of the most flattering comments he would receive.†

---

* The doctorate is believed to have been proposed by a St. Andrews professor who had lived in Philadelphia and been a Junto member.
† When Franklin prepared to return to America in the autumn of 1762, Hume wrote, "I am sorry that you intend soon to leave our hemisphere. America has sent us many good things, gold, silver, sugar, tobacco, indigo, etc., but you are the first philosopher and indeed the first great man of letters for whom we are beholden to her."

In all, Franklin was gone nearly three months, and he reckoned he had traveled fifteen hundred miles. Having left on August 8, he resumed his Craven Street ledgers on November 2.

FRANKLIN WAS THRILLED WITH LIFE IN LONDON. In the autumn of 1761, he was able to obtain one of the scarce tickets to Westminster Abbey to witness the coronation of King George III, which must have been a delight for the man who still had faith in the Patriot King. Still, Franklin's official tasks remained onerous. Parliament had appropriated £200,000 to partially reimburse the various colonies for their share of military spending in prior years, and as primary agent for Pennsylvania, Franklin was responsible for the complex financial arrangements. When the money finally became available in November 1760, Franklin tried to deposit the roughly £30,000 that was Pennsylvania's share in the Bank of England and let Pennsylvania authorities draw checks on the account for purchases in England. But the bank refused to take money from one man and let others draw it out, so Franklin had to assume the double duty of both depositor and payer.

Blocked by the Penns' new governor, the Assembly could not risk new legislation to fix matters, so Franklin had to disburse payment orders as they came in and invest the remainder in the hopes of earning the colony some profit. During 1761, Franklin bought stock for £26,900, nineteen shillings, eight pence, which had a face value of £30,000. Almost immediately, however, negotiations for peace with France broke down and a new war with Spain loomed, causing shares to fall. Franklin's holdings suddenly were worth £3,000 less than the purchase price. Despite his warnings to be frugal, the Assembly wrote more checks on the funds than he could cover, and he was forced to take out loans from two banks, the Barclay brothers, and Sargent, Aufrere & Co.

In 1761, Parliament made a second grant, and Franklin tried, over Penn objections, to shift his responsibility to the bankers. Pressed by the proprietors, the Barclays dropped out, but the bank of John Sargent stood by him. The total losses after the debacle was settled came to nearly £4,000. Penn agents in Philadelphia spread word that the losses were due to Franklin's folly and grand living. But Isaac Norris, the Assembly Speaker, assured his agent that the vast majority did not blame him; indeed, Norris continued to send his own money to Franklin to invest on his behalf.[2]

DESPITE HIS MONEY TROUBLES, Franklin continued to challenge Thomas Penn whenever the opportunity arose. About this time he met a great-grandson of Pennsylvania founder William Penn. This young man, named Springett Penn, was descended from Gulielma Penn, William's first wife. Springett charged that his uncle Thomas (half uncle, actually) was trying to cheat him out of his estate in York County, Pennsylvania. One can imagine Franklin's glee as he pushed this cause around the corridors of Whitehall. Unfortunately for the agent, the matter died when Springett did, in 1766.

William Franklin in the meantime was moving up in the world rapidly. Dr. Pringle had become an intimate of the new royal family and of Lord Bute. Lord Bute was a fan of Franklin's and conducted his own electrical experiments. Franklin and his son visited Bute a number of times; indeed, a portrait of the Scottish lord was installed in the Market Street house in Philadelphia as proof of the great man's friendship.[3] William was suddenly advanced as a prospective royal governor for the colony of New Jersey. Probably through the same Dr. Pringle's good offices, both Franklins were hauled up to Oxford University in April 1762 for honorary degrees. Franklin received a doctor of civil laws and William a master of arts.

But there was little joy for Franklin. There was no immediate prospect for a royal charter for Pennsylvania. The king, busy trying to install his own party into power, could not pay much attention to a complaining colony. And the parliamentary elite was not about to oust a lawful proprietor and make King George even richer. It became clear to Franklin that it was time to return to Philadelphia. Sadly, that meant giving up ties throughout Britain and Europe that he might never revive again. It meant returning to a more subdued life at home; his career in public life there must surely be at an end. He also could expect bitter rebuke from the pro-Penn forces for his successes, and reproaches from his own allies for his failures. His implacable Philadelphia foe, William Smith, had been in London when Franklin received his Oxford honors and wrote in protest of it; Smith spent the rest of his stay saying that Franklin had lost all support in Philadelphia and probably feared going home. It was a dismal prospect.

Moreover, Franklin was not pleased by William's choice of wife. The son was engaged to Elizabeth Downes, the thirty-year-old daughter of a rich Barbados planter, but Benjamin had hoped his son would marry Polly Stevenson. Perhaps he had wanted William to return with him to Pennsylvania to a more modest future in the law, but his son chose to reach higher. William would receive his royal seals as governor in September.

Perhaps Franklin's displeasure had to do with an overriding disappointment in his mission. Instead of boosting Pennsylvania (and the rest of America) in the eyes of England's leaders, he had seen hostility and resentment build. The complaining colonists appeared to many in Parliament as being more interested in their prosperity than in the security of the empire. Franklin had invested much of his considerable prestige in his cause and was stung when he was denied a hearing on a royal charter.

Then there was the prickly Franklin sense of self. He knew that his friends Dr. Pringle and Lord Bute had taken a hand in securing the royal governorship for William and that they meant well. But he could not help being doubly insulted: Was this not an attempt to placate Franklin, and at the same time a snub—giving to the son what should have been the father's? In any event, when Franklin was thwarted in anything, he could turn cold in an instant. He cut William and his fiancée off abruptly.

In haste he turned over Pennsylvania's affairs to the new agent, his friend Richard Jackson. He packed, settled his accounts, and was out of London to Portsmouth in August, even though William was to be married in just a few weeks. He languished in port until nine other merchantmen and a warship could be assembled in convoy for the slow trip west to Philadelphia.

He expected a gloomy homecoming after five years away.

Chapter 10

Rejection and Return

"**I** got home well the first of November, and had the happiness to find my little family perfectly well, and that Dr. [William] Smith's reports of the diminution of my friends were all false," Franklin wrote to his friend William Strahan upon his return to Philadelphia in the autumn of 1762. He added with some pride:

> My house has been full of a succession of them from morning to night ever since my arrival, congratulating me on my return with the utmost cordiality and affection. My fellow-citizens, while I was on the sea, had at the annual election chosen me unanimously, as they had done every year while I was in England, to be their representative in Assembly, and would,

they say, if I had not disappointed them by coming privately to
town, have met me with five hundred horses.[1]

He did receive a hero's welcome from his supporters, although
his enemies were quick to enlarge on the disgraceful tales about the
expense of the mission, the lavishness of Franklin's life in London,
and his supposed lascivious pursuit of women. Great emphasis was
put on the risk that he had imposed on Pennsylvania's future with
his political campaign for a royal charter. As the winter weeks
moved pleasantly into the Christmas holiday season, Philadelphia
in 1762 must have been in its full glory. With more than 25,000
inhabitants, the town was the largest in America. While it was not
London, it was a welcome respite for the returning traveler.

Not that Franklin gave himself up completely to leisure and the
punch bowl after his return. He entertained no thought of retiring
from public life to a quiet, contemplative existence. Turmoil bubbled
around him. He moved at once to refute the misspending charges
laid against him. Two enemies, the disgruntled cleric William Smith
and the upwardly striving William Allen, had spread lies throughout London from 1760 onward and now returned home to continue
their campaign on the Penn family's behalf. He also had to win firm
support for his campaign to have the king take back the Pennsylvania grants and turn it into a Crown colony. Only Assembly
Speaker Isaac Norris and Joseph Galloway, a political ally of
Franklin's, knew how serious he was about a royal charter, and both
men were initially skeptical.

Franklin laid the accusations to rest when he presented his
accounts to the Assembly when it convened in the new year. To
everyone's surprise, he claimed only £714, ten shillings, and seven
pence in expenses for the five years in London. This in no way
reflected the true cost of his mission; it barely covered the room
and board paid to Mrs. Stevenson. Just how much Franklin spent

of his own money, or whether he received support from other sources, remains an open question. His books were something of a muddle and may have been redrafted to fit the circumstances. The fact remains that he tried to return more than half of the original £1,500 stipend. But the Assembly refused to accept it and further added £2,214 and ten shillings for a total payment of about £3,000 plus the £714 he had already spent. To his intense satisfaction, he received a formal vote of thanks for his service. Among the committee members who examined the accounts and signed off on them was enemy William Allen. Once an ally, Allen was the son-in-law and protégé of Andrew Hamilton, Franklin's old patron. Now the colony's chief justice, Allen had hopes for a grander future under the proprietors since his daughter had married the latest governor, John Penn, son of Richard Penn and eager surrogate for his uncle Thomas.

John Penn was thirty-three, weak and lazy, but at least initially he seemed anxious to avoid clashes with the Assembly. After all, the war was nearing an end, and surely things could get back to normal soon. Franklin at first was willing to give him the benefit of the doubt. He wrote of Penn:

> He is civil, and I endeavour to fail in no Point of respect; so I think we shall have no personal Difference, at least I will give no Occasion. For though I cordially dislike and despise the Uncle, for demeaning himself so far as to back bite and abuse me to Friends and to Strangers, as you well know he does, I shall keep that Account open with him only, and some time or other we might have a Settlement; if that never happens I can forgive the Debt.[2]

The civility could not last for very long, but Franklin was distracted by other, more pressing matters. First, as soon as spring made the roads passable, he was off on another of his marathon journeys; based on the postal reforms he had seen in England, he set out to improve the intercolonial postal delivery network he had instituted six years before. In all, he would travel more than sixteen hundred miles on horseback and be away until November. In April, he journeyed to Virginia for a month to meet his new partner in the office, John Foxcroft, and inspect the mail system to the south. After returning briefly to Philadelphia, he set out for New England. Now that Canada was a British possession, he had to set up a systematic mail packet service from New York to Montreal. He also required the express riders to travel day and night between Philadelphia and New York and later from New York to Boston, halving the delivery time. In the midst of this, he visited William and his new wife, now installed in New Jersey. Apparently, they patched up the relationship, at least to the point of restrained cordiality.

It was an awful trip, however. Franklin suffered two painful shoulder injuries when horses he was riding threw him. Even though his daughter, Sally, had traveled with him on the northern part of the trek and was there to comfort him during his two convalescent delays, Franklin was now fifty-seven and slow to mend.

WHEN FRANKLIN RETURNED TO PHILADELPHIA, the political turmoil of 1763 confronted him head-on. King George's first choice for prime minister, his old tutor John Stuart, now Lord Bute, had come to power with the ouster of Pitt and had quickly secured a peace with the French and Spanish that looked so concessionary that wags dubbed it "the peace that passeth understanding." Yet the king and Lord Bute had recognized a hard truth: England was near bankruptcy after one hundred years of nearly unbroken warfare at home and abroad.

The great weapon in the English economic arsenal had been an ability, unique among the European powers, to finance the government's debts through London's private banking system, dominated by the Bank of England. But now that debt was twice the level of what it had been at the start of the century, and the Britons were the most highly taxed people in the world. Something had to give.

The Treaty of Paris of February 1763 was nothing more than a card game in which the participants passed around pieces of territory according to the strengths of their hands. The French, who had lost the war, got back the sugar islands of Guadeloupe and Martinique and some of the lost regions of India. England got Canada and all the French territories east of the Mississippi; Spain got the French territory on the west bank of the river; the Spanish ceded their colony of Florida to the British and got back Cuba in exchange. Territories in Africa and India were given back or kept as part of more complex bargains. To English merchants, it looked like a sellout; to the London mob, anything short of total capitulation by Louis XV was a good cause for a riot, and riot they did. Jackboots (an obvious pun on the king's prime minister) were burned in effigy.

Worse occurred back in America. The Indian tribes who had allied with the French were both angry and afraid. The French had never tried to grab their land. French traders were content to exchange iron goods, guns, and rum for furs; now English settlers would come into the Ohio Valley and take away vital hunting grounds. Indeed, the English had already taken fourteen French forts that ringed the Great Lakes all the way to Detroit. In early spring, these forts were the first to be attacked in a general Indian uprising that was blamed on an Ottawa chief named Pontiac.* After the first assaults, only Fort Detroit, Fort Pitt (formerly Duquesne), and Fort Ligonier were standing in the west. By June,

---

* The uprising is known as Pontiac's Rebellion, although it seems that other Native American leaders actually planned and executed the campaign.

everything else north to Fort Niagara was in smoking ruins. Farm families on the frontier fled with what they could carry or were killed where they stood. Savagery was the order on both sides. General Lord Jeffery Amherst, the British commander, made the infamous suggestion of sending blankets infected with smallpox to the warring tribes. Safety in Pennsylvania lay no farther west than Carlisle.

Amherst correctly estimated that as many as ten thousand British regulars would be needed to secure permanently the new extended frontier, and it would take a long time to put those troops in place. In the meantime, the settlers formed guerrilla bands out of anger and fear; these were largely Scots Presbyterians from Cumberland County and the Paxton and Donegal townships in Lancaster County. They put little trust in the king's troops and none at all in the local authorities safe in Philadelphia; their reprisals against the Indians took no notice of whether the tribes were peaceful or warlike. During Christmas 1763 a band called the Paxton Boys conducted a series of murderous raids on peaceful Christian Conestoga Indians near Lancaster, butchering young and old with hatchets; a number of the victims had been under the protection of Moravian elders, but to no avail.

In the new year of 1764, the Paxton Boys grew to more than six hundred and began to move on Philadelphia with an ill-formed idea to force troops and arms out of the city for a final massacre of the Conestoga Indian communities. Franklin was a special target of the vigilantes, for he had written another of his famous pamphlets that moved public opinion; he bitterly denounced the murders as a crime unknown in any part of the so-called barbaric world "except in the neighbourhood of the Christian white savages of Paxton and Donegal!"

Again, Franklin was the leading organizer of Philadelphia's response. An impromptu militia of war veterans was put together on a moment's notice; Franklin refused John Penn's offer of the colonelcy and enlisted as a common infantryman.

By early February, the Paxton Boys had reached Germantown, just eight miles from the city. John Penn panicked. The governor, Franklin recalled with satisfaction, "did me the honour, in an alarm, to run to my house at midnight, with his councillors at his heels, for advice, and made it his headquarters."[3] Franklin and three other men went out to negotiate with the band's leaders and convinced them to abandon their reprisals and allow the Assembly's militia to secure the frontier.

Franklin took immense satisfaction in his leading role. He wrote to his friend Dr. Fothergill afterward, "And within four-and-twenty hours, your old friend was a common soldier, a councillor, a kind of dictator, an ambassador to a country mob, and, on his returning home, nobody again."[4] This was understatement, for it ignored the fact that John Penn was bitterly mortified at his failure to exert leadership at a critical moment. He blamed Franklin for sparking the public criticism that the governor had done nothing to stop the first murders and then had run in panic at the moment of crisis. "All hopes of happiness under a proprietary government are at an end," Franklin wrote.

John Penn wrote to his uncle Thomas, "There will never be any prospect of ease and happiness while that Villain [Franklin] has the liberty of spreading about the poison of that inveterate malice and ill nature which is deeply implanted in his own black heart."[5]

The governor was further galled in the spring of 1764 when Speaker Isaac Norris, in ill health, resigned his seat and Franklin was elected to the Assembly chair (though not without vocal opposition). Franklin found that the character of Pennsylvania's political alliances had changed dramatically in the time he had been away. Even the Quakers were more sharply split than usual. Many of the pacifist Friends had followed the custom of the meetinghouse and withdrawn from politics when the votes went against them. This reduced their power in the Assembly, and new voices began to fill the hall.

The question of whether a royal governor should replace the proprietors brought out in sharp relief the broader political division. Some of the defense Quakers and the Moravians favored the shift to Crown rule. The large and growing Scots-Presbyterian population opposed it, fearing that a royal governor would bring a Church of England authority with him. Others opposed the switch due to their aversion to the plan's champion, Franklin. Penn allies were quick to remind the Germans that Franklin had called them "Palatine boors," and the Scots bristled at his labeling the Paxton mob "Christian white savages." Smith and Allen sponsored libelous pamphlets and a rash of anonymous doggerel, including one pamphlet that accused Franklin of allowing William's mother, allegedly the house servant Barbara, to starve to death and to be buried in an unmarked grave.[6]

Another sneer accused:

> Franklin, though plagued with fumbling age,
> Needs nothing to excite him,
> But is too ready to engage
> When younger arms invite him.

Events back in London had not helped Franklin's cause. In the autumn of 1763, King George III issued an edict that barred settlers from moving west into the new lands just vacated by the French. The king's motive was twofold. He wanted to placate the warring tribes to the west and to keep his own subjects closer to the settled areas, where their prosperity might be taxed more efficiently.

George III was in trouble. The Earl of Bute had been forced from office in August 1763 not only because of the outcry over the peace terms but also because he had the temerity to impose a tax on that English staple, hard cider. George Grenville, brother-in-law of Pitt, took his place. Grenville made it clear that the American colonies were going to have to start paying considerably more taxes than they had in the past. The Seven Years War had cost the British £350,000 each year for the North American operations alone; this did not count the hundreds of thousands of pounds Parliament had granted the colonies to repay what the colonies themselves had raised—supposedly voluntarily—on the king's behalf. Now ten thousand regulars would have to be based in this expanded holding, and Grenville knew his cupboard was bare.

Agents of the new prime minister began to heat up the already existing public resentment in England by charging that in all the wars from Queen Anne onwards, the Americans had been slackers, smugglers, and misers even when their own defense was involved. The accusation had enough truth to it to sting American sensibilities, particularly for men like Franklin who had risked quite a bit in the war. But it also was true that some colonies were so politically divided—Maryland, to name one—that they often failed to raise a militia in time for the fighting. Others—Pennsylvania, to name another—usually were years behind on their money contributions to the war effort. New Englanders were particularly adept at smuggling to avoid paying the king's duties—of 14,000 hogsheads of molasses brought in to the region's ports for the rum distilleries in 1763, all but 2,500 were from French sugar islands in the Caribbean.[7] As for George III's decree to restrict settlers east of the sources of rivers that flow into the Atlantic, the land-hungry immigrants simply kept heading west, and colonial officials wrote protests based on the "sea-to-sea" grants that were part of some of their original charters.[8]

In the face of growing evidence to the contrary, Franklin continued to think the young king was the best hope for Pennsylvania.

He built support for a petition from the Assembly to the Crown and set the annual election in October as a referendum on Penn rule. In the meantime, he pressed his agent friend in London, Richard Jackson, to pursue the inheritance claims of Springett Penn against Thomas Penn. If this second-front operation were to succeed, Franklin had no doubt that Springett would be happy to sell the colony to the king.

But this raises an important question. George III had little enough money to keep his kingdom afloat; how could he afford the hundreds of thousands of pounds it would take to compensate Thomas Penn for the loss of a prosperous colony? The young king, moreover, believed his ministers' complaints about the conduct of the colonists during the late war. The king by his own lights was no reformer and by instinct recoiled at the idea of taking a colony just because its inhabitants were dissatisfied. What is surprising is that not even Franklin's bitterest foes thought to use any of these points against his argument that the king was benevolent and would be a lighter weight to bear than the proprietors. George III was still the Patriot King to most Pennsylvanians, even if his ministers were wrongheaded.

As the 1764 political campaign moved into the summer, there was ominous news from London. Word arrived a month after the event that on April 5 Grenville had won a bill from Parliament called the Sugar Act to impose duties on lumber, foodstuffs, molasses, and rum imported into the colonies from non-British possessions. Although it cut in half the sixpence per gallon duty on molasses, the colonists seethed at another provision of the bill to send many more customs inspectors to America to crack down on smugglers. Established New Englanders whose fortunes were based on evading the revenue men—John Hancock, for one—were outraged.

On April 19, Grenville turned the screws again. Parliament approved—and the king signed—an act that forbade the colonies from printing paper money. The prime minister also announced that he intended to introduce a bill in the near future that would impose a stamp duty on all legal documents, newspapers, stationery, and other paper products, including playing cards, used in the colonies.

From the British point of view, none of these impositions was onerous. The Sugar Act alone would raise only £60,000 a year, with a similar sum expected on the stamp levy. The Currency Act helped support sterling and prevented debtors from using cheap colonial money to pay off their creditors. Surely loyal subjects of the king would see that these were merely overdue reforms.

Instead, the colonies were seized by fear and anger. Shrinking the money supply, raising taxes, and cracking down on profitable trade relationships with the Dutch and French in the Caribbean could throw the American provinces into an economic depression before peace was really secure. Then there was a real concern that the new king and his government were prepared to wipe away many of the liberties and powers granted to the colonial legislatures in the charters from previous kings. The furor found its center in Boston, which was hardest hit by all the new levies. A thirty-nine-year-old lawyer named James Otis aroused the merchant community and the mob by denouncing "taxation without representation." Massachusetts's leaders urged other colonies to join their boycott of British luxury goods, which began in August.

Pennsylvania was not far behind in the fury generated by Grenville's acts. Franklin's advocacy of a royal charter became a confusing issue. The king was popular, but his government—especially Grenville—was not. As for the Penns, they still coasted on the reputation of their founder father with older citizens. Others saw them as part of the callous London elite.

John Penn saw the frustrations of the Germans and the Scots as a way to overturn the antiproprietary majority in the Assembly and oust Franklin and his lieutenant, Joseph Galloway. He opened his uncle's purse wide. Pennsylvania's German and Scots-Irish communities had their own complaints about taxation and representation and did not need much prodding by the governor. Of course, out of the Assembly's thirty-six seats, only ten were allotted to the five most distant counties; the remaining twenty-six went to delegates from the three "home" counties and Philadelphia.

Franklin knew the October election would be a close one but was confident that public outrage at the young governor's conduct toward the Paxton Boys, plus other abuses he had committed during his brief term, would weigh heavily in the minds of the voters. He turned his attention to the conduct of the king and his ministers in bearing down heavily on the colonies. He wrote to his friend Peter Collinson soon after the Sugar Act was passed:

We are in your hands as clay in the hands of the potter; and so in one more particular than is generally considered, for as the potter cannot waste or spoil his clay without injuring himself, so I think there is scarce anything you can do that may be hurtful to us but that will be as much or more so to you. This must be our chief security; for interest with you we have but little. The West Indians vastly outweigh us of the northern colonies. What we get above a subsistence we lay out with you for your manufactures. The cat can yield but her skin. And as you must have the whole hide, if you first cut thongs out of it 'tis at your own expense...and who knows but in time we may find out where to get cloth?—for as to our being always supplied by you, 'tis folly to expect it. Only consider the rate of our increase, and tell me if you can increase your wool in that proportion, and where, in your little island, you can feed the sheep. Nature has put bounds to your abilities, though none to your desires. Britain would, if she could, manufacture and trade for all the world; England for all Britain; London for all England; and every Londoner for all London. So selfish is the human mind. But 'tis well there is One above that rules these matters with a more equal hand. He that is pleased to feed the ravens will undoubtedly take care to prevent a monopoly of the carrion.[9]

Franklin's stubborn anger at the Penns was fueled by fresh offenses. The new governor was again blocking the Assembly's efforts to use tax revenues to finance the military operations against the Indians. Penn no longer demanded that the proprietors be exempt from taxation, only that they be taxed at the lowest possible rate on all their lands—raw or developed. Just before its spring recess, the Assembly sent a warning to Penn. The message, probably written by Franklin, threatened that if any harm came to the colony because it could not supply its own troops, the blame "will undoubtedly add to that load of obloquy and guilt the proprietary family is already burdened with, and bring their government (a government which is always meanly making use of public distress to extort something from the people for its own private advantage) into (if possible) still greater contempt." On the same day the Assembly voted to take to the people the question of whether "an humble address should be drawn up and transmitted to His Majesty, praying that he would be graciously pleased to take the people of this province under his immediate protection and government."[10]

THE CAMPAIGN'S FINAL WEEKS WERE VENOMOUS and violent. Parades turned into brawls, in which Franklin's friends among the craftsmen—including a five-hundred-strong guild known as the White Oaks—broke pro-Penn skulls with gusto. Franklin himself was the target most often libeled by the anonymous pamphlets, but both sides offered plenty of slander. He and Galloway managed the campaign for their loyalists—known as the Old Ticket—and they lined up old and handicapped voters who could be dragged to the polls at the last minute. The New Ticket managers laid on wagons to bring their reserves in from Germantown and beyond if need be.

The ballot boxes opened at nine A.M. on October 1 at the State House in Philadelphia. All day long the voters poured into the city on foot or horseback. At three the next morning, the New Ticket forces tried to end the balloting but were pushed out of the voting room and down the stairs. Franklin sent his agents through the streets to bring in his reserve of infirm voters in sedan chairs and stretchers from all parts of town, while the New Ticket wagons began rolling into town by midmorning of the second day. When the polls finally closed at three in the afternoon, more than four thousand votes had been cast.

Franklin and Galloway lost their seats from the city districts by a mere fourteen votes, but the Old Ticket held its majority in the Assembly. On October 26, the reconvened Assembly chose Franklin to rejoin Richard Jackson in London to present the petition for the royal charter to the king and to lobby in Parliament against any future taxes. Pennsylvania's treasury was empty thanks to John Penn's stubbornness, so the Assembly called for voluntary contributions. In a few hours £1,100 had been raised, but Franklin took only £500 of it and rushed off to pack.

Did he even bother to discuss the matter with Deborah? Probably not. He left her in charge of a new three-story brick house he was having built, which would not be finished until 1766.* On November 7, 1764, Franklin and three hundred friends set out on

---

* The house was built on the south side of Market Street between Third and Fourth Streets.

horseback to meet his ship at Chester. Favorable winds matched his racing spirits, and the ship reached the Isle of Wight in the astonishing time of thirty-one days. He went directly to London and banged on the door at Number 7 Craven Street until he was admitted by a startled maid. Mrs. Stevenson was not at home and had not expected him. But no one was happier at that moment than Franklin.

Franklin as he was during his brief return to Philadelphia in the early 1760s. Note the bells to the left, which were connected by a wire to his lightning rod and would ring whenever the wire was charged.

Chapter 11

Back to London

$\mathcal{W}$hile the center of Franklin's public life remained in Philadelphia forever, his heart at this moment was in London and at Number 7 Craven Street. He at once set out to revive his old network of friendships and to build the contacts he needed to get a hearing before the young king's new government. In short order the Stevenson house rang with music and laughter as men of importance and charming women called on the celebrated American.

In one sense he was being unfaithful to Deborah. During his first five-year mission in the metropolis, his letters to her had moved from the affectionate and homesick to the perfunctory. But in another sense Franklin was showing his compulsion to compartmentalize his life. Once back in America in 1762, he had settled in quickly enough and begun to build the rather grand new home that would be his final retirement place.

Franklin was a fairly new hybrid—not an Anglo-American, as his father had been, but an American at his core with a thick English veneer. He dealt with this conflict in his nature at first by separating each part of his identity and wavering between the two. He had this in common with others who became ardent revolutionaries. Many of the Founding Fathers lived their lives as copies of the English country squire and gentleman soldier—Washington is a good example. Others seized the certainties of English law to define their careers and character—witness Adams and Jefferson.

But Franklin differed from his fellow revolutionaries in two key ways. First, he was a constantly evolving identity, a person who in his youth had easily shrugged off most of his Boston Puritan heritage. Second, he spent most of the years leading up to the Revolution in London. London was a city he loved, and it formed a large part of his identity. Other Founders might consider themselves Virginians or New Englanders first and Englishmen second, but Franklin's ties were more complex.

Yet, even when in England, Franklin did not identify completely with the Mother Country. He managed to keep a cold eye on events back in Philadelphia as well as on what was going on in London. He often flattered English and Scottish friends whenever he was back in Philadelphia with letters announcing his intention to "settle up" in the colonies and move back across the Atlantic for good—providing that he could "convince the good Woman to overcome her fears of the voyage." In truth, there was never any question of the Franklins' moving to England, and everyone among his friends knew it. Deborah had always been his "plain country Joan" who would have never fit into London life. Although she had been more firmly in the middle classes than he was when they married, she had built her own circle of family and friends that filled her days when her husband was off somewhere else. Also, Deborah had too much dignity to risk embarrassment among the snobbish gentry of England, nor would she do anything to hold back his advancement. She had another strong suit that is often overlooked. While she had plenty of evidence that her husband could be distracted by prettier faces, she knew that she was the Mrs. Benjamin Franklin he wanted and no other. She counted on this to eventually draw him home again. Her tragedy is that there was not time enough for her.

Her husband's stays abroad could not have been pleasant for Deborah by any means. His flirtations with other women were a constant irritation, however secure she may have felt. Franklin did not help matters by making sure she knew what he was up to. Just after the American's arrival in London in 1757, William Strahan wrote Deborah a complimentary, yet teasing, letter that also contained a sharp dart. The much quoted letter ("I never saw a man so perfectly agreeable to me…") contains a warning that is often left out:

> Now madam, as I know the ladies here consider him in exactly the same light I do, upon my word I think you should come over, with all convenient speed to look after your interest; not but that I think him as faithful to his Joan, as any man breathing; but who knows what repeated and strong temptation, may in time, and while he is at so great a distance from you, accomplish.[1]

This has been taken to hint that Franklin had immediately gotten entangled in a romance on his arrival. It is just as likely that Franklin himself prompted the comment, for he was not above tweaking his wife into jealousy. But were there other genuine romances on Franklin's part? Was Deborah ever really in jeopardy of losing her husband? What was going on at Craven Street?

MRS. STEVENSON FROM THE FIRST TREATED FRANKLIN like a guest, nursed him during his illness, and prepared his favorite dishes. Later she developed a deep proprietary affection for him and ultimately, during this second, ten-year stay in London, accompanied him to dinners and social occasions in Deborah's rightful place. Friends who wrote him routinely sent their regards to her as more than a formal courtesy. Once Franklin left England for good, a year after Deborah's death in 1774, there was even some discussion of Mrs. Stevenson's coming to Philadelphia to join him. But there were several reasons why that was never practical. For one, the position offered was only as a housekeeper, not as a wife. Besides, she would never have given up her independence and property. Then, too, wartime Philadelphia would not have welcomed her.

Margaret's daughter, meanwhile, was somewhat prim, but by all accounts, Polly Stevenson adored Franklin, and he responded with deep affection and none of the roguish teasing he reserved for other admiring young women. She soon moved out of the Craven Street house to care for an ailing aunt, but she took up a long-running correspondence (173 letters) with Franklin that fed his need for intimate affection and his delight in instructing an alert young mind. The correspondence was a continuing tutorial on hydraulics, the radiation of heat from the sun, heat from friction, celestial speculation, and much more, but the letters also reveal the correspondents' love and affection for each other.

At the same time, Franklin's letters to Polly sounded a familiar theme—the benefits of marriage and childrearing. To the point, he constantly schemed to marry his own children off to the children of other friends—his Sally to the son of William Strahan, his William to Polly, and later his grandsons to young noblewomen in France. Marriage to Franklin was one of the key ingredients in achieving personal virtue and happiness. Urging marriage also gave him a safe escape in case his expressions of affection might be taken amiss.

He also advanced the fiction in his letters that Polly and other young women friends were his daughters. Indeed, Polly Stevenson did become a kind of daughter to him. During the Revolutionary War, once she was widowed, Polly and her children made the risky journey to stay with Franklin in France for a while. After the war, she and her family joined him back in Philadelphia. Polly and Sally Franklin, his real daughter, were beside his bed when he died.

In a way, then, the Stevenson women formed a surrogate family, filling in for the wife and daughter he had left behind. But what of other women? A legend persists that Franklin was a sexual athlete whose promiscuity would have brought him public ruin in today's moral climate. During his life his enemies used his sexual reputation as fodder for bitter attacks. William's birth was an easy weapon. William's own illegitimate son would soon be spotted in London. But it is too glib to dismiss his open admiration for women as the randy behavior of an old goat or, worse, to portray him as an oppressor of women. It also is true that there is no hard evidence that he ever had a sexual encounter or romance with any other woman after he married Deborah. Still, a more speculative assessment may give us a glimpse into his elusive inner character.

First, Benjamin Franklin did love the company of women. We know this because he told us in his *Autobiography* that he could as happily chat up a tavern wench as he would later flatter a French countess. He had a special weakness all his adult life for younger women who were beautiful, bright, and inquisitive. The obvious attraction of youth and beauty for an older man surely were at work here. But there was something more, for many of these women were strongly drawn to him as well, and indeed, most of Franklin's relationships outside his marriage lasted throughout the lives of most of these women.

While it can be argued that the eighteenth century was a better time for a woman to be alive than previous centuries, it was not by much. Samuel Johnson's cruel sneer, "Nature has given women so much power that the law has very wisely given them little," was considered witty at the time. Women were in bondage at first to their fathers and, if they were lucky, later to their husbands. Most women were fortunate to get any education at all. Middle-class women (such as Deborah Franklin and Margaret Stevenson) had schooling that offered bare literacy and simple mathematics, but more emphasis was put on sewing and cooking. Wealthier women could get tutoring in what might be called the cultural arts of needlework, music, and watercolors.

Franklin knew something about the restraints imposed on the ambitious through the barriers of class, income, and downright snobbery. He would struggle all his life to rise to a position of equality with other men in the world. While many distinguished persons welcomed him as a valued brother, others never let him forget his humble birth.

It is possible, then, to look at Franklin's liaisons as alliances among strivers in a common cause. By helping these women liberate themselves, he was helping himself. In Philadelphia, Franklin had a coterie of intelligent young women, mostly daughters of his establishment friends, who looked to him as a guide in their intellectual development. If they wanted more than the rudiments provided by their parents, they had to get it for themselves. A surprising number did so.

These were well-to-do women to be sure. Many could afford to spend time in London, where literary salons were far more open and diverse than the French ones upon which they were modeled. Many also benefited from the salons sprouting in Philadelphia and other American towns. Young women could gather in congenial homes and help educate each other; the salons also provided an eager audience for American artists such as painter Benjamin West and poets Francis Hopkinson and Nathaniel Evans. Franklin, in turn, learned much from these fledgling artists and advanced a number of careers by getting their names known in London.

There is little prospect that he would attempt any familiarities other than roguish teasing with girls who were of the first families of the colony; if the girls did not rebuke him, their families certainly would have ruined him. The story of Franklin and his devotees also sheds some light on his relationship with Deborah. Although hardly a dull woman, she had early achieved what she set out to become, the secure wife of a prominent husband. She ruled her domain unchallenged. If she yearned for acceptance at a higher level of society, she never let it show. As for aspiring to finer thoughts and arts, she had little time for either. If her husband wanted to waste time chatting to pretty young girls, more fool he.

Not surprisingly, Franklin drew a similar fan club in England. Some were like the lively Georgiana Shipley, the daughter of one of his closest new friends, Bishop Jonathan Shipley. Georgiana had four sisters, but none doted on Franklin more than she. It was during a stay at the family's summer estate near Winchester that he wrote the first part of his *Autobiography*. The young woman and he exchanged a lively, and occasionally flirtatious, correspondence for a lifetime—during the Revolutionary War she even sent mail to him in Paris through secret channels.

Another part of the Craven Street fan club were friends of Margaret and Polly Stevenson, lively young women such as Dorothy Blunt and Mary Barwell who were in and out of the Craven Street house at will. They were daughters of merchants, and if they were not the intellectual equals of his Philadelphia pupils, they were more fashionable and gay.

And finally, there were what might be called Franklin's projects. Some were distant relatives, including a Sarah (Sally) Franklin, the sickly teenage daughter of an English cousin named Thomas Franklin. Benjamin had met them when he and William went on a sentimental journey through Northamptonshire in the summer of 1758, searching out gravestones and introducing themselves to distant relatives. Thomas showed up at Craven Street with Sally in tow. The girl's mother had died, and she needed more care and schooling than the distraught relative could provide. Franklin put her in the charge of Margaret Stevenson, who oversaw "a little Schooling and Improvement" in the domestic sciences so she could return home and make a good marriage, which she did.

But some Franklin historians, particularly some purse-lipped nineteenth-century ones, have worried over others of the projects. There were the Davies sisters, Marianne, who was sixteen, and Cecilia, eleven. In 1761, the year after the tax victory, Franklin perfected a version of an intensely popular musical instrument known as the armonica. This device originally was a series of glass bowls that were filled with water to various levels. The musician then lightly swirled his moistened fingertips across the tops—as one might do with a wineglass—and produced ethereal music that captivated audiences. Franklin dispensed with the inaccurate water levels and had a glassmaker produce a graduated series of bowls mounted on a spindle through their centers. The spindle was rotated by means of a hand crank or foot treadle and all the musician had to do then was slide his fingers along the spinning bowls to produce the music. Franklin's design swept Europe, and Mozart and Beethoven both composed for it. Franklin trained Marianne to give the first performances; for nearly a decade after that, she and Cecilia (who sang) toured Britain and Europe playing before royal courts. Marianne ultimately had a complete breakdown* that required her

---

* Marianne Davies's collapse might be traced to the effects of lead poisoning. The glass bowls commonly used in armonicas were made of leaded glass and were painted with lead paint in various bright colors for the musician's convenience. Performers frequently licked their fingertips to moisten them before touching the bowls. They often fell ill from various neurological ailments, and this led to the instrument's fall in popularity.

to be confined, due, it was said, to the mesmerizing sounds of the device.

Such was the bitterness of Franklin's enemies that as the Davies sisters attracted fame, his kindness to them was used as proof that they were yet others of his illegitimate progeny. Word quickly reached Philadelphia, and Deborah. Another supposed illegitimate daughter was Judith Osgood, whom a later biographer named as a descendant only on the evidence that Franklin wrote to her as "my daughter"—a form of address he used often with young women— and that he gave her away when she married John Foxcroft, his friend and associate in the colonial postal service.

Since Franklin's ledgers for his London time are handy at the American Philosophical Society in Philadelphia, others have speculated over disbursements to other women and whether they might be in part payments for sexual favors. One such recipient was Amelia Evans, one of Deborah Franklin's goddaughters, who made an unfortunate marriage to a merchant who found crisis whenever he went abroad seeking fortune. Another woman who appears in the London ledgers may have cared for William's illegitimate son, a toddler named William Temple. As a royal governor with a new wife, William Franklin left his father to take care of the child.

It is true that Franklin was very much a man of the eighteenth century, a time of liberated sexual conduct and experimentation that ranged across class and gender. Englishmen read Henry Fielding's ribald satires *Joseph Andrews* and *Tom Jones* and laughed knowingly. As with much of the questing English Enlightenment, everything sexual was up for grabs, in one sense or another.

We do know that Franklin at least once found that his attraction went past the bounds of intellectual striving.[2] During Christmas Week 1754, while on a trip on postal business, he stopped in Boston for a family wedding. His brother John's stepson was marrying the sister of Catharine Ray, a vivacious twenty-three-year-old beauty from Block Island, off the coast of Rhode Island. Franklin was soon to be forty-nine. Something sparked between them.

After the festivities, Franklin accompanied Catharine on a drawn-out journey back to Rhode Island that was broken up by visits to relatives of both in Westerly and Newport. But most of the time it was the two of them jogging along on horseback through the cold days—she, thrilled to have the attention of the famous scientist and public figure; he, entranced by her beauty and her inexhaustible curiosity. He pretended to be able to read her mind, and she called him a "conjurer." With reluctance he finally handed her into a fishing skiff bound for Block Island and stood on the shore looking through his spyglass until she was well out of sight. He had been away from Philadelphia for six months on this trip, but he had not wanted to leave Catharine. After she wrote him a letter of effusive affection, he recalled their reluctant parting:

I almost forgot I had a home till I was more than half-way towards it. Then, like an old man, who, having buried all he loved in this world, begins to think of heaven, I began to think of and wish for home....My diligence and speed increased with my impatience. I drove on violently and made such long stretches that a very few days brought me to my own house and to the arms of my good old wife and children where I remain, thanks to God, at present well and happy.

Persons subject to the hyp [hypochondria] complain of the north-east wind as increasing their malady. But since you promised to send me kisses in that wind, and I find you as good as your word, it is to me the gayest wind that blows and gives me the best spirits. I write this during a north-east storm of snow, the greatest we have had this winter. Your favours come mixed with the snowy fleeces, which are as pure as your virgin innocence, white as your lovely bosom—and as cold.

But let it warm towards some worthy young man, and may heaven bless you both with every kind of happiness.[3]

Probably the best take on the Franklin-Ray affair comes from Claude-Anne Lopez, who has devoted a lifetime of scholarship at Yale to the man. "A romance? Yes, but in the Franklin manner, hovering between the risqué and the avuncular, taking a bold step forward and an ironic step backward, implying that he is tempted as a man but respectful as a friend."[4]

Yet the love was real enough on both their parts. A stream of letters passed between them for the rest of their lives. Hers were full of effusive expressions of love and questions that had come to mind. Franklin responded warmly but more cautiously. She would send cheese she had made and sugarplums that, she hinted to him, she had kissed before packing. He sent her books and advice on how to be a good woman and what kind of good man to marry. He also took the precaution of making sure that Deborah knew of his friendship with the young woman. Whatever she guessed, Deborah kept to herself, and the two women exchanged cautious greetings and occasional small gifts.

Catharine and Benjamin did not meet again until 1763, by which time she had married William Greene* and had two of her six children; they met on only two other occasions. Yet when Franklin was eighty-three, the memory of their horseback tutorial was fresh in Catharine's mind when she wrote, "I impute a great part of the happiness of my life to the pleasing lessons you gave me in that journey. Among the felicities of my life I reckon your friendship, which I shall remember with pleasure as long as that life lasts."[5]

But did Franklin need more than an idealized platonic love? Perhaps. Did he seek it inside the Craven Street house? Probably

---

* William Greene became the wartime governor of Rhode Island.

not, if Margaret Stevenson had anything to say about the matter. It is unlikely she would have gambled her own freedom and station in an affair with her tenant, and she certainly would have put a stop to any serious affair with anyone else inside her own home. Polly particularly would have been out of bounds, for with the prospect of an inheritance, she could make an excellent marriage on her own without having to seduce the much older Franklin.

Yet when Charles Willson Peale, the painter, paid an impromptu visit to Craven Street sometime in 1767, he sketched as an amusement a young lady sitting in Franklin's lap giving him kisses. The plump man in the chair is clearly Franklin; the girl is deliberately vaguely drawn. Was it Polly Stevenson? Perhaps not, for she was very prim and moral. Whoever it was, it had to have been in jest, for Franklin was no fool to allow such an indiscretion to be captured unless it was innocent.

But put the question another way. Was Franklin at this stage likely to take a mistress—with all the attendant complications and risks—or to seduce some young woman who sought his company or his aid? The most probable answer is no. He had learned of the peril of mistresses long before from his run-in with James Ralph's hatmaker. Also, more important, he did not have to. To put it bluntly, if in fact his physical passions were still as compelling as they had been when he was a young man, we have ample evidence that he knew how to satisfy them. Brothels that catered to discreet gentlemen were so convenient and numerous in London that every bookstall had directories on sale for the new arrival. Franklin would scarcely have needed a guide by then any more than when he had been a young printer. It would have been of no more importance to him to stop by one after a dinner meeting of one of his philosophical societies than it would have been to linger at a bookstall. And those visits would certainly have been solitary

Charles Willson Peale's sketch of a young lady sitting in Franklin's lap.
The girl is deliberately vaguely drawn.

because so many of his friends were Quakers and others of stern moral attitudes. As always, however, there is no hard evidence.

The sexual urge was as important a part of the makeup of Benjamin Franklin as it was for any of our Founding Fathers. But while it may be disappointing to some, it is more likely that his more public passions drove him at this point in his life. Women, like everything else, had various important roles in his life, but he was too adept by now to let them get mixed in with more important desires.

CERTAINLY FRANKLIN HAD LITTLE TIME FOR ROMANCE when he arrived at Craven Street in December 1764. Almost at once, another "cold" forced him to bed, where he stayed for most of the month. But more important, he had a plan. Unfortunately, as hindsight makes clear, he was too focused on triumphing over the Penn brothers and too confident of his own powers of persuasion. As a result, he failed to see the problems with his idea. He would learn how wrong he was.

Chapter 12

Countdown to Revolution

In 1764, when Franklin arrived in London for his final stay, America and Britain had begun to walk slowly toward the revolution and war that would lead to separation. History never is inevitable, but there were compelling reasons why neither the colonists nor the king's government could retreat along the way.

The Seven Years War had left most of northern Europe in a shambles. Frederick the Great estimated that Prussian casualties, both military and civilian, were in excess of 300,000. The total deaths in Europe may have been four times that. France was financially ruined and gripped by droughts. Victorious Britain was staggered by a £120 million national debt and faced with a collapse in international trade. Seven years' worth of East India Company tea lay rotting in London warehouses. Country squires and city mobs alike refused to pay a penny's more tax to bail the government out. Worse, the king's war ministers estimated the cost of employing ten thousand regular soldiers to guard the new expanded boundaries of North America at £200,000 a year.[1] The money just was not there.

For their part, the Americans had more than an ideological interest in preserving their unique charter freedoms from Parliament's taxing grasp. Under the loose arrangement to which the colonies had grown accustomed, the king would annually make a formal request to each colony for money to support military operations in North America. The assemblies would answer the request (after some delay) either by collecting and remitting scarce sterling or by issuing new provincial money that would be redeemed with interest at a set date in the future. That money, being legal tender, often was offered to pay debts and customs duties back in England, even though it generally was worth half of sterling.

Thus, the status quo was an issue not merely of political principle but also of cold, hard cash. By shutting off the money supply, by taxing directly, and by cracking down on the profitable, albeit illegal, trade with French sugar colonies, Parliament was doing more than just raising a reasonable sum from its ungrateful subjects. It threatened the economic underpinning of the whole North American experiment.

The postwar depression that gripped international trade hit Boston immediately and then inexorably spread south to the other major port cities. As markets dried up for tobacco, cotton, indigo, and rum, colonial merchants defaulted on debts owed to London traders. American ships, which could haul 28,000 tons of goods to London each month, lay idle at anchor while four thousand seamen grumbled and starved. Prominent merchant houses went bankrupt, smaller suppliers reeled, and planters watched their crops rot and their slaves grow restive in idleness.

Independence was furthest from American minds. Samuel Adams, a Bostonian who had failed as a brewer and a tax collector, became one of the earliest agitators to urge resistance to the new taxes and restraints. But even Adams could say with perfect sincerity, "I pray God that harmony may be cultivated between Great Britain and the Colonies, and that they may long flourish in one undivided empire."[2] Money aside, most Americans wanted a restoration of the same *English* rights guaranteed to their cousins across the sea. The historic restraints on American trade, which required all goods shipped to and from other nations to pass through London brokerage houses, plus the limits on what kind of goods could be made, were irritations but perhaps justifiable market protection.

But in Britain, a representative and a voice (however diffuse) in Parliament's debates were guaranteed prerequisites to being taxed by Parliament. Let the king request money from the colonial assemblies in the old way, or, perhaps better, let a new way be found for America to pay its share of the empire's costs while still preserving its cherished rights.

Franklin's mission included finding this new way, if one was possible. Officially, the Pennsylvania Assembly had sent him to obtain a royal charter and to lobby against future taxes. But he had come to London with another, secret objective in mind. He had not even put this other plan to paper—as he usually did—nor had he discussed it with Galloway or any other allies in the Old Ticket party. His estrangement from Pennsylvania had hardened more during his time in Philadelphia. The new Scots and Irish immigrants to the west were rapidly overtaking the Quaker–English merchant alliance. This was no time to try to win a political mandate for what was a problematical tactic. Besides, Franklin himself had toughened to the point where he believed he alone could deal with the ministers in London.

Although the details remain sketchy, the main thrust of Franklin's proposal was that the colonies would issue a single American currency. The colonial assemblies would collect taxes to redeem the money; each colony would receive a share of the money issue equal to its tax levy. This money could be used to pay British taxes, and in addition the king's government could use it to purchase the supplies needed to maintain the new regiments in America. Thus the king would get a guaranteed flow of funds and the colonies would preserve their rights. This was a variation of the *representation by taxation* theme Franklin had advanced ten years earlier at the Albany Congress.

During his month-long convalescence from the "cold" that felled him on his arrival in London, Franklin had long strategy discussions at the Craven Street house with his friend and coagent, Richard Jackson. During Franklin's time in Pennsylvania, his lawyer friend's star had risen. Jackson not only was a member of Parliament but also held the important post of private secretary to Prime Minister George Grenville. Grenville, as was common, kept the ministries of Treasury and the Exchequer for himself. He was something of a financial expert but knew little about America. Jackson had given Franklin ample inside information about the prime minister's tax plans, and in addition he would ensure that the appeal for a royal charter would win the most sympathetic hearing possible.

The trouble was that Jackson was skeptical of Franklin's two objectives. He was convinced that Grenville would oppose a royal charter because it would cost too much. What the prime minister wanted was more money coming out of America, not less. Moreover, the king was bent on establishing personal rule over Parliament, just as the Whig majority was determined to add to its own power. Any prime minister had to show himself to be firm and resolute, or scores of other politicians lurking in the corridors of power would trip him up. Overturning an established proprietor would set every colonial interest from India to the Caribbean against him; giving the colonies their own money would spark a revolt in the House of Commons.

Grenville's worries about his grip on power were well founded. America was not the only problem facing the ministries. Taxing the colonies was part of a larger effort to control the vast wealth coming out of India, which was the sole proprietorship of the powerful East India Company. Fractious Ireland was no more pacified by having its own parliament than Scotland was comfortable fifty years after being forced into the British union. The last Stuart rising in 1745 was still a fresh memory.

Jackson's arguments reflected widely held attitudes, but Franklin was slow to realize this. He was not a lawyer and so did not reach for legalisms. Rather, he was a negotiator, a dealmaker, who relied on finding solutions that benefited all parties involved. Surely some way could be found to increase revenues from the colonies without jeopardizing their time-honored guarantees of self-government. Part of such a solution might well mean shifting Pennsylvania into Crown colony status, which itself would increase the king's cash flow. Jackson was skeptical, and he had reason to be.

Another reason for Franklin's optimism was that the taxes and restraints that Grenville had already imposed had not yet aroused public outrage back in the colonies. Most colonists were unsure about what the new requirements meant. Some colonies were affected by particular levies more than others. It was hard to assess how this new proposal that tax stamps be affixed to all documents would work, especially since the details were not known. Franklin's attitude was that everything was negotiable. Unfair taxes could be amended. If the colonies were really to be hurt, the pain would be felt quickly enough back in England, and amending would follow. Surely George III and Grenville would realize that, with the population of America doubling every twenty-five years and prosperity growing even faster, England's best interests lay in long-term conciliation. One of the articles of faith of the Enlightenment was that progress was inevitable.

THE PRIME MINISTER WAS PERFECTLY WILLING to conciliate the colonials as long as more American revenue resulted. So on February 2, 1765, Franklin and the other agents met with him in the Treasury offices at Whitehall. Grenville confirmed that his new budget bill would include a stamp duty on paper items sold in the colonies. When the agents protested, Grenville smoothly asked them if they had a better way. He in no way intended to weaken the provincial assemblies, he said, and if they could provide him with a way to raise the sums he needed, he would consider it. In the meantime, the budget bill went forward to the House of Commons a few days later.

Franklin and Thomas Pownall, his old ally from the Albany Congress and now a retired royal governor, came back to Whitehall on February 12 with the common currency scheme, which was predicated on Grenville's rescinding the previous year's ban. The prime minister retorted that the measure had been adopted at the urging of Virginia merchants, who were unwilling to accept currency made by the New England colonies to settle debts. An American money would be no more acceptable. The Stamp Act legislation moved through the Commons with very little debate. Only Colonel Isaac Barré, a member who had fought with General James Wolfe at Quebec, defended the colonial resistance to being taxed, uttering a potent phrase that the colonial Americans were the "sons of liberty" who had brought more value to Britain than they had cost.

Here Franklin fell into a trap. Thomas Whately, another of Grenville's secretaries, called him to Whitehall after the act was passed on February 27 (and scheduled to go into effect November 1). The prime minister, Whately said, wanted to ensure that American anger was assuaged as much as possible. Did Franklin think it better to appoint people already in the colonies as official agents to sell the stamps, rather than send agents over? He did. The arrival of British customs inspectors and other enforcement officials was causing enough of an uproar. Then, Whately asked, could Franklin recommend some capable men for the job? Franklin gave him the name of an ally in Philadelphia and a prominent friend in Connecticut. What he did not know was that Whately had already asked the Penn brothers for their nominees, and Thomas Penn, sensing it could do him further harm, wisely declined the honor.

The violent backlash to the new tax throughout the colonies caught everyone by surprise, Franklin especially, but also the government, and even many Americans. The fifty-five kinds of documents that were to require a tax stamp before use were not big-issue items that would burden the colonists. Stamps for everyday items such as newspapers were half a penny. Expensive stamps for wills and land titles were one-time costs to most. Yet the publication in late spring of the stamp list and the names of the agents appointed to sell them on commission sent mobs into the streets everywhere. As so often happens, those with not much to lose were among the loudest voices. Patrick Henry, a twenty-nine-year-old country lawyer, roused the Virginia House of Burgesses with his famous "if this be treason" speech.* From Boston, Samuel Adams and physician James Warren began to organize a formal protest group called the Sons of Liberty to threaten the stamp agents and keep citizens from using the stamps.

---

* Henry concluded by saying, "Tarquin and Caesar each had his Brutus, Charles the First his Cromwell, and George the Third—" At this point, the House Speaker cried, "Treason!" and Henry resumed, "—may profit by their example. If this be treason, make the most of it." See James Trager, *The People's Chronology* (New York: Henry Holt, 1994), 1765.

More established colonists cautiously reserved judgment but were quickly overwhelmed by the public outcry. The speed with which the reaction spread throughout the still distant colonies was remarkable. By early summer the call had gone out for each colony to send delegates to a Stamp Act Congress in New York in September. The organizers hoped to win support for a total boycott of all British imports that required a stamp or other duty. Within weeks, the normal business of courts, land transfers, and other public matters began to shut down. Those officials who tried to enforce the new rules were threatened by mobs, and the new stamp agents were forced to resign in fear of their lives. Franklin's appointees were among the prime targets. So was Franklin's reputation, especially after he sent a number of letters in the spring to friends urging them to make the best of the bad laws while he worked for repeal. Rumors spread that he had recommended the hated tax to Grenville and that he was angling for higher office in London as a reward. In September, daily demonstrations in Philadelphia began to threaten Franklin's home on Market Street. Deborah sent Sally to New Jersey to stay with her brother, but she refused to budge herself. Relatives brought guns to the house, and they dug in until eight hundred sturdy mechanics who belonged to the White Oaks came to defend their fellow craftsman's family and sent the mob packing.

Although he was alarmed at the violence back home, Franklin had reason to hope he could win repeal of the hated act. He pleaded with his supporters throughout the colonies to remain patient and peaceful, but it was uphill work. Every ship from England seemed to the colonies to bring news of fresh impositions. Hateful writs of assistance allowed customs agents to force their way into homes and warehouses to search for smuggled goods. Trial by jury before the Admiralty Court, which heard smuggling cases, was suspended. In May, the Quartering Act ordered all colonies to provide barracks and full supplies for the British troops on their way to America;

until barracks could be built, arriving soldiers were to be quartered in private homes. All regions objected, but the main burden fell on New York, where the bulk of the regiments were to be billeted. Until then, New York had been the most ambivalent of the colonies about resistance, since it saw the interests of Massachusetts and Virginia as being separate from its own. Now New Yorkers were eager converts to the cause.

Franklin refused to panic. In July, Grenville was forced from office for reasons unconnected to the budget debate. Charles Watson-Wentworth, the second Marquis of Rockingham, succeeded him. Although inexperienced in government, the thirty-five-year-old Rockingham was known to Franklin as the leader of the reform wing of the Whig majority. This meant he had a precarious hold on the government and was confronted by an old guard under Lord Grenville. But he had the tacit support for the time being of William Pitt, who was in the country recuperating from gout and an emotional collapse. Many of the young men who supported Pitt were brought into the ministries. Most important for Franklin, the new head of the Board of Trade was the thirty-four-year-old William Legge, Lord Dartmouth. Both Rockingham and Dartmouth were sympathetic to the American plight but had no immediate remedies in mind. Grenville's dismissal did mean Richard Jackson's removal, but replacing him was Edmund Burke, a young Irish-born member of Parliament who was vocally opposed to the Stamp Act.

During this time, Franklin's public activities were strangely quiet. He launched a personal lobbying campaign aimed at specific members of the Lords and Commons to repeal the Stamp Act and to loosen some of the more repressive antismuggling measures. In a rare letter of that time, to his Scottish friend Lord Kames, he explained, "I was extremely busy, attending members of both Houses, informing, explaining, consulting, disputing, in a continual hurry from morning to night."[3]

But his lobbying and the stream of pamphlets and papers that came out of Strahan's printing house were largely anonymous. Franklin had been stung by critics on both sides of the Atlantic who were offended by his being a Crown official (he still was deputy postmaster) and a colonial agent at the same time. He was aware of suspicions that he was playing both ends against the middle, so he wisely made his argument, not himself, the main issue before the men he had to reach.

Carl Van Doren unearthed in the Franklin Papers collection at the American Philosophical Society a sketchy outline drafted by Franklin that emphasized the message he delivered in his frequent audiences with Rockingham and Dartmouth and the other members of Parliament:

> We do not dispute your power. We know we cannot in any form support a contest with you. Not only in arms, etc., [are you] our superiors infinitely; but in abilities of mind, knowledge, cultivated reason, etc. We cannot subsist without your friendship and protection, etc. But the greater you are, the more we are in your power, the more careful you should be to do nothing but what is right.

From this deliberately obsequious beginning, Franklin then outlined three remedies that would bring the colonies back to order and provide the government with expanded taxes. There was nothing new here. The colonies could be allowed specific numbers of seats in the House of Commons. Alternatively, he raised the old Albany Plan of a common American council that would levy taxes to raise needed revenue from the colonies. Third, he put forward the paper money scheme.

None of these proposals would go anywhere. The English majority in the Commons despised the Welsh and Scots members, and the separate parliament scheme was being tried in Ireland without success. As for a currency rival to sterling, it flew in the face of the mercantilist faith in tightly controlled markets.

Although he could not put it in such blunt terms, the American boycott of British imports was his most effective argument. The colonists showed themselves resolute and united to an extent that astonished and unsettled the British. As a result, Franklin's influence as the leading American representative in London grew even as his proposals were put aside. During the Christmas recess, petitions from the British manufacturing community began to flood into London. Birmingham iron founders reported that their shipments to the colonies were off by 90 percent and that ten thousand of their workers had been laid off. American orders were being canceled in Liverpool and London, and payments had stopped coming on goods already sent. British workers took to the streets, and threats of insurrection spread from America to England. But the parliamentary revulsion against the riots and the extralegal Stamp Act Congress paralyzed the Rockingham government, and the Grenville faction was determined to enforce the measures, as were the adherents of the king.

THE LOGJAM BEGAN TO BREAK IN JANUARY 1766 when, to everyone's surprise, William Pitt returned to the House of Commons. Drawn and leaning on a cane, Pitt was obviously ill but determined to speak for an outright repeal of the Stamp Act. "If I can crawl or be carried, I will deliver my mind and heart upon the state of America," he said. Even though he was Grenville's brother-in-law, he faced off against him in the debate on enforcement or appeal.

Pitt's speech in the House on January 14 (Franklin watched from the gallery) is considered one of the monuments of Commons debate. Speaking without notes, he observed that Parliament's right to tax residents of Scotland and Wales did not begin until those regions were formally brought into union. He also noted that the American colonies produced £2 million a year in trade profits for Britain. That flow of income could be left free to greatly expand or it could be taxed unfairly and thereby reduced. Moreover, he argued, it was dangerous to drive the colonists to resistance when both France and Spain still were active enemies in North America. He also connected the liberty enjoyed by the colonists with that enjoyed by Englishmen at home. "I rejoice that America has resisted," Pitt declared. "Three million of people so dead to all feelings of liberty, as voluntarily to submit to be slaves, would have been fit instruments to make slaves of the rest." Yet he concluded, "Let the sovereign authority of this country over the colonies be asserted in as strong terms as can be devised, and be made to extend every point of legislation whatsoever; that we may bind their trade, confine their manufactures, and exercise every power whatsoever—except that of taking money out of their pockets without their consent."[4]

Pitt was offering the members a way out of their dilemma. With the assent of Rockingham, Burke and other aides began to urge Parliament to a remedy that would quiet the Americans while still asserting the government's power to rule over the colonies. First, though, the angry members had to be convinced that the rebellious colonists were worthy of being conciliated. Colonial officials were having their houses burned; customs agents were being tarred and feathered. The king wanted firmness, not conciliation.

As the debate raged, petitions that London merchants had gathered from manufacturers piled up in both houses. Pressure built for the House of Commons to hold a hearing for witnesses. Chief among them was to be the American agent Benjamin Franklin, who would take all questions about the loyalty of the colonists.

ON FEBRUARY 13, 1766, FRANKLIN PRESENTED HIMSELF at the historic Commons chamber and was ushered to the bar that faced the Speaker's chair. Parliament waited as a committee of the whole.

The first questions came from friendly members and clearly had been set up in advance to allow Franklin to argue that the colonies already were heavily taxed. He also noted that the money raised by stamps would be spent not for troops in the old colonies but for military needs in Canada and Florida. Grenville, the former prime minister, cut into the friendly questioning to get to the issue at the heart of the debate:

> *Grenville:* Do you think it right that America should be pro-
> tected by this country and pay no part of the expense?
>
> *Franklin:* That is not the case. The colonies raised, clothed,
> and paid, during the last war, near 25,000 men and spent
> many millions.
>
> *Grenville:* Were you not reimbursed by Parliament?
>
> *Franklin:* We were only reimbursed what, in your opinion,
> we had advanced beyond our proportion, or beyond what
> might be reasonably expected from us; and it was a very small
> part of what we spent. Pennsylvania, in particular, disbursed
> about £500,000 and the reimbursements in the whole did not
> exceed £60,000.[5]

Repeatedly Franklin stressed that the Americans were loyal to Britain. "They were governed by this country at the expense only of a little pen, ink, and paper. They were led by a thread." Yet, he maintained, the colonists would submit neither to these new taxes imposed by Parliament nor to the reduction of their rights before the law—the English law. The final questions summed up the American mood for the members:

Q: What used to be the pride of the Americans?

Franklin: To indulge in the fashions and manufactures of Great Britain.

Q: What is now their pride?

Franklin: To wear their old clothes over again till they can make new ones.

Within a month, Parliament had repealed the Stamp Act. A day after voting for repeal, it passed a Declaratory Act, which at first was ignored in the transatlantic jubilation. The act reasserted in blunt terms the power of the king—with the consent of Parliament—to make laws of all kinds, including taxes on the British colonies "in all respects." For the moment, Franklin was treated as a triumphant orator, which he knew he was not; there were few flashes of wit during the grueling examination, which was the longest public speaking engagement he ever made. But he had reminded Parliament, and the public that read published transcripts, that the real threat in the Stamp Act could be found in the empty warehouses and ships tied up along the Thames.

He enjoyed the gratitude of the Rockingham Whigs and took understandable satisfaction in the news that his name and that of the king were now regularly toasted and cheered throughout America. His critics were silent, and many even repented ever doubting his sincerity. More important, the riots and protests quieted at once and the boycott withered. He was able to have Mrs. Stevenson go shopping with him and select a new gown for Deborah, plus yards of satin ("eleven shillings a yard"), a silk negligee, a petticoat for Sally, a Turkish carpet for the dining room, tablecloths, and a box of cheeses. Franklin teased his wife that he hoped some of the cheese "may be left when I come home."

Yet Franklin had failed in his original mission, and he knew it. Ousting the Penns from their hold on Pennsylvania was a dead issue. So was the currency scheme. As for America ever having representation in Parliament, he wrote to a friend in May:

> The parliament here do at present think too highly of themselves to admit representatives from us.... It would certainly contribute to the strength of the whole if Ireland and all the dominions were united and consolidated under one common council for general purposes, each retaining its own particular council or parliament for its domestic concerns.... But this should have been more early provided for.[6]

Now it was too late for such a reform.

NEVERTHELESS, IT WAS TOO SOON FOR FRANKLIN to return to Philadelphia. Though he asked to come home in the summer, the Assembly instead reappointed him for another year. The Assembly wanted him there because, once more for reasons unconnected with America, the Rockingham government collapsed in August. Franklin and the Pennsylvanians must have been much cheered when Pitt, now an earl in the Lords, was brought back to power by a grumbling King George III. After having avoided him years before, the new chief minister sought Franklin's advice in private on colonial policy matters. As much as was possible with Pitt, a friendship developed. The agent thought he no longer would have to rely on friendly secretaries but instead could go directly to the source of power. Pitt was still frail, however, and had none of the stamina of a decade earlier. Like many strong men, he often surrounded himself with weaker underlings, and in this case he unwisely kept on a number of key Rockingham allies. People wondered when he passed over control of the Exchequer to Charles Townshend, a viscount who was as arrogant as he was brilliant. But Franklin took heart that the job of secretary of state for the colonies went to William Petty, Lord Shelburne, another young Pitt protégé who was talented and devoted to the American cause.

During the autumn and early winter of 1766, however, Pitt grew sick again and avoided London. Shelburne's plans to relieve the Americans were stalled inside the Privy Council, and Townshend emerged as the leading figure among a weak collection of ministers. The king did not mind this much and was pleased when Townshend boasted in January 1767 that he could come up with as much money as could be gotten out of those recalcitrant Americans and thereby reduce taxes on English estates.

The Townshend Acts deliberately tore down all the reconciliation that had taken place the year before. In addition to pressing customs officials to ferret out smuggling more aggressively, the acts empowered Royal Navy vessels in American waters to stop shipping to and from ports. Instead of direct taxes, Townshend's Exchequer imposed duties on tea, glass, paint, oil, lead, and paper imported into the colonies, with the goal of raising £40,000 a year.

FOR THE NEXT EIGHT YEARS, FRANKLIN FOUND himself fighting a frantic rearguard action, as Britain seemed bent on pushing the colonies either to subservience or to rebellion. One of the agent's problems was finding a stable group of ministers to win over to the American cause. When Townshend died in the summer of 1767, he was replaced by Frederick, Lord North, a Tory loyalist of the king. He had been brought in as Pitt frantically tried to shore up his majority in both houses. Frustrated, Shelburne resigned that autumn, and by December, Pitt himself was gone from office. He was replaced by the Duke of Grafton as King George moved to get control of the ministries and have his own parliamentary majority to do his bidding.

George III's determination for personal rule is one of the reasons Franklin's efforts were doomed to failure from the outset.

The more members of Parliament saw the potential rewards in backing the king, the less inclined they were to be sympathetic to America's problems. Grafton's ministry merely tightened the screws further. Eight warships and two battalions of British regulars were sent to Boston to quiet the agitation there. When the Massachusetts Assembly proposed that other colonies cooperate in joint resistance, Parliament ordered the resolution rescinded or the legislature would be dissolved.[7]

As a result, the spirit of resistance in America was quickly rekindled. New York's Assembly flatly refused to appropriate the funds to support the troops, and those unlucky enough to be housed in private homes were subjected to countless abuses. Rebellion and independence began to be discussed in the press and in public debates. Royal governors in Massachusetts and Virginia complained that their edicts were being ignored. High court officials and senior administrators were assaulted, as were prominent loyalists. The Sons of Liberty movement spread, and liberty poles were put up and draped with pennants that urged resistance and defiance. Customs duties plummeted, and what trade there was went to the French, Spanish, and Dutch islands in the Caribbean.

The Grafton ministry lasted no longer than Pitt's had. In January 1770, King George III at last got his hands on the reins of government—after a fashion. He named Lord North as first minister of the Treasury and put in place an administration that would last the twelve years until the final hours of the American Revolution. North was totally loyal to the king in the first years. He had been a godson of George's father, Frederick, the Prince of Wales. He had been one of the few boys allowed to be an acquaintance of the young prince, and they were very much alike in temperament—easygoing personally but obstinate when crossed and absolutely committed to building royal power. North shared another key trait with the king—both despised the general public and popular opinion. He boasted that while in Parliament he had never voted in favor of a single popular bill—indeed, he had even supported the infamous cider tax plan.

Early on, North was dubbed a lackey of Lord Bute, who still remained the king's mentor. But in fact, it was the king who began to micromanage the government during this time. North refused to be called prime minister, saying the position did not exist. Instead, the king appointed men to head the various ministries who would do his bidding.

As with previous governments, other issues intruded on Franklin's ability to get his message through to Whitehall. Parliament began to focus on growing scandals over the East India Company's administration of India. When London mobs (egged on by radical politicians) demanded publication of parliamentary debates, the matter stalled in debate and riots broke out. In the violence, a mob assaulted Lord North, destroying his carriage and stealing his hat as a trophy.

However much he may have sympathized with the plight of ordinary Englishmen who were struggling to achieve some of the rights already enjoyed by the colonists, Franklin instinctively disapproved of mob rule and public violence. Anarchy unsettled him as much as legalisms frustrated him. So he carefully kept away from the dominant English rebel of that day, a disaffected member of Parliament named John Wilkes. So virulent were Wilkes's harangues against King George (from the sanctuary of the House of Commons floor) that he had been expelled and had had to flee to France for a time to escape imprisonment. But now he was back; his Middlesex district repeatedly reelected him to Parliament, but the king denied him his old seat.

Wilkes fanned controversies other than the tyrannical ambitions of the king. Bread riots in London looted government grain stores. Scandals arose about adulteration of food; grain merchants mixed chalk, alum, and bone ashes in flour to make it whiter. All the while the East India Company continued to defy government efforts to exert control over its operations, even though it was in deep trouble: each year ten million pounds of tea arrived in London, but its high price dampened demand. Franklin described the mood to a friend:

> The residence of the king is now a daily scene of lawless riot and confusion. Mobs patrolling the streets at noonday, some knocking all down that will not roar for Wilkes and liberty; courts of justice afraid to give judgement against him; coal-heavers and porters pulling down the houses of coal merchants that refuse to give them more wages; sawyers destroying sawmills; sailors unrigging all the outward-bound ships, and suffering none to sail till merchants agree to raise their pay; watermen destroying private boats and threatening bridges; soldiers firing among the mobs and killing men, women, and children; which seems only to have produced a universal sullenness that looks like a great black cloud coming on, ready to burst in a general tempest.
>
> What the event will be God only knows. But some punishment seems preparing for a people who are ungratefully abusing the best constitution and the best king any nation was ever blessed with, intent on nothing but luxury, licentiousness, power, places, pensions, and plunder.[8]

Even at this point Franklin put his faith in the king. But the reality was that in the mind of the king, America was an irritant, not a crisis. He instructed his ministers to placate the colonists if they could but to remain firm and in command regardless. Franklin watched with growing concern as the new decade arrived, with each month seeming to bring some fresh offense against the colonies. Each offense provoked ever more violent reactions back home. His old metaphor of the wind roiling the waves took on a new and ominous prospect.

For the first time, Franklin began to doubt his ability to work out a peaceful solution that would be equitable to both sides. The dominion status that he had argued for so assiduously might not be the answer after all. American liberties were too important to be compromised. Well before anyone in America, he began to muse about a final separation if justice failed. This thought must have horrified him.

Chapter 13

The Death of a Dream

$\mathscr{T}$he North administration forced Franklin to abandon his hopes for reconciliation. This, of course, meant giving up his faith in King George III. He could no longer ignore the absolute determination of the king and his ministers to wring tribute out of America. It was clear that the king's attempts to control the colonies were doomed to failure. Yet war—and it would be a civil war—was too horrible a catastrophe for Franklin to embrace.

Franklin's volumes of correspondence with colonial leaders convinced him a sea change was occurring; America was transforming at a pace beyond all comprehension. Britain's ability to govern this new land without the consent of the governed was fast disappearing. Despite the king's ban, Virginians were pushing in droves over the mountains into Tennessee, and Daniel Boone led a band of Carolina settlers into far Kentucky, into Indian lands the king had guaranteed to the tribes.

By 1770, there were 2.2 million inhabitants in the Atlantic colonies, 600,000 more than ten years before. In 1700, Pennsylvania had been the fifth most populous colony; now, with 240,000 citizens, it ranked behind only Virginia with its huge slave population. These new colonists were not satisfied merely to till the soil. Not only had the colonies outstripped England and Wales in iron production, but also new craftsmen were turning out pottery, furniture, and metal goods (Paul Revere was just one of many silversmiths) that competed with what Britain could offer. American vessels now dominated the Atlantic whaling industry and were creating a new source of fuel energy; one fleet of fifty ships in 1768 actually sailed as far as the Antarctic. Pushing for change was a rising new generation of political leaders who had no fond memories of Mother England or its Patriot King. After 1770, this group grew in numbers and steadily became more militant. Franklin was left in the uncomfortable position of continuing to seek peaceful reconciliation as he became more radicalized by the determined arrogance of the king and his government.

Even as he became America's leading voice in London, Franklin was well aware that many radicals were suspicious of his relative moderation. In London he faced two brothers from the famous Lee family of Virginia, Arthur and William Lee. They were rich, talented, haughty, and suspicious. Arthur, the greater schemer of the two, was both a physician and barrister and had publicly supported the radical politician John Wilkes. When Wilkes became mayor of London in the early 1770s, Arthur became a sheriff and William an alderman. Both brothers were noted participants in the routs and orgies that Wilkes and his friends enjoyed. Arthur Lee published such fierce attacks on the North ministry that Samuel Adams encouraged him to apply for the job of agent for Massachusetts.

When a majority of the Boston radicals chose Franklin instead, Adams secured for Lee the uncomfortable post of being agent-in-waiting should Franklin return home. Both brothers would confound and vex Franklin for the next ten years. Another problem for Franklin (and friend of the Lee clan) was John Dickinson, a Philadelphia lawyer who in 1767 began to publish a series of articles titled *Letters from a Farmer in Pennsylvania*. The two differed mainly in their political makeup: Franklin was the negotiating radical, Dickinson the cautious legalist. Dickinson had opposed the attempt to wrest Pennsylvania's charter from the Penns, arguing (correctly) that the colony could expect no better rule from the king's ministers. In the *Letters*, which were popular on both sides of the Atlantic, he conceded a point that Franklin never gave up: Britain had a right to rule its American possessions, and that power extended logically to Parliament through the king. Nevertheless, Dickinson drew a line at London's ability to tax the colonies at will. Though he disagreed with Dickinson's larger point, Franklin had a collection of the articles printed in London at his own expense because he and Dickinson both saw that, instead of mob violence, an intercolonial boycott of British goods was the best hope of achieving justice from the king.

But Franklin could not concede the Whig conviction that Parliament had the power or right to tax specific colonies directly. It was this point that he and his dear friend Strahan argued over constantly. Strahan was now chief printer for the king and had used his position to press for repeal of the Stamp Tax, but he rejected the notion that Parliament had no right to levy the tax in the first place. In fact, he argued that Parliament could impose new taxes in the future. In a letter to his friend, Franklin stated that Parliament could say what it wanted about the right to tax, provided it never *exercised* that right, adding, "and we shall continue to enjoy *in fact* the right of granting our money with the opinion now universally prevailing among us, that we are free subjects of the King, and that fellow subjects of one part of his dominions are not sovereigns over fellow subjects in any other part."[1]

New voices began to echo Franklin's conclusions. In 1768, British customs officials in Boston seized John Hancock's sloop *Liberty*. The thirty-one-year-old Hancock had inherited a fortune from an uncle who had profiteered on supplies sold to the British troops in the late war, and he was busy adding to that wealth by smuggling wine into the port. The seizure provoked both a mob riot and an anti-importation agreement among the merchants. It also propelled Hancock into a rivalry with Samuel Adams and Dr. Joseph Warren for leadership of the resistance movement. John Adams, a thirty-five-year-old country lawyer cousin of Sam Adams, was making a name as a compelling orator at mass meetings and in the courts of Boston. In Virginia, Patrick Henry found himself being overshadowed by a newly elected member of the Burgesses. Thomas Jefferson, just twenty-six, had begun a series of pamphlets on the causes of discontent in Virginia; the pamphlets were read throughout the colonies with enthusiasm and in Whitehall with unease.

Something very important was going on, and Franklin was quick to spot both the promise and the hazard. The ability to communicate political thoughts to a wide audience in a short period of time was producing an American consensus. Philadelphia alone now had nearly two dozen print shops, and Franklin's still popular *Pennsylvania Gazette* had half a dozen weekly competitors.[2] Throughout the colonies, the emerging leaders shared secret political views and tactical information in newly formed committees of correspondence. Older leaders were shouted into silence or slowly recruited to the coming confrontation.

The young radical voices also were intent on being heard in London, and their still ambivalent provincial governments stepped up their representations in the great metropolis. They flooded

Parliament and the ministries with petitions for relief and remonstrances against the increasing injustices. Well up to the eve of the Revolution, most of those who urged resistance still held some hope that their message could win reform.

Franklin became the medium of choice. In 1768, Georgia appointed him as agent. The next year, the New Jersey assembly (not Franklin's son, the governor) chose him as well. In 1770, he became the representative of the most estranged colony of them all, Massachusetts. He took no pleasure in warning his new clients that the horizon looked darker to him than it did to the most disenchanted mind at home. In a 1771 letter to Massachusetts Speaker Thomas Cushing and Samuel Adams, he warned:

> I think one may clearly see, in the system of customs to be exacted in America by act of Parliament, the seeds sown of a total disunion of the two countries, though as yet that event may be at a considerable distance. The course and natural progress seems to be, first, the appointment of needy men as officers, for others do not care to leave England; then, their necessities make them rapacious, their office makes them proud and insolent, their insolence and rapacity make them odious, and, being conscious that they are hated, they become malicious; their malice urges them to a continual abuse of the inhabitants in their letters to administration, representing them as disaffected and rebellious, and (to encourage the use of severity) as weak, divided, timid, and cowardly. Government believes all; thinks it necessary to support and countenance its officers; their quarreling with the people is deemed a mark and consequence of their fidelity; they are therefore more highly rewarded, and this makes their conduct still more insolent and provoking.
>
> The resentment of the people will, at times and on particular incidents, burst into outrages and violence upon such offices,

and this naturally draws down severity and acts of further oppression from hence. The more the people are dissatisfied the more rigour will be thought necessary; severe punishments will be inflicted to terrify; rights and privileges will be abolished; greater force will then be required to secure execution and submission; the expense will become enormous; it will then be thought proper, by fresh exactions, to make the people defray it; thence the British nation and government will become odious, and subjection to it will be no longer tolerable; war ensues, and the bloody struggle will end in absolute slavery to America or ruin to Britain by the loss of her colonies; the latter most probable from America's growing strength and magnitude.

I do not pretend to the gift of prophecy. History shows that by these steps great empires have crumbled heretofore; and the late transactions we have so much to complain of show that we are in the same train, and that without a greater share of prudence and wisdom than we have seen both sides to be possessed of we shall probably come to the same conclusion.[3]

Given that the above was written four years before Lexington and Concord, it is an astonishingly accurate précis of how the American Revolution came to happen. In Franklin's view, English arrogance was turning into greed and malice. Now that he was the undisputed voice for America in London, officials targeted him—and feared him—even more. The North ministers, wary of his close ties to English radicals who fanned public discontent, clumsily tried to flatter him into cooperation or threaten him into submission. One could flatter Franklin up to a point, but he could not be threatened to any effect. Nor could he be bribed.

Both the Grafton and North ministries dangled various prospects of high office before him. He was offered the sole postmastership of the colonies, then threatened with being dismissed; he smiled and was noncommittal to both. Although Franklin was successful at making money, it was never an overriding objective. Money had grown tighter after 1766, when his profit-sharing deal with David Hall came to an end; he had simply outlived the annuity he had planned to make his final few years comfortable. Now he had to write Deborah cautionary letters about expenses. Even so, when Sally Franklin was set on marrying a lackluster merchant named Richard Bache, a marriage of which he disapproved, Franklin gave the couple £500, urged them to move into the Market Street house with Deborah, and offered to help them set up a store. Of course, his multiple agent jobs eased his financial worries, for they brought him £1,500 a year on top of the money Pennsylvania had allotted. Therefore, he was in a position to ignore such blandishments as when the Privy Council mentioned his name for deputy to the secretary who controlled the American colonies.

By 1770, THE FOUR BRITISH REGIMENTS THAT HAD been sent to quiet Boston had had little effect; four more regiments followed. Moreover, because of the colonial boycott, the Townshend taxes had produced nowhere near what they were supposed to. The cost of the soldiers was fifty times the tax revenues they were to exact.

So once more conciliation was the order of the day. And once more it was done clumsily. Over the warnings of King George, Lord North pushed through a repeal of all of the Townshend levies except the one on tea. North kept the tea tax to uphold Parliament's power to tax, and he reasoned that it would not arouse much controversy because the tax was actually less than it had been before the Grafton government had taxed tea. But Grafton's tea law also had provided that the tea be sold directly by American agents of the company, instead of passing through the local merchant wholesalers. Rather than calming public opinion, the tea law enraged the business community, and tea became symbolic of all the other dissatisfactions.

And there were plenty of other dissatisfactions. The Virginia governor dissolved the House of Burgesses, but it continued to meet in private and urge the continuation of the boycott on all goods. To quiet Massachusetts, North recalled the hated governor, Sir Francis Bernard, and replaced him with Thomas Hutchinson, who was known for wangling lucrative offices for relatives and advancing his own cause in London at the expense of the colony. The net result was even deeper anger in the colonies and even less money coming in. As Franklin had predicted, imposing greater force had come at great cost to Britain.

Franklin's dealings with Lord Hillsborough, the secretary responsible for American affairs, reflected the government's changing attitude toward the colonies. When Franklin had come with petitions from his new client, Georgia, Hillsborough took them promptly to the king. Yet soon enough, Hillsborough would only deal directly with the colony's assembly. And when Franklin came in 1771 to present himself as the agent for Massachusetts, the secretary refused to receive the authorization letter from the Massachusetts Assembly. Hillsborough claimed that Governor Hutchinson had written a letter refusing the appointment; he called triumphantly for John Pownall, the secretary to the Board of Trade, to confirm the existence of the letter. Yet when Pownall arrived, Lord Hillsborough was embarrassed to be told that Hutchinson had given no such veto. After a heated exchange in which Hillsborough angrily thrust the appointment document back at Franklin, the agent showed a bit of his temper. He recalled later that he said:

> I beg your lordship's pardon for taking up so much of your time. It is, I believe, no great importance whether the appointment is acknowledged or not, for I have not the least conception that an agent can *at present* be of any use to any of the colonies. I shall therefore give your lordship no further trouble.[4]

With those words, Franklin withdrew. In a letter he wrote a few weeks later, he stated, "I have since heard that his lordship took great offence at some of my last words, which he calls extremely rude and abusive. He assured a friend of mine that they were equivalent to telling him to his face that the colonies could expect neither favour nor justice during his administration. I find he did not mistake me."[5]

In these years, violence began erupting more often in the colonies. Just after Lord North took control of the government, Sons of Liberty in New York brawled for two days with British regulars, resulting in the first bloodshed of the struggle. On the same day that Parliament voted on Lord North's bill to repeal all but the tea tax, March 5, 1770, a squad of British soldiers in Boston fired into a threatening crowd, killing four men. The Boston Massacre, as it is forever known, sparked rage on both sides, even though most of the soldiers (some of whom were defended by John Adams) were acquitted at their trial. In May 1771, North Carolina farmers known as the Regulators tried to shut down the colonial courts to protest Parliament's taxes, but loyal militia crushed the revolt at Alamance Court House.

Small wonder, then, that Lord Hillsborough treated Franklin's growing role as America's agent as an affront and a threat. It seemed that every time the British government attempted to soothe colonial unrest, fresh violence resulted in the colonies; Franklin had to have a role in this.

Nevertheless, Hillsborough could surprise Franklin. In August 1771, Franklin set out with his friend Richard Jackson on his most ambitious tour of the British Isles to date (both as a public relations exercise and to survey what support might come to the American cause from the disaffected Irish and Scots), and when he visited Ireland he unexpectedly ran into Lord Hillsborough, whose title was in the Irish peerage. Although Hillsborough had earlier that summer harangued William Strahan about Franklin's being an enemy of the king, the secretary was suddenly most congenial and cordially invited him to visit the lord's estate when he journeyed northward to Belfast. Unwilling to offend, Franklin stayed at Hillsborough's estate for days and was squired around the countryside to see the sights. All the while the secretary tried to flatter him with earnest requests for advice on how to deal with the angry colonists.

Franklin wrote to Massachusetts Speaker Thomas Cushing after he returned to London:

> He seemed extremely solicitous to impress me, and the colonies through me, with a good opinion of him. All which I could not but wonder at, knowing that he likes neither them nor me; and I thought it inexplicable but on the supposition that he apprehended an approaching storm and was desirous of lessening beforehand the number of enemies he had so imprudently created. But if he takes no steps towards withdrawing the troops, repealing the duties, restoring the castle,* or recalling the offensive instructions, I shall think all the plausible behaviour I have described is meant only, by patting and stroking the horse, to make him more patient while the reins are drawn tighter and the spurs set deeper into his sides.[6]

Franklin was not at all surprised to find that when they both returned to London some weeks later, Hillsborough's enmity quickly revived.

THE REST OF FRANKLIN'S JOURNEY WAS MORE PLEASING. After Ireland, he and Jackson pushed over to Scotland and into the embrace of his

---

* Castle William in Boston fortified the harbor entrance and was the British stronghold.

friends in Edinburgh. He stayed with the philosopher David Hume, who was now sharply critical of the American protests yet unwavering in his hospitality and regard for Franklin. There were side trips to visit Adam Smith, who was working on the early drafts of the cornerstone of modern economics, *The Wealth of Nations*. Franklin also visited his jurist friend Lord Kames, and while there he confirmed what he had suspected—government agents were reading his mail, and some letters he had written to Kames had never arrived at all.

Franklin had always loved to travel, but he particularly appreciated this trip because it offered him privacy in his conversations. He was well aware that eavesdroppers targeted his regular club and coffeehouse meetings and that his friends were subjected to veiled threats because of him. Yet in Ireland or Scotland he felt free to voice his concerns about the coming split with Britain.

The trip lasted until the end of November. But his marathon journeys were taking a toll. He was sixty-five. The smoke of London irritated his lungs, and his gout often put him to bed for days. He still rose at dawn and did an hour of nude exercises with the windows thrown open, and he had begun to use light weights, which he swung about to get his pulse up from sixty beats a minute at rest to above one hundred. But nowadays, he confessed, he often went back to bed for a nap before dressing for breakfast.

He was getting old and, probably for the first time, genuinely homesick. Sally and Richard Bache had produced a grandson named Benjamin, and Deborah's letters were so full of the toddler that Franklin teased her with having forgotten him. That winter, Deborah suffered a stroke that impaired her understanding and memory. She began a slow decline in health. He talked constantly of returning home after this or that measure was through Parliament. In the spring he talked about sailing home on the fall packet; in winter he promised to come home in the spring.

Instead, as the years moved toward revolution, his travels in any direction except home accelerated. He had gone to Europe twice with Sir John Pringle. On the first trip, in 1766, he was elected to the Royal Academy of Sciences in Göttingen, Germany. The next year he spent a long visit in Paris with the French science academy; he was presented to King Louis XV and met the highborn friends who had pushed his electricity discoveries onto the world stage. In 1769, he returned to Paris, where the main interest was the transit of the planet Venus in front of the sun expected in June 1770, which touched off the first international effort to observe such an event systematically. Observatories had been set up and manned wherever the planet's passing could be seen, including in Philadelphia. The French, he also found, were interested in the political schism developing between Britain and America. He wrote to a friend:

> All Europe (except Britain) appears to be on our side in the question. But Europe has its reasons. It fancies itself in some danger from the growth of British power, and would be glad to see it divided against itself. Our prudence will, I hope, long postpone the satisfaction our enemies expect from our dissensions.[7]

France continued to honor Franklin and circulate translated editions of all his scientific writings. In 1772, he joined his friend Pringle as one of eight foreign associates of the French Royal Academy of Science.[8] Yet for all the genuine affection Franklin felt for his friends in France, Germany, and elsewhere in Europe, he never mistook their enthusiasm for things American as being completely separate from their own narrow national interests. Even at that early date, whatever discomfited Britain encouraged Europe—especially the French.

Franklin brought new ideas back from France that changed his thinking. While in Paris he had been introduced to François

Quesnay, the physician to King Louis and founder of a new school of economic thought. The Physiocrats, as they came to be known, developed the first challenge to the mercantilist, beggar-thy-neighbor policies of the moment. Quesnay and others argued that the source of all wealth was the land and that prosperity was founded on agricultural abundance. This notion fit nicely with Franklin's own attitudes about the inherent wealth of America, where land was cheap and fertile. His Scots friend Adam Smith was working along similar lines. This new faith in the economic promise of America made it all the harder for Franklin to abandon the notion of a reformed commonwealth relationship with Britain. Surely the natural laws that the Enlightenment was setting down for the first time would force all governments to change for the better.[9]

BACK IN CRAVEN STREET, FRANKLIN'S STUDY-LABORATORY was crammed with experiments on everything from the steam engine to new textile loom designs to plant hybrids. In 1771, before he set off for Ireland and Scotland, Franklin escorted Dutch botanist Jan Ingenhousz* to Birmingham and Manchester, where they shared experiments with the Lunar Society.†

The year before that trip, in 1770, Franklin had found himself drawn into the mysteries of anatomy and medicine. His beloved Polly Stevenson had written that she had met a young physician and had decided, though he did not know it yet, that she would marry him. William Hewson was one of the leading surgeon-anatomists of his day. When the newlywed Hewsons moved into the Craven Street house in September, the doctor opened his own

---

* Jan Ingenhousz was a Dutch plant pathologist who outlined the principles of photosynthesis. While in England he worked with Joseph Priestley to use plants to purify air through oxygen.

† The Lunar Society's name came from the fact that the group met on days when there would be a full moon, so the members could get home at night without accident. Punch was served at these learned meetings.

school to dissect cadavers for the education of young medical students. Historians working on the Franklin House project surmise that Hewson took over the first floor dining room for his operating theater. Craven Street was an ideal location for such a school. While dissecting itself was not illegal, it was a hanging offense to dig up a body buried in consecrated ground. Yet there was a shortage of bodies, and bands of "resurrectionists" were happy to meet the market demand, bringing their cargoes down the river and up the short distance to the basement kitchen door in the dead of night.

This led to something of a sensation 225 years later when workmen were digging out the foundations of the Craven Street house to stabilize it before an extensive restoration. Prying up a flagstone in the basement kitchen floor, they discovered the complete skeletons of ten human adults and fully twelve hundred bones of children, and animals of all kinds. Many were colored with ink for instructional purposes.* There is no evidence that Franklin ever observed, let alone participated in, a dissection. But one wonders whether he could have resisted the temptation to explore an unknown world.

The normally crowded Craven Street house became more populated than ever with the medical students tramping about the place. Polly Hewson soon gave birth to a son, Billy; Franklin doted upon the boy as a surrogate for Benjy Bache back in Philadelphia. The house still held his cousin Sally Franklin, and two nephews from New England, Jonathan and Josiah Williams, soon joined them. Jonathan became a private secretary and aide to his uncle and took over his increasingly complicated (and onerous) bookkeeping chores. Margaret Stevenson often went away to visit her sisters, and in her absence Polly assumed command. This gave Franklin a

---

* After an examination of the bones, the London police coroner decided in 2000 that no foul play was involved. No excavation of the rest of the floor was undertaken.

chance at another of the literary whimsies he so enjoyed. Despite all the other claims on his time, he produced a series of full newspapers, the *Craven Street Gazette,* that mocked the stiff, formal language of the *Court Circular,* which chronicled the public appearances and journeys of the royal family.

The *Gazette* dubbed Margaret Stevenson "Queen Margaret," and Polly was "Lady Hewson" and the "lady chamberlain of the household." Franklin lampooned himself as "Dr. Fatsides" and "The Great Person." The anecdotes in each issue portrayed a household in chaos, as much to tease Polly as to make Margaret ashamed to have abandoned Franklin. He also included bogus letters to the editor and equally funny responses. The newspaper was studded with other features such as "Marriages. None since our last, but Puss begins to go a-courting. Deaths. In the back closet and elsewhere, many poor mice."[10]

There were many new friends who would be important assets once the Revolution came. One was Caleb Whitefoord, a wealthy Scots Madeira merchant who kept his shop and home at Number 8 Craven Street. Whitefoord, a witty writer of political satires, became Franklin's devoted companion on his daily rounds through the city. Another devotee was Massachusetts native Edward Bancroft, a writer and scientist who had discovered new textile dyes. This new acolyte was a born intriguer who had contacts high in the government, and he was flattered that Franklin used him as a spy in the corridors of Whitehall. Both men would play crucial diplomatic roles in the coming war.

The most influential friend Franklin made in these years was the most senior lord in the British nobility, Sir Francis Dashwood, the Lord Le Despencer—popularly known as "Hell Fire Francis." Dashwood was a high Tory with a deep personal loyalty to the Earl of Bute and King George. He was a knowledgeable and devoted antiquarian who helped found a number of learned societies that studied the art and architecture of ancient Mediterranean cultures. At the same time, he was one of the most dissolute and licentious of men in a time when England was among the most libertine nations in the Western world.

FRANCIS DASHWOOD WAS JUST TWO YEARS YOUNGER than Franklin, but their lives could not have been more different. He had inherited his baronetcy when he was sixteen and had at once plunged into a frenzy of drinking and sexual escapades that made him notable even among other libertines. When Franklin first came to London to work as a printer, Dashwood was the talk of the town for a scandalous grand tour he had made of Europe, Turkey, and Russia. He and many other young bloods joined clubs devoted to sexual experimentation and (often at the same time) virulent mockery of Roman Catholic ritual. These were publicly known as "Hell Fire Clubs" after a group so notorious for its debauchery that it was suppressed in 1721 by royal edict.

Dashwood took his tastes to an exotic extreme. In 1745, he founded a mock religious brotherhood known variously as "The Knights of St. Francis of Wycombe" and "The Franciscans of Medmenham." He renovated a ruined Cistercian monestary on the banks of the Thames near Marlow and turned his own home at West Wycombe, near Oxford, into a fantasy estate where guests could disport themselves in secret garden hideaways.[11] There the "monks" practiced their sacrilegious rituals that mocked Roman Catholic liturgy, and of course they held their sexual romps, with masked aristocratic ladies and high-priced London prostitutes.*

---

* Visitors may tour the grounds of the Dashwood estate at West Wycombe Park as well as the ornate caves Sir Francis dug out of a chalk hill nearby. The side passages and rooms of the caves were supposed to be the location of many of the orgies. A wax museum is there now, including a scene of Sir Francis in conversation with Franklin, who visited the caves in the early 1770s. Visitors are free to speculate on how conducive the damp, chilly caves would have been to sexual romping.

The two dozen regular members of the society were, in fact, the leading challengers to the Whig ascendancy in Parliament. Among the early initiates were Frederick, Prince of Wales, and the Earls of Bute, Sandwich, and Carhampton. John Wilkes belonged for a time but was expelled for behavior that shocked his friends; he later published an exposé of the order. The ascendancy of George III brought the elevation of many of the monks, but it spelled the decline of the brotherhood. The society continued to hold summer gatherings intermittently, but age and discretion cooled the monks' ardor.

Dashwood joined the Earl of Bute in his ill-fated ministry, as chancellor of the Exchequer. William Pitt later appointed him postmaster general, a position he held until his death in 1781. Thus he was Franklin's patron, and, although he was a slow convert to the American cause, he protected the agent's hold on the American postal system until his final return to Philadelphia at the outset of the Revolution in 1775.

Franklin began to visit the West Wycombe estate in the summer of 1773. By then, he and Sir Francis were close friends, and the American reveled in the company of other guests, including leading poets and polemicists as well as his old friend Jonathan Shipley, the bishop of St. Asaph. Franklin wrote to his son, William, of his visit: "I am in this House as much at my Ease as if it was my own, and the Gardens are a Paradise. But a pleasanter Thing is the kind Countenance, the facetious and very Inteligent Conversation of mine Host."[12] It is unlikely that Franklin enjoyed any wild orgies, if only because Dashwood had installed his longtime mistress and their children in the place and had settled into a sedate domesticity.

Franklin's visits to Dashwood opened a second front. He was blacklisted at court (the king now despised him as a troublemaker) and stalemated at Whitehall. Through back channels, the agent tried to convince the British government to roll back the punishments being meted out to the colonies. He published anonymous satires that attempted to show the British the folly of their ways. While his humor was still evident, there was a new sharp edge to these pieces that showed him willing to provoke where he once sought to convince.

The first satire, which appeared in the *Public Advertiser* in September 1773, was a direct jab at Lord Hillsborough. It pretended to be advice Franklin had given to the minister when he took office. *Rules by Which a Great Empire May Be Reduced to a Small One* satirized in twenty rules how the government had mismanaged the colonies. They were familiar complaints but in a novel form. Among the rules he playfully advised were: send inferior men to govern; ignore the complaints of the governed; harass the colonies with your own taxes rather than accept their voluntary grants of money; use the troops sent to guard the frontier to oppress the people; and misappropriate money raised for the defense of the colonies. By following these rules, Britain was sure to "get rid of the trouble of governing [the colonies] and all the plagues attending their commerce and connexion from henceforth and for ever."[13]

While this deliberate rudeness caused a stir, the next satire was such a clever hoax that it was taken as true. Just before heading off for a two-week stay with Dashwood, Franklin published *An Edict by the King of Prussia*, a parody of King George's claims to rule the American colonies directly. Adopting the voice of Frederick the Great, Franklin proclaimed that Britain was founded by colonists from Germany and had not paid much in taxes:

> And whereas we ourself have in the last war fought for and defended the said colonies against the power of France, and thereby enabled them to make conquests from the said power in America, for which we have not yet received adequate compensation... we do hereby ordain and command that duties be laid on all goods exported from Britain or imported into it, and

that all ships to and from Britain touch at our port of Konigsberg, there to be unladen, searched, and charged with the said duties.[14]

He later wrote to William:

> I was down at Lord Le Despencer's when the post brought that day's papers. Mr. Whitehead* was there too, who runs early through all the papers, and tells the company what he finds remarkable. He had them together in another room, and we were chatting in the breakfast parlour, when he came running in to us, out of breath, with the paper in his land. "Here!" says he, "here's news for ye! Here's the King of Prussia claiming a right to this kingdom!" All stared, and I as much as anybody; and he went on to read it. When he had read two or three paragraphs, a gentleman present said, "Damn his impudence. I dare say we shall hear by the next post that he is upon his march with one hundred thousand men to back his plan." Whitehead, who is very shrewd, soon after began to smoke it, and looking in my face said, "I'll be hanged if this is not some of your American jokes upon us." The reading went on and ended with abundance of laughing, and a general verdict that it was a fair hit; and the piece was cut out of the paper and preserved in my lord's collection.[15]

Both pieces were instant successes. The *Advertiser* reprinted the *Edict* for weeks afterward, and demand forced even Strahan to publish copies in the *Chronicle* and in the *Gentleman's Magazine*. Franklin was pleased by the reaction—"the general sense of the nation is for us," he wrote to Speaker Cushing. The king's closest

---

* Paul Whitehead was a political satirist who served as Dashwood's secretary.

advisers were not amused. Dashwood later included Franklin in a party going to Oxford to see Lord North's appointment to an honorary post at the university. When the entourage stopped over at the Wycombe estate on the return, North was so deliberately rude to the American that the prime minister's wife sat and chatted with him to lessen the embarrassment.

When Franklin returned to London from Wycombe in the autumn of 1773, he undertook his most risky political gamble ever. It would get him thrown out of England for good and hasten the march toward revolution. This was hardly what Franklin had in mind, but it would fix his reputation back in America as one of the stalwarts of the Revolution.

Chapter 14

To the Brink of War

$\mathscr{I}$n the final years of his frustrated embassy in London, Franklin's personality and tactics sharpened. Pennsylvania's struggle to counter the proprietors' impositions was subsumed in the broader colonial struggle with King George and Parliament. To the frustration of conciliators back home, Franklin was now slow to submit colonial assemblies' petitions for redress. Since these remonstrances only angered or prompted harsher reprisals, he saw little use in them.

He began to show a cold hardness and to take broader risks. He had to confront the unhappy fact that while he was successful at winning friends who could influence public opinion, most of these admirers had little clout with the few who held direct power. His scientific and philosophical friends sympathized but could do little.

His Tory friends who did have the king's ear smiled and urged patience.

As he had predicted, deliberate misinformation from royal governors and other appointees in America was prompting harsh policies. Like generals on the losing side of a war, they bombarded the king's ministers with complaints of plots and with demands for harsher laws and for more resources for enforcement. The litany was the same: Most Americans were still deeply loyal to Britain and her king, but a few conspiratorial malcontents who had only their own interest in mind stirred the mobs and resorted to unlawful violence. Chief among these was that corrupt and licentious rascal Benjamin Franklin, who was personally directing what amounted to rebellion from his luxurious remove under Whitehall's nose.

It was easy for the series of prime ministers to believe this simplistic explanation of the American troubles since they were distracted by other troubles. A new war with France and Spain was a possibility. Domestic upheavals grew more violent, and the economy stagnated. Despite Franklin's most aggressive presentations and personal lobbying, the power elite at Whitehall trusted the heated accusations from their appointees on the scene more than the protests of this annoying man who seemed to haunt their outer offices. Franklin also realized that although most leaders of the American colonial resistance disliked their governors and other high officeholders, they scarcely appreciated the damage these officials in their midst were causing.

IN JUNE 1772, THOMAS WHATELY DIED. Whately was the private secretary of Lord Grenville who had lured Franklin into naming American agents during the Stamp Act crisis seven years before. Whately had served both Grenville and North and had carried on private correspondence with a number of colonial officials in order to make himself more knowledgeable and influential. Much of this correspondence had been shown to Lord Grenville and remained in the official files. It would become the focus of an intense struggle.

In August 1772, Lord Hillsborough lost his post as secretary and blamed Franklin for his fall. In truth he had fallen into a trap he had set for Franklin and some others who wanted to build a new colony on the Ohio River, in what is now West Virginia. Hillsborough had urged Franklin and the other promoters (including some powerful English noblemen) to increase their land request to twenty million acres. The secretary had assumed that the claim would be rejected, but to his mortification, the king and the Privy Council gave preliminary approval for the grant. When he tried to block it, the powerful shareholders forced him from office. Hillsborough went, protesting bitterly.* He was replaced by William Legge, Lord Dartmouth.[1] Franklin and Dartmouth were old friends from the young nobleman's days as head of the Board of Trade in 1767, when the Rockingham ministry repealed the Stamp Act. When Dartmouth returned to London that October, he formally recognized Franklin as agent for Massachusetts, something that Hillsborough had steadfastly refused to do. At that time, Franklin had a petition from the Massachusetts General Assembly protesting the recent decision to pay its governor, Thomas Hutchinson, directly from London—which removed what controls the local government had over the powerful executive.

Hutchinson was one of the most despised of all the men who had presided over that fractious colony. A native New Englander, descended from a long line of Puritan merchant ship owners, Hutchinson had remorselessly clawed his way to power and placed relatives in lucrative positions to an extent that enraged the public even in that age of nepotism and self-advancement. His son-in-law,

---

* The land titles were never officially conveyed to the company, and as the Revolution drew near, the plan died.

Andrew Oliver, was now the lieutenant governor. When in 1770 Lord North allowed the East India Company to sell its surplus tea directly through its own agents in the colonies—cutting American import houses out of the trade—Hutchinson ensured that many of the jobs went to relatives. At their October 1772 meeting, Franklin proffered the Massachusetts petition, but Dartmouth asked him, as a favor, to withdraw it. The king would surely reject such a petition at that point, so early in Dartmouth's tenure; the new secretary asked for more time to prepare the ground. Franklin, sensing he had a chance to revive his influence in high places, readily agreed to put the petition back in his pocket for the time being.

Then a strange thing happened. No one is really sure when, but about this time, Franklin came into possession of a packet of letters written to Thomas Whately between 1767 and 1769. Six of the letters were from Hutchinson when he was lieutenant governor and chief justice, and four were from Oliver when he was secretary of the province.[2] They were inflammatory in the extreme. The two Massachusetts officials pleaded for an even firmer policy against the protestors, begged for more troops, and complained that they could not carry out their duties because of the plots laid by a small clique of radicals. Hutchinson's last letter was the most explosive; it stated, "There must be some abridgement of what are called English liberties" in Massachusetts. These clearly were letters that Whately had passed on to Prime Minister Grenville, who not only studied them but also showed them to a wide circle of friends, including Franklin's old agency partner Richard Jackson.

Letters were currency in the political arena of that day. Franklin knew that his letters to radical friends in England and Scotland were intercepted and copied as closely as his writings to his son and his Philadelphia lieutenant Joseph Galloway. For years he had been careful to write nothing that would put him at risk, legally, if showed publicly. But he was not above jabbing at his enemies in private letters, full knowing that they would be reading the insults as well. A year before Hillsborough's downfall, Franklin wrote to Massachusetts Speaker Thomas Cushing a brutal assessment of the "Character of the present American Secretary." Hillsborough is, Franklin said,

> proud, supercilious, extremely conceited (moderate as they are) of his political Knowledge and Abilities; fond of everyone that can stoop to flatter him, and inimical to all that tell him disagreeable Truths. This man's mandates have been treated with Disrespect in America, his betters criticized his Measures, he is censured and despised, which has produced in him a kind of Malice against the Colonies.[3]

Hillsborough kept a copy of that insult, plus a dozen others, in his files for some future revenge against Franklin.[4]

Communications that were strictly confidential went by trusted merchants or sea captains bound for home. In turn, Franklin, through his friend Edward Bancroft and other spies, did a healthy trade in buying letters or copies of government memos—anything that might help the colonial cause. The Hutchinson-Oliver letters were such a topic of open gossip that he must have learned of them easily.

A puzzle remains as to who gave him the letters. The best bet is that it was one of the Pownall brothers. John Pownall remained in the prime minister's secretariat, while Thomas Pownall, himself a former Massachusetts royal governor and foe of Hutchinson, was one of Dartmouth's close advisers and an ardent advocate of putting British-American relations back on the old sound footing. A side issue is whether Dartmouth had a hand in the affair.

In December, Franklin sent the letters to Thomas Cushing, and they got through unmolested. In a cover letter Franklin stressed that he wanted Cushing to show the letters only to a small group of Massachusetts leaders. They must know how perfidiously the governor and his aide had behaved. He also argued that this was proof that not all their troubles emanated from the king and Parliament.

But could Franklin have been so naïve as to believe that the letters would be kept under such close control? Or did he perhaps hope that the letters would disgrace Hutchinson on both sides of the Atlantic and thus give Dartmouth leverage within the king's government? With so much of Franklin's correspondence sidetracked into government files, how did these explosive letters get by Dartmouth's spies? Or was Franklin so frustrated that he deliberately threw a bomb into the middle of the stalemate in hopes that something would break loose?

In any event, Boston exploded. During the spring of 1773, the letters were repeatedly copied and circulated hand to hand in Boston. By June, public demand was so strong that Cushing had to lay the letters before a General Assembly already in a rage over the new tea laws. The Assembly quickly petitioned the Crown for the removal of both Hutchinson and Oliver.

In the minds of the people, the Hutchinson-Oliver letters became mixed in with the outrage over the tea duty issue and other British offenses. When an armed revenue cutter ran aground off Rhode Island, a mob burned the ship. In May, tea ships were turned back from the docks in Boston, New York, and Philadelphia. Other cargoes remained in warehouses. Later, in October, a cargo ship was burned at Annapolis. John Hancock, who had switched to importing tea from merchants in the French, Dutch, and Danish islands in the Caribbean (illegally, of course), found himself on the edge of ruin again.

In July, Hutchinson obtained a copy of Franklin's letter to Cushing and sent it to Dartmouth, who took the private position within the government that it bordered on treason. Strangely,

Franklin was not publicly denounced as the sender of the letters although throughout London there was widespread speculation that he was the source. If Dartmouth had been involved in the plot, he now had to cover his tracks. He might be charged with suborning a Crown postal official who himself might be arrested. He also had been actively seeking Franklin's advice on how to respond to the public uproar over the tea duties and how to coax both the king and Parliament out of their resentful mood. In any event, Dartmouth ordered General Thomas Gage, the army commander at Boston, to get the original of Franklin's letter so he could be prosecuted on criminal charges, but Cushing had prudently destroyed it.

For a while things simmered, and Franklin continued to build his friendships within the Bute-Dashwood circle and to lobby for the removal of Hutchinson and Oliver. Though he had said he would sail home by the autumn packet, he decided to stay on to watch what happened. With Parliament adjourned until January, he took a holiday trip to Twyford to visit his friend Bishop Shipley.

In the meantime, Thomas Whately's brother William grew exceedingly angry. William Whately was a banker to the government and the executor of his late brother's estate. Since the Massachusetts petition specifically cited the letters to his brother, he was accused of having allowed them to fall into colonial hands. Affronted, he searched most of the autumn for someone to challenge. He found John Temple, a distant relation of Lord Grenville who had lost his job as a colonial customs official because of Hutchinson.[5] To the delight of the coffeehouse crowds, the two exchanged increasingly insulting letters in the newspapers. Temple denied everything; Whately grew more abusive. Friends of Hutchinson added their own accusations, and finally the November 29 issue of the *Public Advertiser* denounced Temple.[6]

The resulting duel on December 9 was pure comedy. Neither had ever fought before. They first fired pistols at each other and missed.

Then they flailed with swords, sliding about the muddy field in the twilight. Whately was felled and cut a number of times before onlookers rescued them both. Newspaper ridicule and public laughter prompted Whately to talk of another challenge.

This was too much for Franklin, watching from Twyford. He had tried to head off the first duel by sending the newspapers anonymous letters exonerating Temple. A second duel was unthinkable. On Christmas Day he wrote to the *Public Advertiser* confessing that he alone was responsible for sending the letters to Boston.

FOR A WEEK, FRANKLIN REMAINED QUIETLY CONFIDENT that he would not suffer for his actions. He wrote to his son, William, that "I grow less concerned about censure when I am satisfied I act rightly," and he told Cushing that he was not much afraid of what the government could do to him.

In truth, however, Franklin was caught in a trap, and the North government was quick to take advantage. Just days later, on Saturday, January 8, 1774, he was notified that the Privy Council would take up the Massachusetts removal petition on the next Tuesday. On short notice he also was informed that Hutchinson and Oliver would be represented by legal counsel at the hearing. This would not, it seemed, be a straightforward examination of the petition on its merits. Franklin probably was not surprised, nor should he have been. At that hearing, Franklin asked for, and received, a delay until January 29 so he could obtain a barrister to represent him and the Assembly.

Just days before the rescheduled hearing, one of John Hancock's ships docked in London with news that would shock the city. On the night of December 16, Samuel Adams and a small group of men disguised as Mohawk Indians forced their way aboard a merchant ship and threw 342 chests of tea (valued at £9,650) into Boston Harbor. At first, American reaction was muted. Those who still hoped for some reconciliation and reform, including George Washington, condemned what became known as the Boston Tea Party. But as similar destruction followed in other ports, its popularity increased.

Once news reached England, the outrage was instant. Franklin publicly denounced the destruction of the tea and at one point offered to cover the losses out of his own pocket, but to no avail. British blood was up and the scapegoat was at hand.

On Saturday, January 29, Franklin returned to Whitehall to face whatever would come from Hutchinson's lawyers and Alexander Wedderburn, the king's solicitor general. Wedderburn was the archetype of the Georgian place seeker; he was willing to take any side as long as it advanced his own interests. While the king and his ministers might disdain him, they had to acknowledge that he had a razor wit and a viper's tongue in the courtroom. The petition was irrelevant; Wedderburn was to destroy Franklin once and for all.

FRANKLIN PREPARED HIMSELF CAREFULLY, as if for sacrifice. He wore his most ornate and longest full wig. He dressed in his best, a suit of dark Manchester velvet with a spotted pattern. As an accessory, he brought along a long cane that was famous among his scientific brethren.*

The hearing was to be in the Cockpit, a smallish hall in the government palace where the Stuart kings once fought their specially bred fighting roosters. The public crush outside the door was enormous, but Franklin's accompanying supporters—Arthur Lee, Edmund Burke (now New York's agent), Edward Bancroft, Joseph Priestley, and a young admirer named Jeremy Bentham—fought their way to standing-room positions inside.

---

* Franklin often filled the hollow staff with oil; he would then wave the cane over wind-rippled waters. By releasing the oil, Franklin would appear to calm the troubled waters and thus would baffle his audience.

Franklin's lawyer was John Dunning, himself a former solicitor general. He advised Franklin to leave the arguing to him and that the agent was not obliged to answer any of Wedderburn's questions. Thirty-six Privy Council members took their places on chairs behind a wide table. This was an extraordinarily large group of attendees, and most had come for gleeful sport. There were some somber friends, such as Lord Le Despencer and the out-of-office Lord Shelburne, but to be sure there were many more enemies, including Lord North and a gloating Lord Hillsborough. The throngs who packed the room, outraged by the colonists' tea party as well as by how Franklin had stolen the Hutchinson-Oliver letters, were eager to see Wedderburn savage the American agent.

The session in the Cockpit lasted about two hours by most recounting. The first half was taken up with a reading of the petition and the letters in question. Dunning spoke briefly to remind the noblemen that this was a humble petition of grievance from loyal subjects and nothing more. During this, Franklin stood quietly by the fireplace at one end of the long room. He was composed and confident to all outward appearance.

Wedderburn, a small man with quick movements, commenced his attack at full force. He paced the length of the long table at which the council members were seated. He shouted and pounded on the table. The issue was not the petition but the perfidy of Dr. Franklin (the honorary title being used as a barbed weapon of derision). Wedderburn compared Franklin to Zanga, an African murderer in a popular tragic poem who declares:

> I forged the letters; I disposed the picture,
> I hated, I despised, and I destroy.*

---

* From *Revenge*, by Edward Young.

Wedderburn warmed to the attack:

> My lords, what poetic fiction only had penned for the heart of
> a cruel African, Dr. Franklin has realized and transcribed from
> his own. Here is a man, who, with the utmost insensibility of
> remorse, stands up and avows himself the author of all.... I
> ask, my lords, whether the revengeful temper attributed, by
> poetic fiction only, to the bloody African is not surpassed by
> the coolness and apathy of the wily American?[7]

Wedderburn tried to make something of a legal argument. But he
kept coming back to Franklin. It was the "wily" agent and his
"junto of six persons" back in Boston who were duping the "innocent, well-meaning farmers which comprise the bulk of the
Assembly." It was Franklin alone who led the Boston radicals; he
was "a first mover and prime conductor...the actor and secret
spring...the inventor and first planner of the whole contrivance."[8]
The solicitor general charged that Franklin's real ambition was to
become Massachusetts governor himself, which was patently
ridiculous. As the second hour drew to a close, he began to repeat
himself, and the Privy Council members lapsed from their initial
merriment and laughter into a bored resignation.

Franklin remained motionless and without expression. He was
now sixty-eight, and it must have taken all his strength just to get
through the physical ordeal, let alone the emotional punishment.
Ralph Izzard, a South Carolina planter who resided in London, said
later he would have struck Wedderburn if he had been attacked so.
Some of Franklin's friends walked out of the Cockpit in visible
shock. The agent himself merely turned at the adjournment and
walked slowly out of the room, pausing to shake hands without
comment with a few well-wishers. Then he went back to Craven
Street and sanctuary. On Monday he was formally informed that he

had been removed as deputy postmaster general for the American colonies. Not even Dashwood could stand in the way of the king as he began to crack down on America in earnest.

Outside in the streets of London the talk was not of Franklin's alleged perfidy but of the viciousness of Wedderburn's attack. As Carl Van Doren has pointed out, Franklin made the right decision to remain silent even while Wedderburn slandered him and shredded his reputation: "If Franklin, exposed to this lightning of abuse, had made the most far-sighted calculation, he could not have chosen a shrewder behavior. He did not have to choose. In emergencies men behave, not according to what they later reflect would have been wise, but according to their characters at the time. Franklin already had the instinct to be patient under stress, the habit of magnanimity, and the schooled knowledge of the world which made him realize that the longer Wedderburn went on the sooner his words would come to be held against him, as so much injustice and inhumanity."[9]

WHILE FRANKLIN IN HIS SOUL HAD ALWAYS BEEN a man alone, he now felt real isolation. Craven Street was an unhappy, often empty place. Cousin Sally Franklin had gone home to her father in the north, and nephew Josiah Williams had returned to New England. In May 1774, William Hewson cut himself doing an autopsy, contracted septicemia, and died. A distraught Polly shortly bore her third child, a daughter, and sat forlorn in her mother's house.

Though he kept a strict control over his life and feelings, Franklin needed the support and affirmation of admiring friends. After the session before the Privy Council, Franklin encountered an uncomfortable coolness at his favorite coffeehouses and clubs, and although many of his friends expressed their loyalty, others— among them his oldest and closest confidants—drifted away. Strahan, his beloved "Scotch Straney," disapproved of Franklin's actions, and besides, he felt the weight of his government job. Sir

John Pringle, the favorite traveling companion, was now fully occupied as the British army's chief health officer and with the preparations for a larger military presence in the colonies. Arthur Lee, vexing and impatient, abandoned Franklin. Against the older man's wishes, Lee went to France and Italy that spring expressly to sound out possible alliances that could help the colonies if war—now no longer unthinkable—should flare with Britain. Franklin still wanted no part of war and resolutely turned away all confidential approaches from French diplomats stationed in London.

Meanwhile, King George III and Lord North tried to bring the rebellious and ungrateful colonies to heel. While Massachusetts was the main target of what came to be called the Coercive (or Intolerable) Acts, nearly every other colony felt the blow. This was a proven method to crush rebellion; many of the men in the North government had begun their careers breaking Scotland's final bid for freedom less than thirty years before.

Parliament closed the port of Boston to international commerce until the destroyed tea was paid for. So many troops landed that one out of five Boston inhabitants wore a red coat, and General Gage was named the colony's acting governor (Hutchinson was given a sinecure back in England). Parliament forced a new constitution on Massachusetts and vastly reduced its Assembly in power and status. Another act took away the right to local trial for smugglers and dissidents, and provided that some cases could be moved to England. Other colonies—New York particularly—were hit with tougher rules about housing soldiers. The final blow came with the Quebec Act, which extended religious liberty to the French Canadian population but then drew the boundary of Canada's major province southward so that it blocked any hopes of westward expansion by colonies from Connecticut to Georgia.

Franklin watched the time for peace slipping away. He had seen the devastation of war twenty years earlier on the frontier and knew that a full civil war could bring cruel havoc to America. But he also knew what no one else in London could acknowledge. In such a hateful war, America would ultimately prevail. It would not be enough for King George to defeat a rebel army; the impossible test would be for Britain to restore the kind of government control that it had enjoyed before the French and Indian War. No force could do it.

Rumors that he would be arrested and imprisoned whirled about him. William Whately filed a civil suit against him, but it was more an annoyance undertaken at government prodding than a real danger. Oddly enough, even though the Hutchinson letters affair ended Franklin's effectiveness as a lobbyist in the corridors of Whitehall, he became the celebrity of the day among London's social and political elite. It had never occurred to the British nobility until now that their subjects across the sea were sincerely disaffected or that they had the courage or the resources to resist. Separation, once unthinkable, became a real threat. Franklin became the symbol of this threat, and they clamored to hear his views.

In late 1774, various opposition factions within Parliament began a last attempt to reconcile with the colonies. Once again, William Pitt, now Lord Chatham, came out of retirement, seeing opposition to the war as a way to rebuild his majority and to checkmate the king. He invited Franklin to his country estate at Hayes and had him devise a plan that could be acceptable to the ministries and the American revolutionaries. Meanwhile, Lord Shelburne, who hoped to succeed Pitt as head of the reformers, was working on other members of the back bench.

Franklin and his allies saw an opportunity to pull back from the brink of war. Merchant banker David Barclay and physician John Fothergill told Franklin to refine the plan he had given Pitt so that they could pass it on to Lord Dartmouth. Dartmouth himself tried to approach Franklin; whatever the role this erstwhile friend had played in the American agent's recent disgrace, he was, it seems, still willing to help Franklin approach Lord North. Dartmouth went through the Howe brothers—Admiral Lord Richard Howe, who would command the Royal Navy's war fleet during the coming war with the colonies, and General Sir William Howe, who would become the British army's commander in chief. The brothers had strong ties to America and saw advantage in being peacemakers, since the king and Lord North were suddenly uncertain about the prospect of a distant civil war that almost certainly would bring the French and the Spanish into the contest.

By November 1774, several versions of Franklin's seventeen-point plan for reconciliation were in circulation at Kensington Palace and Whitehall. Franklin and Arthur Lee, now back from France and Italy, had also presented their case by publishing a flood of pseudonymous pamphlets and privately circulating other, more daring essays. The conditions were clear: Massachusetts must pay for the destroyed tea, but the British must withdraw troops not needed to protect the frontier; civilian rule must be reestablished and fortifications in the port cities (like Castle William in Boston Harbor) returned to local control; an American Congress must be established with power to legislate on intercolonial matters; Parliament must cede its power to rule and tax to this new legislature; civil liberties must be restored; oppressive duties and trade restraints must be negotiated.

In truth, it all was quite impossible.

On Christmas Day 1774, Franklin was playing an enjoyable game of chess at the home of Lord Richard Howe's sister when the admiral presented himself and opened a new round of negotiations. It became clear by January that neither Lord North nor the king would seriously consider any of the plans Franklin had authored.

TERRIBLE NEWS CAME IN EARLY FEBRUARY 1775. Franklin learned that Deborah had suffered another stroke in December and had died. She had held on alone, always steadfast and loyal, for nearly the last half of their marriage. Now she was gone, and he must have felt both loss and guilt. His letters revealed nothing of his feelings, however.

At the same time, his estrangement from William became an open breach. In his letters, Franklin urged his son to look beyond his royal governorship and consider returning to his farm to make his living; it was obvious to the father that the son would pay a price as part of the punishment that the king would mete out. But William refused the advice. His father had made him what he was: ambitious, proud, and very much a loyal British-American. He was a good governor and a popular one. It was too much to expect him to throw everything over just because of his father's downfall.

It was, in fact, King George and Lord North who gave Franklin the final nudge he needed to go home to Philadelphia. In September 1774, the First Continental Congress had met in Philadelphia and drafted a final appeal to the king to roll back his punishment and bring the colonies back into their old relationship with the Crown. All autumn and winter, however, the king had received appeals for even tougher measures from appalled royal governors and well-known Loyalists. On January 19, 1775, King George opened Parliament with a speech announcing that all the colonies were in criminal resistance and disobedience. In February, the various petitions and pleas were dumped on the House of Commons table to be ignored. On February 9, Parliament voted (over the eloquent objections of Pitt, Shelburne, and Bishop Shipley) to urge the king to declare Massachusetts in open rebellion.

Franklin's final days in London were essentially spent as a rearguard action. Pitt's ornate coach was parked outside the Craven Street house on many days as the men tried to refine an acceptable compromise. But North and the other ministers were resolute, and even Dartmouth finally gave way and apologized for having been too pro-American. Parliament quickly passed a bill to send six thousand more soldiers to Boston and then enacted a total embargo on all trade with New England. The Newfoundland fisheries were declared out of bounds to American trawlers.

Of course, these were all moot gestures, for the closing of the port of Boston had brought a flood of money, food, and other essentials from sister colonies as far away as South Carolina. Life in New England was stark, but the colonists would survive. Franklin's plan for colonial union had been achieved in fact, if not in law.

MANY OF HIS FRIENDS' MEMOIRS CONFIRM that Franklin was on the ragged edge of his nerves at this time. He sometimes would be found in tears, and other times he would rage at some minor slight from the ministers. He became insulting in his final communications to the government, so much so that his friends often intercepted them lest he finally be imprisoned.

Knowing he was being watched, he studiously avoided contact with France's chargé d'affaires in London, despite the fact that the diplomat, Joseph-Mathias Gérard de Rayvenal, had arranged Franklin's visits to the French scientific community. Instead, he began clandestine talks with Dutch and French friends who could privately inquire about what tangible aid might be forthcoming from their governments.

These often overlooked contacts, which began in late 1774, mark the true beginning of Franklin's preparations for a war that now seemed unavoidable.

French historian Henri Doniol, in his five-volume survey of his government's secret archives, concluded that Franklin organized a gunrunning effort in Holland, France, and Spain to move military equipment to secure Caribbean ports, from which it could more easily be shipped into the colonies.[10] Franklin used trusted American ship captains who plied between London and continental ports to carry verbal messages or letters in cipher. He employed friends and relatives as go-betweens to hasten negotiations with Britain's enemies. His contacts included old scientific correspondents such as Charles F. W. Dumas, an old friend in Amsterdam, and leading merchants such as Sieur Montaudoin of Nantes.[11] His nephew Jonathan Williams visited such French friends as scientist Jacques Barbeu-Dubourg, who had translated and published Franklin's electrical discoveries in French, and Samuel du Pont de Nemours.

Barbeu-Dubourg played an important role by going to the French foreign minister, Charles Gravier, the Comte de Vergennes, and opening direct exploratory talks. Montaudoin was equally important. He was not only head of the wealthiest trading family in France but also a member of the French Royal Academy of Science and a Mason. In France, unlike England, Freemasonry attracted both philosophers and the rising merchant class, just as it had in Philadelphia.

While French officials were deliberately noncommittal, Dutch and French merchants needed little prompting. A year before Franklin's first contacts with them, merchants were sending large stores of canvas, bolts of cloth, leather, powder, and shot to the Dutch haven of St. Eustatius and other smugglers' paradises in the Caribbean, speculating that an American rebellion would mean profits and revenge for England's competitors. By early 1775, merchants from France and Spain were traveling across the Atlantic to see just how far the colonists meant to go with their protests.

Since the king had rejected all attempts at reconciliation, Franklin committed to sailing home at the end of March 1775. He spent his time saying good-bye to friends like Caleb Whitefoord and his spy Edward Bancroft. There were final meetings with Edmund

Burke, who planned to make a last appeal in the House of Commons against the coming war. Franklin spent his last day in London, March 19, with Joseph Priestley, who now divided his time in London between being Lord Shelburne's political adviser and conducting his research into gases (which would yield the first description of oxygen).* They spent the day reading the latest newspapers from America, with Franklin marking pieces for Priestley to insert in the London periodicals.

On March 20, he left London in a post chaise with his fifteen-year-old grandson, the newly renamed William Temple Franklin, whom everyone called Temple. Five days later the pair sailed from Portsmouth. During the first half of the calm six-week journey, Franklin immersed himself in a letter to William recounting the final negotiations with the ministers. As they drew closer to America, he began to measure the water temperatures and proved that the Gulf Stream was warmer than the seawaters on either side of it.

Franklin kept his mind busy so he would not have to confront the uncertain welcome that awaited him at home. Who would even care that he was coming home at last?

---

* Priestley became such a political radical that he was forced to emigrate from Britain to America after the war. He lived near Philadelphia from 1794 until his death in 1804.

Franklin in London, during his final mission in that metropolis.

Chapter 15

Revolution

*F*ranklin and grandson Temple landed in Philadelphia on May 5, 1775, and went at once to the house on Market Street that he had had built but had never seen. He was weary and depressed at having failed to stop a war that began while he was at sea. On April 19, Massachusetts militiamen had clashed with British troops at the battles of Lexington and Concord.

Sally and Richard Bache and the two young grandsons welcomed the travelers as cheerfully as they could. But Deborah's memory produced a sad reserve in them all. Franklin knew that both William and Sally resented him for not coming home to ease her final days. Feeling a rare burden of guilt, he spent several weeks resting, rarely venturing out of the house.

within a day or so of his arrival, he faced another matter close to his heart. Son William came from his farm near Burlington, New Jersey, along with Joseph Galloway, Franklin's long-serving political lieutenant. They came in secret, stayed for dinner, and drank late into the night. They heard all Franklin had to say about the obdurate attitude of the British ministers and his prediction that any reconciliation was impossible. Galloway had just resigned as Speaker of the Pennsylvania Assembly and could be selected as one of the colony's delegates to the Second Continental Congress that was to convene in a few days, but he wanted to avoid the horrors of a civil war and was moving into the Loyalist camp. Nor would William listen to his father's plea to resign his governorship and publicly stand for independence. William had resisted such urgings from his father before, and he did so again. He simply could not abandon all he had worked for and been successful at. His father was old and embittered. William was forty-five and still had a full life to look forward to, perhaps even a title and an estate in England. The next day, William returned to Burlington with his son, Temple, in tow.

The uncomfortable exchange with William and Galloway showed Franklin that he was well ahead of his countrymen in his determination for independence. As he would soon discover, most of the new American leaders still hoped for an unlikely justice from Britain. He had never enjoyed being in front of the parade, and now was no exception.

Franklin's rest did not last long. The Pennsylvania General Assembly unanimously elected him as one of five delegates to the new session of Congress. The rout at Lexington and Concord, in which the militiamen had forced the redcoats to retreat back to Boston, had energized the patriots and dumbfounded the British, who had been sure of a quick end to the insurrection.

On May 9, the delegates from the Carolinas, Virginia, Maryland, and Delaware were escorted into Philadelphia by mounted troopers and greeted by bells, bands, and fifteen thousand cheering citizens—half the city. The southerners dazzled the spectators with their showy clothing and retinue of brightly costumed slaves. The next day, the delegations from Massachusetts, Connecticut, and New York were treated to identical fanfare. The Yankees were more soberly dressed, but the crowd pressed close to spot John Hancock and the two Adamses.

Pennsylvania's Assembly ceded the first floor of the State House to the Continental Congress, but it did not halt its own business. On the floor above, the Assembly commenced debate about a new constitution and a reorganized provincial government. Franklin soon was appointed to the colony's Committee of Safety, which was responsible for readying the colony in case of attack. He was not yet well enough to haul himself up the State House stairs, so official business was brought to his study.

Every new arrival called on the Market Street house to hear the latest news from London and to ask Franklin the two questions that burned in their minds: Was separation from Britain inevitable? And, more important, could America win in such a struggle?

With much sadness he answered the first question affirmatively; King George and the North ministry were determined to punish all resisters in the colonies and impose an even harsher rule.

But, he emphasized with calm assurance, America would prevail. For one thing, he knew (because his allies within the government had showed him the confidential data) that the British army of 1775 bore little resemblance to the triumphant force that had fought the French and Spanish all over the world in 1763. There were only about 45,000 able-bodied soldiers (both infantry and cavalry) in the entire empire.* At least one-third of those troops were in England

---

* This does not count troops the East India Company maintained in its own army to protect its holdings.

and Scotland, keeping order and guarding against a French invasion,[1] while others were committed in Ireland, Gibraltar, and the West Indies.

For a brief moment, the patriot militia had the upper hand. By June, General Gage, who had begun the year with about 4,500 troops, had an occupying force of 6,500 supported by a fleet of warships in Boston Harbor. But on April 23, four days after Lexington and Concord, the Massachusetts government called 13,600 militia to arms, and units from Connecticut, Rhode Island, and New Hampshire soon swelled the camps around Cambridge to 15,000. Better still, the quickly formed patriot fleet of armed merchant ships and smuggling schooners proved surprisingly effective in blocking supplies to the British garrison. Between August and November 1775, only one provision ship reached Boston. Franklin argued that it would take a long time for King George to recruit, train, and transport any larger force, let alone an overwhelming one, even assuming he could find the money.

Franklin also recognized that within the House of Commons there was growing opposition to any prospective war. The country squires might roar for victory, but the merchants and manufacturers saw an economic catastrophe looming. Pitt and his adherents saw a return to power if they could cast the king's policies as a threat to English liberties at home and as leading to a transatlantic civil war. America could have its independence if it was resolute enough.

But Franklin knew that America had only a small window of opportunity. Britain had eight million subjects—more than three times as many people as in the colonies—and so the Americans could not hold the advantage in military manpower for long.[*] Nor

---

[*] In fact, the British capacity to produce troops for the American war exceeded expectations. By 1778, twelve new infantry regiments were raised and seventeen more were added by 1780, in addition to four dragoon regiments. This amounted to twenty thousand new troops in the field, not counting the thirty thousand Hessians that were sent over.

could the unconnected and trade-dependent colonial economies compete with Britain's financial resources.[2] While the king might not be able to control the colonies as he had, given time his armies could seize enough control over vulnerable regions—New England and the southern colonies—to prevent the Americans from uniting.

In those early summer weeks of 1775, Franklin could reveal the real truth to only a chosen few, and many of them were unwilling to grasp his point. America needed immediate financial and military aid from some other source. France, long the colonists' bitter contestant for the continent, was the best, perhaps the only, bet. Britain must be delayed from bringing its full weight for as long as possible. And *if* the fledgling nation could develop new customers for its trade exports, it could pay for needed war technology—particularly gunpowder, arms of all kinds, and shot. Then the colonies would have an advantage, for Franklin had no doubt that Americans would be more resolute in defense of their way of life than the British people would be in forcing control over them.

Though Franklin was convinced, his colleagues were not yet ready to confront the hard choices of an alliance. Indeed, they had not even embraced the notion of independence. After the loss at Bunker Hill on June 17, a general uncertainty deepened. When the Second Continental Congress elected George Washington as commander in chief that month and ordered him to the defenses around Boston, the Congress was being flooded with increasingly pessimistic reports and pleas for arms, clothing, and, most of all, gunpowder. It was all overwhelming for men who had been planters or lawyers but never war strategists.*

---

* The Second Continental Congress sat from May 10, 1775, until the Articles of Confederation went into effect on March 2, 1781. At least one-third of the 342 men elected in that period served in either their state militias or the Continental Army during their terms in office. Often only three dozen members were available to transact a mass of minute clerical and administrative business, and the Congress's decisions were constantly in conflict with those of local governments and senior military commanders.

AFTER BEING AWAY FOR MOST OF THE PAST twenty years, Franklin found Philadelphia a radically different place. In his early days, he had boasted that he knew the name of every freeman and slave in the city. He had been the premier practitioner of the most important new technology of the age and had risen to high prominence. Now Philadelphia, with a population of 37,000, was the second largest city in the British Empire; in a city with two dozen print shops, Franklin was just a memory as a printer (his old partner, David Hall, had died in 1772). He knew few people on sight, and initially almost no one recognized him.

He was sixty-nine, a widower; his health was not what it had been. Most of his early friends and colleagues were dead or in retirement. Even his old ally Galloway was gone from the city, having decamped to his country estate because he was suspected of being a spy for the Crown. Old enemies were being replaced too. That old nemesis, Thomas Penn, would be dead before the year was out.

Franklin knew few of the men who were debating this dangerous venture. When he had first sailed as Pennsylvania's agent in 1757, George Washington had been twenty-five, John Adams twenty-two, Thomas Jefferson fourteen, and James Madison only six. Most were not well traveled; Adams, now forty, had never been out of Massachusetts before he attended the First Continental Congress in 1774. Fewer had any military experience, which made Washington's surveying of the frontier and time in battle all the more unique.

But Franklin brought to Philadelphia two qualities that were in as short supply as gunpowder. He had vast experience and a strength of character that was unprecedented. His bubbling sense of humor and absurdity now peeked out from behind a deliberately serene and confident surface. He used wit as a tool—or a weapon. His temper no longer got the better of him, but rather he knew precisely when to show anger to serve his purposes. His science trials had taught him patience. The world acclaim and his friendship with the great minds of his time had brought him an elevating confidence. The arrogance and dishonesty of the king and his ministers had convinced him of the corrupting power of privilege. He had emerged from his twenty years of challenge more in control of himself than he had thought possible. He was ready to help his "home country" become a new nation—and more than anyone else, he was confident that America could indeed be an independent nation.

To his surprise, Franklin was not an irrelevancy to this new generation of leaders. In the minds of these strangers, he was the personification of the American Revolution. His persecution by Wedderburn before the Privy Council the year before had erased people's doubts about his motives. He was also unique among his countrymen in his world reputation. He was by far the most traveled and experienced citizen in the ways of courts and kings. Samuel and John Adams might have burned more hotly for liberty, Thomas Jefferson might have had the better reasoning to argue the cause, but Franklin, simply because he had thirty years' more accomplishment than they, was the light that outshone all the others.

Not everyone was especially pleased at this. The Adams cousins and the Virginia aristocrats Richard Henry Lee and Francis Lightfoot Lee chafed at Franklin's seeming imperturbability. They knew he believed in independence because he had told them so in private, and yet he would not join them in haranguing the other members of Congress into an immediate break with England and a full state of war.

John Adams particularly was miffed when Franklin did not try hard enough to stop John Dickinson from drafting, and securing the votes for, one last appeal to King George III. In the Olive Branch Petition of July 8, 1775, the Congress expressed its loyalty to the king and begged him for relief from the injustices imposed by a misguided Parliament. This conciliatory measure, signed by nearly all those who would sign the Declaration of Independence a year later, essentially argued that all could be restored if the king would just step back from the brink. Yet Lord Dartmouth, alert to the mood of King George, did not even bother to give the petition to him. A few days after the petition arrived in London, on August 23, the king declared all thirteen colonies to be in a state of rebellion that must be crushed. Later the Royal Navy blockaded the eastern seaboard to cut off the principal American port cities and bring the colonies into submission.

In July, Franklin again irked the war hawks by using valuable time drafting a complicated proposal to the king for a federal union of all English colonies, including America, Canada, Ireland, and the West Indies. When the Congress refused even to consider the proposal, he blithely cannibalized its essential elements into an early draft of the Articles of Confederation. Despite support for the Articles from Jefferson and others, a vote was delayed. The main sticking point was a dispute over whether power in the Congress should be equally shared by the colonies or made proportional to population. In addition, Franklin's style of government offered too much direct democracy for those who longed for a republic of gentlemen farmer-philosophers (the Lees and Jefferson) or of university-educated men devoted to the written law. But there really was no time to hammer out an alternative, so the plan was shelved for the time being. A final draft by John Dickinson was ultimately adopted and was fully ratified by the states in 1781.

Franklin's attendance at the Congress debates was regular enough, but it was clear he had no taste for the ornately phrased and long-running speeches that were the mark of an eighteenth-century orator. John Adams sniffed that he often saw his older colleague asleep in his chair during the debates. Thomas Jefferson long afterward recalled, "I served with General Washington in the legislature of Virginia before the Revolution, and during it with Dr.

Franklin in Congress. I never heard either of them speak ten minutes at a time, nor to any but the main point which was to decide the question. They laid their shoulders to the great points, knowing that the little ones would follow of themselves."[3]

Franklin was extremely busy employing his two best skills, plotting strategy in private and writing documents for public purposes. On July 15, he submitted a resolution declaring that the colonies would trade America's goods and foodstuffs with anyone who would provide war supplies. It was held back by a majority not yet ready to challenge Britain so directly. He also arranged through Philadelphia financier Robert Morris to bankroll a covert raid on Bermuda to purloin an unguarded stockpile of gunpowder.

At the end of July he brought forward the report of a committee he had chaired to organize an American postal system, since nearly everyone was boycotting the Royal Mail. The next day he was made postmaster general, with a salary of a thousand dollars plus a budget to hire administrative staff and to appoint postmasters and mail carriers. By August 30, he had published routes that extended from Savannah, Georgia, to Portland, Maine. He made his son-in-law, Richard Bache, who was not prospering, comptroller for the service, while he donated his own salary to buy necessary supplies for the soldiers languishing at the siege around Boston.

More and more claims on his time were made. Because of his experience, Franklin was in charge of designing the colonies' new paper money. He drafted Washington's address to the troops when the general took command of the Continental Army at Cambridge. He also got involved in defense issues. Franklin was named to a committee to promote the making of saltpeter for gunpowder. He designed a sharp-pointed pike that could be manufactured in large quantities (even with the colonials' long rifles, most battles, especially the rout at Bunker Hill, were decided at close quarters by the bayonet charge). He placed a system of iron spiked barriers along the narrow approaches of the Delaware River to prevent the Royal Navy from raiding Philadelphia; a system of lighthouse keepers and pilots allowed American shipping to pass freely through the barriers.

Although he was often plagued by gout, boils, and general fatigue, Franklin's public business forced him out of his home sanctuary. He wrote to his friend Priestley in London:

> My time was never more fully employed. . . . In the morning at six I am at the Committee of Safety. . . which . . . holds till near nine, when I am at the Congress, and that sits till after four in the afternoon. Both those bodies proceed with the greatest unanimity, and their meetings are well attended. . . . It will scarce be credited in Britain that men can be as diligent with us from zeal for the public good as with you for thousands per annum. Such is the difference between uncorrupted new states and corrupted old ones.[4]

This is pure Franklin propaganda at work. He knew perfectly well that his letters to Priestley were being opened and read at Whitehall. As with all of the voluminous correspondence he carried on with his English friends, he played to a wider audience. In a later letter to Priestley, he mocked the enormous cost of Britain's campaign to subdue the colonies: "Britain, at the expense of three millions has killed one hundred and fifty Yankees this campaign, which is twenty thousand pounds a head. . . . During the same time sixty thousand children have been born in America."[5] The gibe quickly made the rounds of London's coffeehouses; there was just enough truth to sting.

DURING THE OPPRESSIVELY HOT SUMMER OF 1775, Benjamin Franklin became better acquainted with the new stars in the patriot cause. He worked with Patrick Henry and James Wilson on the committee to negotiate a treaty with the Indian tribes west of Pennsylvania and Virginia. He also was chairman of the committee made up of Thomas Jefferson, John Adams, and Richard Henry Lee that considered and finally rejected the latest of Lord North's attempts to make the rebels surrender.

Jefferson had come back to town after Washington left, and Franklin took an avuncular liking to this tall, reticent skeptic. There was much to separate them by class, education, and personal habit. Jefferson had received a good education in Williamsburg, was a lawyer by profession and a farmer by vocation. He owned masses of slaves and yet dreamed of a new society of freedom. He was quiet to the point of diffidence, his insecurities often immobilized him, and he was quick to take offense. Franklin had pulled himself up in the world and in the process had rigorously trained his mind and emotions.

Yet there was much to bind them. Franklin and Jefferson were the brightest minds of the American Enlightenment. Like Franklin, Jefferson conducted experiments and made observations on all of nature. He tried to raise every conceivable crop and make every product he needed. He studied the stars and wind. He mused about the Almighty and, like Franklin, sidestepped the patent certainties of established religion in favor of a more difficult quest to find God's mercy. In their moments of pause, did Franklin regale Jefferson with the story of the time he and Francis Dashwood took the Anglican book of common worship and reduced the three-hour ordeal into a more convenient and meaningful format? In any event, in later years Jefferson would take the four Gospels and razor out those portions that he felt interfered with his understanding of the will of Providence. *The Jefferson Bible* is still in print today.[6]

Bonded into friendship or not, the dozens of men of the Second Continental Congress produced an astonishing amount of work. These were men more fit and used to hard work than current generations, yet most recorded in their letters levels of exhaustion they had not known before. John Adams, among his other shared duties with Franklin and Jefferson, was on the strategic committee on the conduct of the war. Jefferson had no fewer than three dozen assignments. Franklin was on ten committees, and when the Congress recessed in August, he spent nearly every day organizing Pennsylvania's defenses, planning the recruiting and training of its militia, and scrounging for lead and salt. When Congress returned in mid-September, he was named to a secret committee to organize the transfer of gunpowder from European merchants' stashes in the Dutch West Indies port of St. Eustatius.

At the end of September, Franklin, along with Thomas Lynch of South Carolina and Benjamin Harrison of Virginia, met Washington in Cambridge to plan the winter campaign and build a permanent army. Most of the militia volunteers who had answered the first calls of the Revolution had enlisted for fixed terms that soon would end. Washington wanted twenty thousand men enlisted for a full year, subjected to better discipline, and supported by better supplies. In four days he and the three visitors effectively created the U.S. Army. They reorganized the corps structure, wrote new articles of war, set rules for prisoner exchange, and established procedures for selling the prizes that the fledgling navy captured.

Franklin returned home by way of Warwick, Rhode Island, where his sister Jane Mecom had sought refuge once the British had shut the port of Boston. To his delight, he found her staying with his old love Catharine Ray Greene. The reunion was doubly sweet now that he was alone. Jane gladly came home with him for a visit, and he took along Catharine's ten-year-old son to put him in school in Philadelphia. He had found the Baches welcoming and affectionate but too absorbed in themselves to offer him the unquestioning love he needed. So he built a small new family just for a short time.

ON HIS RETURN, FRANKLIN WAS PLEASED TO FIND that Congress was closer to seeking foreign help. In November, he was named to a Secret Committee of Correspondence "for the sole purpose of corresponding with our friends in Great Britain, Ireland, and other parts of the world." The four other members were Harrison, Dickinson, Thomas Johnson of Maryland, and John Jay of New York. Historians mark this committee as the foundation stone of the U.S. State Department. They also might well mark it as the start of the country's first foreign intelligence service. All the tools of the spy craft were used—ciphers, invisible ink, secret couriers, and covert operations never to be recorded in any history. Washington at this early date was proving that the Americans were adept, even superior, at establishing military intelligence throughout the war zone. Franklin and his committee were just as skilled in the foreign arena.

Several events pushed the ambivalent majority in Congress toward action. British naval raiders launched a series of attacks that burned Charleston, Portsmouth, and later Norfolk. In addition, Congress learned that the British would soon receive an influx of new troops. King George had, as Franklin had expected, been unable to enlist enough new troops at home, so to everyone's surprise he simply rented what he needed. The first seventeen thousand soldiers had been leased from his cousins in Brunswick and Hesse-Cassel at slightly more than £7 per head.[7] The prospect of their arrival meant that America had to find foreign help as quickly as possible.

Franklin's cautious outreach to the French in 1774 had paid off. In December, within days of the Secret Committee's formation, the first official French secret agent arrived in Philadelphia, sent by the Comte de Vergennes. It was a pure clandestine operation. Achard de Bonvouloir made contact with Franklin through a French bookseller in the city, and the committee members arranged to meet with him in a house on the outskirts of town, each coming alone at night after the streets had quieted. Bonvouloir had only verbal instructions, but the Americans were cheered by the message from the French government. Vergennes and Louis XVI were supportive of the bid for independence and hoped to build a trade relationship that was mutually profitable.

During those December meetings, Franklin and the committee convinced the agent that Congress had already made up its mind for independence (it had done nothing of the kind). The Americans stated that the young nation would oppose any peace that did not completely sever ties with Britain and call for withdrawal of the occupying force. This was not true either, but it was what Vergennes wanted to hear. There was no point in helping America, even covertly, and risking war with Britain, if the Americans suddenly were to cave in and come to terms with their old masters.

France could not risk supporting America until its Atlantic ports were declared open to the world—itself a declaration of independence. But Congress dared not make that declaration unless it was sure of French aid. Early in December, Franklin deputized Arthur Lee, still in London, to go to Europe and make confidential, but official, soundings as to what help might come from other nations. Word of this was sure to get back to Vergennes, suggesting the Americans were indeed in earnest. Franklin sent personal letters to every contact he had abroad—including Dumas and Barbeu-Dubourg, as well as Spanish princes who shared his science interests and many other correspondents from Italy to Russia.

By the early months of 1776, the general public had come to favor independence, at whatever cost. In January 1776, Thomas Paine published his pamphlet *Common Sense*, and it swept the doubts from most minds. Using firm logic and soaring language, Paine convinced the city merchant and the backwoods farmer that they had a common cause worth dying for. Franklin had met Paine in England a year or so earlier and had sent letters of recommendation with him when Paine immigrated to America. Yet even Franklin was astonished when Paine's creation sold 100,000 copies and took its place among our national founding documents.

Paine wrote, "We have it in our power to begin the world over again," and Americans thrilled.[8] But there still was so much to do.

The Continental Congress appointed Franklin to the committee responsible for drafting a declaration of independence. The committee also included Thomas Jefferson (the primary author of the document), John Adams, Roger Sherman, and Robert R. Livingston.

Chapter 16

Declaring for Liberty

By March of 1776, Franklin was so busy with the Secret Committee that he was forced to resign from his Assembly positions. That same month, Congress appointed a former member from Connecticut, Silas Deane, as official trade negotiator to Europe; he was to seek war supplies in exchange for popular American exports such as tobacco and rice. Franklin wrote out detailed instructions about how Deane was to go about making clandestine contact with French officials. Deane ignored them.

At about the same time, Franklin, now seventy, was assigned to a mission that historians generally judge to have been the most quixotic of that hasty time. He was to go to Canada and convince the French majority that they were better off becoming the fourteenth state in the new union than staying a British possession. Franklin had long argued that Canada was rightly part of the American colonial structure. Now it should be part of the new nation.

From Philadelphia the prospects looked bright enough. Led by General Richard Montgomery and supported by that able field commander, Colonel Benedict Arnold, an American invasion of Canada had begun in August 1775. By November, the Americans had captured Montreal and were laying siege to Quebec.[1] The large French population had shown no particular desire to be reunited with their old homeland, and Congress reasoned that a union with Canada could not only add new territory and eighty thousand new citizens but also block Britain from any sortie into New England.

Franklin was accompanied by three leading Marylanders: Samuel Chase, a prominent public agitator for independence, and two of the colony's leading Roman Catholics—Charles Carroll, a wealthy planter, and John Carroll, a Jesuit priest (who would later found Georgetown University). The journey was an unrelieved disaster from start to finish. The commissioners began their nearly four-hundred-mile trek while winter still gripped the Great Lakes. By horse, sailboat, and sometimes sled, they slogged up the Hudson River and Mohawk Valley, then rowed across icy Lake George and portaged to Lake Champlain. A month later, they finally arrived, sodden and exhausted, at Arnold's headquarters in Montreal.

The situation they found was not good. Sir William Howe, who had replaced General Gage, had pulled the British military out of Boston for Halifax, where he would refit, reinforce, and link up with naval support. He was to break the siege at Quebec and recapture Canada.* Montgomery had been killed and Arnold was badly

---

* Howe's plan was to send a force under royal governor Sir Guy Carleton and General John Burgoyne to push the Americans south into New York. In the meantime, he planned to move his own wing south to capture New York (which he did) and catch Washington in the middle of the two armies. Some military historians argue that by splitting his forces and losing control, he ensured the disaster that befell Burgoyne at Saratoga on October 17, 1777.

wounded. During the long winter the unpaid, underfed Americans had run amok among the population—that is, those who had not deserted and gone south. That spring, nine thousand British and German troops arrived in Quebec, forcing a disastrous American retreat that did not halt until the troops reached Fort Ticonderoga in October.

Politically the situation was hopeless. When King George in 1774 had issued the Quebec Act, which recognized the French Canadians' right to Catholic worship, nearly all of the American assemblies had issued resolutions filled with anti-Catholic rhetoric. The Canadians had not forgotten. Nor were Quebec's English residents any help. At most there were only four hundred, and half of them were so fiercely loyal to Britain that a family that housed Franklin and his colleagues was forced to flee south when its guests went home in May 1776.

Without Father Carroll's constant help, Franklin probably would have died from exposure and exhaustion on the return trip to Philadelphia. He later quipped in a letter to George Washington that he had been too ill even to have an attack of the gout. Once he recovered a bit, the gout struck his joints so severely that he was confined to bed for the first weeks of June. As he had done so often before, he worked his way back to health.

THE FINAL STEP TOWARD BREAKING with Britain was at hand. Pennsylvania's Assembly was so divided on the matter that it gave up in despair, leaving the matter to its delegation to the Continental Congress. But the delegates themselves were divided—of the seven delegates, only two (Franklin and John Morton*) were initially for independence—and it required a majority decision to cast the colony's single vote in Congress. The Assembly dissolved shortly

---

* John Morton (1724–1777), a surveyor, had succeeded Galloway as Speaker in March 1775.

afterward, and a convention to draft a new constitution for Pennsylvania would open in July.

Other colonies were not so reticent. In April, colonial legislatures began to instruct their representatives to vote for independence. On June 7, Richard Henry Lee of Virginia sponsored a resolution before the Continental Congress declaring, "These United Colonies are, and of right, ought to be, free and independent states."

In calling for independence, the New Jersey Assembly ordered the arrest of its governor, William Franklin. Benjamin Franklin remained silent when Congress ordered his son sent to confinement in Litchfield, Connecticut, where he would be held for two years. He ignored all pleas from William's ailing wife, who ended up dying destitute in New York two years later. This was Franklin at his coldest. While he maintained good relations with friends in England, such as Strahan, who worked loyally for his enemy the king, Franklin could not forgive his son for putting his career ahead of his duty to his father. So he turned away. He no longer had a son.

THREE DAYS AFTER LEE PROPOSED HIS RESOLUTION, Congress chose Franklin, John Adams, and Thomas Jefferson to draft a declaration that would explain to the world what American independence was all about. Roger Sherman of Connecticut and Robert R. Livingston of New York also were on the committee but apparently were too busy to offer much help.[2]

It is safe to say that the Declaration of Independence is a far greater document than its creators dreamed it would be. It is the American testament of faith and a message to all people of the world. People refer to it—especially to the part about "all men being created equal" and the promise of "life, liberty, and the pursuit of happiness"—with greater reliance than they place on the far more authoritative Bill of Rights. Originally, however, the Declaration had two purposes. First, it was a legal argument made for foreign readers. It indicted the king, specifically, for crimes and injustices so cruel that resistance and revolution were justified by the very rules that Englishmen applied to themselves. Second, the document was part of the national discussion as Americans chose just how they would, in Thomas Paine's words, "begin the world over again."

With that objective set by Congress, Jefferson, Adams, and Franklin met the next day to determine the outlines of the document. By common retelling, Jefferson was chosen to write the draft.* He did not have much time. The debate on Lee's resolution was to begin July 1, and the Declaration was to be the centerpiece of that argument.

He did have plenty of material to work with, however. By that time there were no fewer than ninety other "declarations of independence" from New England village meetings, colonial assemblies, militia units, and even a grand jury in South Carolina.³ The most important of these was Jefferson's own draft of the preamble to Virginia's new state constitution—itself a restating of the historic English Declaration of Rights. A second important source was George Mason's Declaration of Rights, which he had drafted for that same Virginia constitutional convention.⁴ Dumas Malone, the Jefferson biographer, rightly notes his "rare gift of adaptation."

John Adams in his later recollections said that he and Franklin were given a first draft within two days. He also recalls the pressure on them: "We were all in haste. Congress was impatient." Haste was necessary for sure. Word had reached them from General Washington that the Howe brothers with their armada and enlarged army were headed to New York in an attempt to split the northern region from the rest of the rebellion.

---

* Adams, late in life, wrongly recalled that he had been asked but had deferred to Jefferson for political reasons.

A whole branch of scholarship has grown up over whether Jefferson can rightly claim on his tombstone to be the "Author of the Declaration of Independence." But it would seem to be valid enough. The extant drafts show some changes by his two colleagues. Franklin made several alterations, including substituting for "We hold these truths to be sacred and undeniable" the more direct "to be self-evident," and sharpening charges of the king's "arbitrary power" to "absolute despotism." But the real changes to Jefferson's creation came after June 17, when the document was circulated to Congress.

One can imagine Jefferson's hurt and dismay as delegate after delegate rose to pick his creation apart phrase by phrase. Yet historian Pauline Maier, who specializes in the Declaration, argues that Congress made his document leaner, more specific, and sharper.[5] Still, for all the cutting and pasting, fully nineteen of the twenty-one accusations Jefferson had made against the king stood. Of the two excised, one accused King George of forcing African slaves on the colonies (which was false), and the other of using agents to incite slaves to rebel against their masters (which was true).

Of all the careless myths about the Declaration, the most pernicious is that the delegates were oblivious to the injustice of asserting that all men were created equal while many remained in bondage to others. On the contrary, slavery was very much on the minds of the Congress, and a demonstrable majority of delegates opposed the institution. In fact, a key part of the revolutionary fervor in America drew with it a commitment against the enslavement of Africans anywhere in the new nation. Both Rhode Island and Connecticut had been quick to enact bans on the slave trade in 1776, while earlier, Virginia's Fairfax Resolves, signed by Washington and others, had called for ending the importation of slaves there. At that same time, a Franklin friend, physician Benjamin Rush, founded the first antislavery society in Philadelphia. Franklin himself had evolved into a committed abolitionist as early as 1772 through his experiences with the schools of Dr. Bray.

The Declaration, in fact, started the real American debate on slavery. Of course, in the most literal sense it evaded the slavery question, since references to that hateful practice were dropped from the final draft. Jefferson's slavery charge was removed and the complaint about insurrections was fudged to include the "domestic" threats from Indians and Loyalists as well. Yet those changes resulted because of debate within the Congress, specifically because of the objections from the South Carolina and Georgia delegations. The Congress was in haste, and there would be time enough to take the issue up again when a more permanent government could be organized.

Still, the changes disappointed Jefferson and Franklin. The older man consoled the unhappy Virginian with a story about a hatmaker named John Thompson who drew up plans for a shop sign with a large hat pictured and the legend "John Thompson, Hatter, makes and sells hats for ready money." By the time his friends were done with their changes, all that was left on the sign was his name and the picture of the hat. Jefferson took the point: Shorter is sometimes better.

THE REAL TEST OF THE DECLARATION HAD BEGUN on July 1 with the start of debate on Lee's resolution for independence. There in that stuffy room, as a summer thunderstorm pounded the windows, John Dickinson, of Franklin's own Pennsylvania, led the opposition side in the debate. John Adams, in one of his great moments, rose for the pro-independence side to deliver a two-hour speech (part of which he had to repeat for late-arriving delegates) that was considered a turning point in the argument. Still, four states hung back. In a preliminary tally, South Carolina was a "no" vote; New York's delegates abstained, for they had not yet received their instructions; Delaware's delegation was split one-to-one, with the third member absent; and Pennsylvania was still divided, with Dickinson and three others present against, and Franklin and Morton for, independence. There must be unanimity among all thirteen colonies if they were to hold themselves out to the world as thirteen united states. Wisely, Congress recessed for the night without taking a vote.

Several things happened during the evening of July 1 to turn events around. South Carolina's delegation caucused and changed its mind. Caesar Rodney arrived dramatically by horseback to tip Delaware into the "yes" column. And somewhere in Philadelphia that night, Franklin used all his powers of persuasion on his fellow Pennsylvanians. James Wilson came over to his side, and, in what had to be a supreme act of sacrifice, Dickinson and Robert Morris agreed to abstain. So Pennsylvania would vote "yes." Twelve states would ratify on July 2, and New York was almost certain to follow suit in a week or so.

Thus, on July 2, Congress completed the heavy business of voting for independence. Two days later, on the date we celebrate as Independence Day, the delegates voted once again, with the same result: twelve states for the Declaration, with one state, New York, abstaining.

No contemporary record shows that at the signing of the Declaration, John Hancock said, "We must be unanimous; there must be no pulling different ways; we must all hang together." Or that Franklin ever replied, "Yes, we must all hang together, or most assuredly we shall all hang separately." It may well be that John Hancock was the only person to affix his signature to the working copy on July 4. Indeed, the actual signing of the Declaration of Independence took place in August, after parchment copies had been printed, and it included some delegates who had not been present on the Fourth of July.

Voting for independence was a momentous decision, but Congress had to press on with other, more important business. The delegates knew that parchment alone would not secure their victory: news arrived on July 4 that the Howes had landed their troops on Staten Island and were threatening the New Jersey coast. After the vote on independence, Franklin, too, pressed on with other business. Indeed, on July 4 he was busy on another committee with Adams and Jefferson, to design the official seal for the United States. They turned out such a fussily ornate product that Congress kept only the motto *E Pluribus Unum* (Out of Many, One) and the Eye of Providence, attributed to Freemasonry. Both still grace our dollar bill.

Pennsylvania duties also demanded his time. In mid-July, Pennsylvania opened its constitutional convention, since the Declaration of Independence had severed ties between Britain and the colonies—and had therefore (and at long last) ended the Penns' charter. The convention elected Franklin president almost immediately, and from that position he directed the writing of the new constitution. Completed over the course of that summer, the document bore his hallmarks—a one-chamber legislature, a three-man executive, and annual elections. Just as the Massachusetts constitution bore the best imprint of its author, John Adams, so did Pennsylvania's show Franklin at his most radical. He was committed to the idea that the broadest number of people should have a direct voice in the affairs of their government. Battling both the Penns and the Quaker elite had left him with a deep resentment of people who sought to rule others. One little-noted provision in his first draft was a state limitation on the amount of wealth a citizen could accumulate—but he quietly put it aside when the opposition threatened to hold up approval of the whole. This was in keeping with his legislative style—to fight for what he believed in but never to block a law's adoption just to get his way.

THE TEXT OF THE DECLARATION OF INDEPENDENCE made its way to the public quickly enough, and it produced the desired effect. The document baffled London. That the Americans were sullen and discontented was well known, but the depth of feeling conveyed in this public statement of grievances was news to many. Lord North was astute enough to know that it was one thing to bring recalcitrant subjects back into the realm but something entirely different to conquer a people that considered themselves a sovereign nation. While King George remained determined, North feared that it would be a long war that he might not be able to win. He still had his majority in the Commons, but it was restive. So was much of Britain.

The Declaration was serving its first purpose: it became a direct appeal to the great powers of Europe to enter into full diplomatic and trade relations with a legally sovereign nation. So for the rest of the summer, Franklin was occupied with Jefferson and Adams, plus Dickinson, Morris, Wilson, and Richard Lee, in laboring over what was to be known as the "Model Treaty." This was to be a template for later treaties of alliance and trade with France and other nations. For all the conviction that the new nation needed the support of powerful nations abroad, the Americans instinctively feared that they would end up swapping one master for another. The Model Treaty stressed that America sought "amity and commerce" with other nations. Gunpowder and shot were needed, not troops that would be hard to expel after victory was assured. The Model Treaty was not an application for submission.

All the while, Franklin kept one eye cocked at Britain. Just two weeks after the Continental Congress declared independence, Admiral Lord Richard Howe sent Franklin a cordial personal letter. First, he informed his American friend that Lord North had publicly commissioned both Howes to offer full pardons to all rebels who gave up (though he did not explain that North had secretly excluded the Adamses, Richard Henry Lee, and Franklin himself from the possibility of pardon). Then he asked whether there was some way to avoid the dreadful costs of war. Howe did not need to remind Franklin that his brother Sir William's army—bolstered by the first Hessian levies—now outnumbered Washington's two-to-one, or that Lord Richard's massive war fleet was waiting to attack.* Let us stop now at the brink and reconsider, he urged. Once he gave the order to advance, it would be too late, and that would be too sad indeed.

Franklin showed the letter to Congress, then in response offered this deliberately harsh rebuke:

> Directing pardons to be offered to the colonies who are the very parties injured, expresses indeed that opinion of our ignorance, baseness, and insensibility which your uninformed and proud nation has long been pleased to entertain of us; but it can have no other effect than that of increasing our resentments. It is impossible we should think of submission to a government that has with the most wanton barbarity and cruelty burnt our defenceless towns in the midst of winter, excited the savages to massacre our peaceful farmers and our slaves to murder their masters, and is even now bringing foreign mercenaries to deluge our settlements with blood.[6]

Using more violent expressions than he had allowed Jefferson to put into the Declaration, Franklin made a number of telling points. It was now too late for peace, he said, for even if the Americans were willing to forgive all the harshness meted out to them, the British people were unlikely to make amends with the Americans. If by peace Lord Howe meant a peace between two equal states,

---

* With thirty battleships and two thousand cannon, plus five hundred transports and store ships, it was the largest British fleet ever assembled up to that time.

then something might be worked out—but they both knew that the king would never assent to that, and that Howe had no power to conclude such a peace. Franklin blamed Britain's "fondness for conquest as a warlike nation, her lust of dominion as an ambitious one, and her wish for a gainful monopoly as a commercial one." He predicted that the war to come would prove as pernicious to Britain as the Crusades had been to all of Europe centuries earlier. Then, at the end, he added a personal justification for his harsh response:

> Long did I endeavour with unfeigned and unwearied zeal to preserve from breaking that fine and noble china vase the British Empire; for I knew that, once being broken, the separate parts could not retain even their shares of the strength and value that existed in the whole, and that a perfect reunion of those parts could scarce be hoped for. Your lordship may possibly remember the tears of joy that wet my cheek, when, at your good sister's in London, you once gave me expectations that a reconciliation might soon take place. I had the misfortune to find those expectations disappointed and to be treated as the cause of the mischief I was labouring to prevent. My consolation under that groundless and malevolent treatment was that I retained the friendship of many wise and good men in that country, and among the rest some share in the regard of Lord Howe.[7]

Despite the strong rhetoric, the Americans' situation looked bleak for the present. The Howe forces overwhelmed Washington's, and it was only by luck that the Virginian was able to bring his troops across the river from Long Island to Manhattan. He had little hope of hanging on.

Instead of following up their advantage, the Howe brothers halted their drive, and Lord Richard sent Franklin yet another plea for parlay. After some diplomatic maneuvering, on September 6 Franklin found himself on another long journey, bound for Staten Island and accompanied by John Adams and Edward Rutledge of South Carolina. It was a tough trip in the heat. The roads were clogged with militia units marching to reinforce Washington. At a crowded inn in New Brunswick, New Jersey, Franklin and Adams had to share a bed. Adams, something of a hypochondriac, would later recall that Franklin urged him to leave the window open to the night coldness and then lectured him on the benefits of fresh air. The Massachusetts leader found the lecture so scintillating that he fell asleep.

Lord Howe and his secretary, Henry Strachey, were all cordiality when the American representatives arrived at his headquarters on Staten Island. But it was clear from the start that the admiral had no direct authority from the king to begin peace talks. Instead, it was out of a remnant of affection for the colonies that he went fishing one last time for some sign that the Americans would relent. In turn, each of the three Americans told him they, and the new nation, would not. After the delegates were rowed back to New Jersey, the Howes renewed their offensive against Washington and drove him out of New York to Harlem Heights and then to White Plains. The hard years of the Revolution lay ahead.

Wʜᴇɴ ʜᴇ ʀᴇᴛᴜʀɴᴇᴅ ᴛᴏ Pʜɪʟᴀᴅᴇʟᴘʜɪᴀ, Franklin found a letter waiting for him from his French scientist friend Jacques Barbeu-Dubourg. The letter assured him (wrongly) that the ministers to the French king were ready to make their favor public. Franklin was dubious and raised an argument within Congress "that a virgin state should preserve the virgin character and not go about suitoring for alliances, but wait with decent dignity for the application of others." He preferred to risk being hanged by going back to England to launch a political peace offensive on King George's home ground. He later conceded that that "might not have been such a good idea." Congress instead named him and Jefferson to join Silas Deane as commissioners to the court of Louis XVI. After Jefferson demurred because of his wife's health, Congress summoned Arthur Lee from London to complete the trio.

Once again Franklin was hurled into battle for his country. This time, to the normal risks of a transatlantic voyage was added the threat of capture by British warships, which would mean certain execution. If he made it across the great ocean, he would be in a foreign land and would have to convince a former enemy of America to take its side. It would be exhausting work with an uncertain outcome. Yet Franklin never hesitated. This was the kind of work for which he had fitted himself. Gone would be the boring sessions in Congress, the petty squabbles that erupted among incompetents. seeking army commissions, the corrupt merchants scheming for profitable contracts. This would be a cold, hard game of wits and determination with men equally matched.

As he was packing, Thomas Story, a special messenger Franklin had hired to communicate with his many contacts in Europe, returned with a bagful of confidential and encouraging letters. In one, the French foreign minister, Vergennes, had agreed to ship £200,000 worth of arms and ammunition from the royal arsenal to a West Indies port. This was the first real proof that the French were willing to help the Americans.

So Franklin hurried to settle his affairs, donate money to the cause, and make a secret exit. He recruited Temple Franklin to act as his secretary. His other grandson, Benjamin Franklin Bache (Benjy), now seven, would come too and be put in school. For security, most of Congress was kept unaware of his schedule, and he quietly slipped aboard the sloop *Reprisal*, which was loaded with indigo to help defray the costs of the mission. On October 26, the ship slipped down through the sunken protective barriers of the Delaware River and into open water.

Once at sea, Franklin began to revive. On this, his seventh crossing of the Atlantic, he dipped his thermometer over the side to map yet another portion of the Gulf Stream. He netted seaweed to check the state of the little crabs nestled there. He paid close attention to the transit of the sun and the strength of the wind. And all the while he was thinking of the work that awaited him in France. Washington was holding the British at bay until help could come. Clearly, the Revolution was at stake.

In an age of elaborate wigs and suits, Franklin adopted a modest dress: simple fur hat, spectacles (at a time when no one wore glasses in public), plain coat. The French saw (and celebrated) him as the true American, the modest Quaker, and Franklin reveled in the image.

Chapter 17

The Diplomacy of War

In a hard pounding voyage, the sloop *Reprisal* flew across the Atlantic in four weeks. Just off the French coast, Captain Lambert Wickes spotted two small British merchantmen. Despite the Secret Committee's strict injunction to the captain not to privateer, Franklin, seeing the opportunity, gave Wickes permission to seize the ships. The action was brisk.

The three Franklins landed on December 3, 1776, and traveled by coach to that capital of French merchant-Masons, Nantes. Still frail from the illnesses that had struck him the previous summer, Franklin found his stamina was not what it had been, and the trip through the rural countryside was worse than anything he had endured on American roads. He had hoped for a secret arrival in Nantes and the chance for quiet recuperation, but it was not to be:

joyous private banquets and public adulation awaited him. It took him until December 20 to arrive at Versailles, a village on the outskirts of Paris, where Silas Deane met him.

It was clear at first glance that Deane was worn to a frazzle by his heavy burden of contracting and political lobbying. Deane had good intentions but was out of his depth among the sophisticated traders and diplomats whose language he did not understand. He had been a schoolmaster in Connecticut and then, thanks to family connections, a middling merchant and indifferent member of the First Congress. He deserved a better fate than befell him later, but he aspired to something he could never be—Franklin's equal in the commission they shared.

For his part, Franklin felt no need to confide in this jolly, indiscreet climber. He knew that, like many of his fellow countrymen, Deane saw his mission as an opportunity to serve both his nation and his own pocketbook. Franklin saw nothing wrong with that, for he still believed that self-interest drove a man's best efforts. He also grasped as few others did that America's ultimate victory depended as much on its economic strength as on the zeal of its citizens.

Above all, a proper resentment of British injustices and a genuine faith in liberty drove the Revolution, not the cupidity of the Founding Fathers. Still, there were material concerns. In little more than a century, America had become a wealthy place, and its citizens saw their material rewards being siphoned off by Britons who had not toiled in their farms, mills, and craft shops. Farmers had grown well-to-do, planters wealthy, and city merchants wealthier still. The Revolution would free this rather formidable economic engine from the British throttle; American products could be sold to a wider world market for what they were worth. While the Continental Army suffered horrendously at the beginning, most patriots outside the war zone found that their economic prospects improved, and their appetites for advancement matched their zeal.

The concept of conflict of interest was virtually unknown in the eighteenth century, and Franklin could be as ambitious as anyone where the marketplace and the political arena intersected. It was his boast that he never sought a political office, never turned one down when it was offered, and never resigned one once he held it. Nevertheless, his relatives were freely given post office appointments that tied into the printing empire he had created. He also saw no conflict in the deals arranged by fellow members of Congress. For instance, partners Robert Morris* and Thomas Willing, the richest of Philadelphia's merchant-trader-financiers, controlled a fleet of twenty-six armed merchant ships that doubled as privateers. The Willing & Morris firm and others that had Founding Fathers as partners (often silent partners) planned to supply Washington's army while transporting their own cargoes in the same ships—costs, insurance, and commissions to be billed to Congress, of course. With thirteen separate state militias plus the Continental Army and Navy to supply, the profit potential was staggering. Names like Hancock, Cushing, Alsop, and Wharton appear both on the Revolution's founding documents and on its bills of lading.

By the same token, Franklin knew that the French merchant counterparts would drive the hardest bargain they could. He, far better than Deane, understood that the same was true of the advisers to King Louis XVI. Deane wanted to demand most favored status partly out of pride, partly out of financial ambition. Franklin disdained that concern, and it would bring criticism on his head later.

---

* Morris would be called the "financier of the Revolution" and be both lauded and damned for it. After he convinced the Secret Committee to appoint his half brother, Thomas Morris, a drunk on the loose in Europe, as the official broker for the exchange of American goods for French guns at the port of Nantes, Thomas promptly fell into the hands of a group of merchants who kept him pliant with alcohol.

FRANKLIN KEPT HIS EYE FIXED ON A NUMBER of objectives that were essential to winning the armed conflict in America and securing the colonies' true independence. His battles were not just with enemies but also with fellow Americans who had vastly different views of the Revolution and their place in it. As had happened often before, Franklin had one set of orders from the Secret Committee and another set of goals of his own. Not only would he be a treaty commissioner and aid seeker, but he also would organize covert operations, guerrilla raids, disinformation campaigns, and propaganda warfare. Moreover, he appointed himself (Congress would have expressly forbade it) America's unofficial ambassador to Britain.

This last was perhaps the most important challenge. In nearly every great war, the combatants use interlocutors to exchange messages that cannot be delivered in the open. In modern intelligence parlance this is called "back-channel communication," but it goes back as far as the popes who mediated between kings in the Middle Ages, and farther in fact. Franklin was determined to keep up communication with his friends in Parliament's opposition party—Pitt, Shelburne, Shipley, Burke, and others. But ultimately he wanted to speak clearly to King George III, to convince him that he could never subdue his rebellious subjects and that it would be to his benefit to let America go free.

Back in Congress, certain factions would have been horrified to learn what he really was doing. These anti-Franklinists sought their own vision of America. They were patriots true enough, these New Englanders and Virginians. But they saw themselves at the hub of a wheel from which all other Americans radiated outward like spokes. They had an instinctive disdain for men of the middle colonies like John Jay of New York and merchants like Morris. Franklin was a natural target. He was too reticent, kept too much to himself to suit the volatile Lee-Adams group. He also was careless of things that mattered to them—appearances of rectitude, reverence for the written law, faith in the superiority of things American. Franklin never was a bookkeeper, as his records from his missions to London proved. He had developed tastes that matched his wealth but not, of course, his humble background. Franklin was needed for the moment, but should be replaced as soon as possible by a candidate from their own ranks. One of these candidates was already nearby—in fact, he would soon be joining Franklin in Paris. His name was Arthur Lee.

Lee and his older brother, William "Alderman" Lee, had remained in London after Franklin had gone back to Philadelphia. Arthur assumed the role that he had hungered for: Massachusetts agent. William dabbled in the colony's trade. Once the radical John Wilkes became lord mayor of London in 1774, the brothers happily joined in the routs and dissipation that were a scandal even to that jaded city. It was at one of the Wilkes circle's fracases that Arthur Lee met one of the most colorful characters of Revolutionary history—Pierre Augustin Caron de Beaumarchais.

This graceful, ingratiating Frenchman had accomplished a great deal in just forty-four years. Starting out in life as Caron, he was such a skilled watchmaker and musician that he attracted the favor of King Louis XV and found his way into the inner circle as a tutor to the royal family. The old king was forever falling in the thrall of one mistress or another, and Beaumarchais was born for coordinating such intrigues. Soon he was conducting more important diplomatic missions for his monarch. When Louis XVI succeeded his grandfather in 1774, he too found this amusing and multi-talented courtier useful.*

When Beaumarchais met Lee in the autumn of 1774, he was interested in Lee's claims to be directing the American resistance

---

* Beaumarchais (1732–1799) was the author of such comedies as *The Barber of Seville* and, later, *The Marriage of Figaro*.

in London. The Frenchman frequently visited London, and their friendship ripened. Both men knew that before Franklin had left in 1775, he had reached out to arms makers, dealers, brokers—anyone from Britain to Portugal who could supply aid to the cause. Lee had been on some of these missions as well, and Beaumarchais dangled a chance for Lee to enlarge Franklin's outreach and to succeed him as quartermaster of the Revolution.

King Louis XVI had ordered a massive modernization of the French army and navy, which meant that French arsenals were jammed with out-of-date cannons, rusting muskets, and disintegrating gunpowder. Beaumarchais boasted to Lee that with his contacts at court, he could secure those arms at bargain prices as long as the American could organize shiploads of tobacco (a premium product in European markets). Therefore, the French government would be repaid for things they were going to dispose of anyway, the Americans would get much needed weapons, and the two men would pocket huge profits.

Lee was dazzled, and one can only imagine his joy when in late 1776 he was named an American commissioner, equal in all respects to the man in whose shadow he had labored all those years. The prospect was not enough though, not for Arthur Lee. He flooded his brothers back in Philadelphia with complaints: Washington's retreats were harming efforts to win aid from France; this drunkard Thomas Morris must be replaced at Nantes (William Lee would be ideal for the position); Silas Deane was a cipher and a fool; Franklin, when he arrived, would be an embarrassment. Some of his letters actually got to Philadelphia, where the coalition of Lees and Adamses circulated them freely. Other letters ended up in British intelligence files.

Arthur Lee argued that Washington should be replaced with someone "of the first rank and abilities." He urged his brothers to oust Franklin and John Jay from the Secret Committee of

Correspondence, for they were "men whom I can not trust. If I am to commit myself to an unreserved correspondence, they must be left out, and the Ls or As put in their places."[1] Some of these letters crossed the desk of General Washington, who noted them without comment and passed them on to Richard Lee.

FRANKLIN KNEW NONE OF THIS AT THE MOMENT. After he met up with Silas Deane, the two reviewed events on both sides of the Atlantic. Deane's news was better than Franklin's. He had supplanted Franklin's scientific comrade Jacques Barbeu-Dubourg in the minds of the French ministers as the chief supply agent for America. Despite the fact that the scientist had generously advanced thousands of livres* in the American cause, Barbeu-Dubourg was an incurable gossip at a time when circumspection was essential to King Louis. More to the point, Deane had secured for the Americans tons of saltpeter and hundreds of thousands of pounds of top-grade gunpowder at considerably below market rates. This was life-giving support for Washington; indeed, by some estimates, 90 percent of all the gunpowder used by the Americans in the war came from France.[2]

Yet Deane had overdone it. He had signed contracts for thirty thousand rifles, two hundred cannon, thirty mortars, thousands of tents, and uniforms for ten thousand more men than Washington had on his rosters. Over the past year he had also concentrated his contracts with Beaumarchais, though Lee did not realize until well into the summer of 1776 that he had been euchred out of position.

In May 1775, the French foreign minister, Vergennes, had convinced King Louis XVI to offer some clandestine support to the

---

* A livre was the French equivalent of the pound but was worth, depending on the time, three-fourths to a half in purchasing power.

Americans. The king had been ambivalent about the whole enterprise, for there was no question of reclaiming Canada, and he certainly did not want an outright war with Britain. But France possessed huge territories in the middle of the American continent and, more important, fabulously wealthy sugar colonies in the West Indies, which Louis knew were absolutely vital to a nation that was still economically weak in the wake of the Seven Years War. And anything that weakened Britain in that hemisphere helped France and secured what it held.

So French merchant ships had begun to carry arms to Caribbean ports, and Nantes merchants had sent other goods on speculation. In December 1775, Vergennes opened serious talks with Beaumarchais and at the same time sent the agent Bonvouloir to Philadelphia to test the mood of Congress. Bonvouloir sent back glowing reports of American readiness to fight, and Beaumarchais won the foreign minister to his grand scheme.

The plan was to create a dummy company financed in equal one-million-livre shares by King Louis, his uncle King Charles III of Spain, and the French merchant community. This company would buy the surplus arms from the royal armories, ship them to the Dutch West Indies port of St. Eustatius and other islands, and let the Americans take delivery in exchange for vastly more valuable American tobacco, rice, and other goods. Beaumarchais promised his king nine million livres' return for his investment of one million.

Even before Deane's arrival, the brokerage firm of Roderigue Hortalez & Cie (Hortalez & Co.) was up and running with Beaumarchais as head. But Vergennes had been explicit. The firm was strictly private, and Beaumarchais and his partners were to bear any losses. On June 10, 1776, Hortalez bankers took possession of one million livres in gold from the French treasury. On August 11, the Spanish gold arrived, and French exporters fell over themselves to make up the remainder.

The arrival of Deane had solidified the organization in French minds. He bore a commission and could sign for shipments to be paid for by Congress. He had brought some cash for other purchases and appeared ready to pledge the credit of Congress for still more.

In London, Lee was apoplectic when he learned of the arrangement. When Franklin notified him that he should join the commissioners in Paris, he was in a poisonous frame of mind.

FRANKLIN REFUSED TO INVOLVE HIMSELF in Lee's complaints against Deane or to assign the Virginian any role worthy of his ambition. The commissioners had a specific, two-part agenda, Franklin reminded them. First, they were to secure a treaty of "amity and commerce" that would constitute French recognition of American sovereign status. That was the harder part of the two stated tasks. Second, the Americans were to get war materiel from the French. In particular, the fledgling American navy needed warships. Of course, Deane had his commission to get arms and he was doing just that. That was all Franklin wanted to know. So the trio settled in at the spacious Hôtel d'Hambourg in the heart of the old Latin Quarter. On Christmas Day, 1776, they went to a service at the nearby Church of St. Germain.

It was hard to make much Christmas cheer for the two Franklin boys. Word had just arrived of Washington's autumn defeats on Manhattan and in Westchester. Things had looked so bad for the Americans that when they had escaped across the Delaware into dire winter quarters, British commander William Howe had halted his pursuit and returned to his mistress in New York, leaving his troops bivouacked in New Jersey. By spring, he had reasoned, there might not even be a Continental Army. Yet on that Christmas Day, Washington led 2,500 of his ragged soldiers back across the river and in a surprise attack at Trenton captured nearly one thousand Hessians.

It would be weeks before Franklin and the rest of Paris learned the good news, but still he was not dismayed. Even as Paris buzzed about Washington's retreat, he sent his first message to the French foreign minister:

> Sir: We beg leave to acquaint your Excellency that we are appointed and fully empowered by the Congress of the United States to propose and negotiate a treaty of amity and commerce between France and the United States. The just and generous treatment their trading ships have received by a free admission into the ports of this kingdom, and other considerations of respect, has induced the Congress to make this offer first to France. We request an audience of your Excellency, where we may have an opportunity of presenting our credentials, and we flatter ourselves that the proposals we are authorized to make are such as will not be found unacceptable.[3]

Over the Christmas holiday, Franklin made sure his two colleagues understood the objectives laid out in the Model Treaty draft he had brought from Congress. This was a single-shot, narrowly focused diplomatic offensive. The commissioners were not, as Lee suggested, to trek about Europe seeking other aid quite yet. The phrase in the introductory letter about their making "this offer first to France" was deliberate and addressed one of Vergennes's fears—that America might make a quick peace with Britain and leave France in jeopardy.

The treaty would be quite specific, Franklin stressed. France's involvement in the war must be limited to trade and aid—the French were to provide no troops and would afterward have no role in the new nation's affairs. If war broke out between Britain and France (and presumably Spain), Congress would not make peace until London came to terms with all allies. America would forswear any ambitions in the West Indies; in exchange, France would not think of reclaiming Canada. Other details, such as fishing in Newfoundland and travel down the Mississippi, were to be negotiated.

The Americans did not have long to wait. On the Saturday after Christmas, December 28, Vergennes summoned them to his chambers for their first interview. The minister was nearing sixty and had done his diplomatic apprenticeship in the confusing corridors of power in Constantinople, Lisbon, and Stockholm. He had surpassed more wily competitors to become the king's chief adviser. Yet when Franklin entered the count's chambers slightly ahead of Lee and Deane, Vergennes was somewhat unprepared.

During his stay in Nantes and his brief outings in the streets of Paris, Franklin had noticed how the French people had reacted to his appearance. He had dressed for comfort on the voyage and left the elaborate wigs and court suits stored in the many trunks he had brought over. Instead, he had worn a thick fur cap that came down to his eyebrows and a plain dark brown coat that had an attachable fur collar. Because his eyesight was failing, he wore glasses (no one at that time wore glasses in public), and he leaned for support on a simple crabtree stick. The effect was tremendous.

The French love to personify great concepts. Their kings could rightly say that they were the French nation, far more so than George III could say that he was England. Voltaire was the French Enlightenment. And here was Franklin, the true American, the modest Quaker (how he laughed at that). See his modest dress, his intelligent gaze, his attractive smile. Franklin knew a good thing and fell in with the fiction. The dress sword, wigs, and fancy coats stayed in the trunks.

Thus Vergennes's first view of Franklin was of a stocky, full-figured man of some age, dressed in a dark suit (but with very white linen), with his own hair hanging back from his receding hairline until it touched his collar. Deane and Lee, who had worn the proper attire of wigs and lace, faded into the background.

Vergennes greeted them all cordially, but he specifically welcomed Franklin as a friend of France, a world-renowned savant, and a valued guest. It was a sad fact that the American delegation could not be officially recognized, he told the commissioners, but the group would receive all the police protection that a legitimate embassy would get. He introduced his first secretary, Conrad Alexandre Gérard, who spoke perfect English. Whenever the esteemed Dr. Franklin had anything to communicate, he was to go directly to Gérard.

The minister took the proffered Model Treaty without comment. It had to be that way, Franklin understood. The French could do nothing that might provoke war with Britain until the Americans had shown themselves capable of winning their contest of arms. And the latest news from America did not inspire confidence. General Washington's retreat from Long Island was not good news, Franklin admitted, but he emphasized that his government was confident of success. The Americans wanted France's aid only to ensure what was inevitable and to lessen the terrible cost of war by hastening its end. Vergennes judged his man acutely. After this first session, he wrote to his ambassador to the Spanish court in Madrid:

> I don't know whether Mr. Franklin told me everything, but what he told me is not very interesting with regard to the situation of his country. The ostensible object of his mission, the only one which he has revealed to me, is a treaty of commerce which he desires to conclude with us; he even left me an outline.... Its modesty causes surprise, because they do not demand anything which they do not already enjoy, at least

from our side. If it is modesty or fear to be a burden to those powers on whose interest they hope to be able to rely, then these sentiments are very laudable; but, could it not be possible that this reserve is the result of a more political consideration? The Americans have felt too much the effects of the jealousy of commerce that animated the English, as not to foresee the consequences which it can and must cause. [I am] Firmly convinced that England would not remain tranquil if the two crowns [France and Spain] would take over the important commerce which England has carried on with her colonies up to now, they [the Americans] perhaps may consider this motive sufficiently strong to effect a rupture between the three powers. This rupture, by changing the stakes of the war, would naturally lead the English to recognize the independence of the colonies which they still withhold, without the colonies finding themselves burdened with an eventual defensive alliance [with France and Spain].[4]

Vergennes was right on the mark. The French and Spanish were being asked to give up any future plans to enlarge their holdings in North America, and to risk likely war with an enraged Britain. In return, the Americans offered nothing more than access to their trade. Yet the Americans knew that "the two crowns" could not stand to see them reunited with Britain—and they realized that the French and Spanish knew it as well.

Vergennes recognized another great truth: "The longer a peace lasts, the less it appears that it will last; peace has now existed for twelve years, and this implies a greater argument against its further stability."[5] This dour assessment meant that France was probably going to war with Britain come what may. And Vergennes knew that Franklin knew that too.

THE MINISTER WASTED NO TIME. On January 3, 1777, he notified Franklin that he was authorizing a secret loan of another two million livres with undefined repayment terms. Franklin was emboldened enough to request eight full-sized warships on January 5, even though France needed every new ship under construction. While he had been circumspect at the first interview, Franklin now laid out in writing his personal agenda, which went considerably beyond what the Secret Committee had authorized:

> Sir: The Congress, the better to defend their coasts, protect their trade, and drive off the enemy, have instructed us to apply to France for eight ships of the line, completely manned, the expense of which they will undertake to pay. As other princes of Europe are lending or hiring their troops to Britain against America, it is apprehended that France may, if she thinks fit, afford our independent States the same kind of aid, without giving England any first cause of complaint. But if England should on that account declare war, we conceive that by the united force of France, Spain, and America, she will lose all her possessions in the West Indies, much of the greatest part of that commerce which has rendered so opulent, and be reduced to that state of weakness and humiliation which she has, by her perfidy, her insolence, and her cruelty, both in the east and in the west, so justly merited.[6]

In just a few days Franklin had done the remarkable—he had surprised Vergennes. The minister could not know that the American had gone far beyond what Congress had authorized, much less that his fellow commissioners had been caught unaware. It was too much, but Franklin had decided to ask for more than he thought he could get at this time and hope that things would change. The jolt to Vergennes was deliberate. Over the holidays, after the British ambassador had lodged a protest at the amount of arms being smuggled to the West Indies, the foreign minister had blocked ships from leaving the coastal harbors. Franklin wanted to break the impasse. Of course, Vergennes would do this time and time again, and when the British relaxed, the French ships would sneak away.

In response to Franklin's request, Vergennes sent Gérard to tell the Americans that the minister could not officially receive such a communication at that time. Franklin immediately sent back an apology for being too brash. It was a grovel but it served its purpose: it placated Vergennes and at the same time showed him that the Americans were willing to go further than he had thought.

Though Franklin's request changed nothing for the moment, the foreign minister would eventually allow the commissioners to buy existing merchant ships and arm them as privateers. In addition, Vergennes would allow American raiders to auction off their prizes in French ports, with proceeds going to the repayment of the loans already granted. He would also hint that there might be future loans.

Considering that he had been in Paris less than a month, Franklin had done well. But it would be a long haul and test all of his resolve and patience. Harder times were yet to come.

Three generations of Franklins: Benjamin Franklin (middle),
son William (bottom), and grandson Temple (top).

Chapter 18

Winning Recognition

$\mathscr{I}$n the two years of 1777 and 1778, Franklin was at his most versatile—juggling tasks, playing the French and British off against each other, and evading the annoyances of his colleagues.

After securing the first loan, he turned his attention to stirring French public opinion for longer-term and ever greater support for the Revolution. It was not hard to do. The announcement that he had landed on the coast had caused such excitement that Vergennes ordered Paris police to suppress vocal support for the American cause in the crowded street cafés. Souvenir makers poured out items bearing Franklin's likeness—with the American wearing the fur hat that had become an instant fashion hit. It was said that every mantel in France had a plaque, mug, or sketch that honored him. The mania so annoyed Louis XVI that he had Franklin's picture put on the bottom of a Sèvres chamber pot and gave it to a mistress who was too enthusiastic about the American Socrates, as he was called.

But Franklin knew that the mob could help him only so much. Political power in France was far more concentrated than in England. In London, his science friends were mostly outside the circle of authority of the ministries or the court, but in France, many leaders of the Enlightenment were of noble birth and played key roles in the king's government. The Parisian salons drew celebrities from the top tier of French life, and if official policy was only occasionally made at these affairs, it was always being discussed and influenced.

So on December 29, the day after his first visit with Vergennes, Franklin accepted an invitation to an after-dinner gathering at the Marquise du Deffand's mansion, Paris's premier salon. Madame du Deffand, once a famous beauty, was now blind and nearing eighty, but she was judged to have the sharpest mind and tongue in town. She was also a devout royalist who openly opposed the American rebellion. Franklin was sure to be chewed up by this old dragon, and her regular guests eagerly awaited the contest. How would the American react to the bad news about Washington's retreat? Would he be arrogant? Defensive? Or, worse, would he try to tease their hostess out of her mood?

The guest list was formidable. France's nobles were arrayed before the American in their most elaborate costumes, while Franklin was dressed simply, in his dark suit, wearing his spectacles, and leaning on his cane. He was pleasant but extremely reticent, for he understood French well but spoke it with an execrable accent and bad grammar. Instead of trying to talk his way into the good graces of the French, he listened. When Madame harangued him, he leaned forward and asked for more understanding. Sometimes he allowed that what was being said might well be true, but he calmly insisted that while no one regretted the break with England more than he, America would prevail. America, he said, would become a better friend to France than Britain could ever be. While it was too much to hope he could have converted the old marquise, his performance was good enough to win him three important friends on the spot. The Duc de Choiseul, who had been the king's prime minister, hoped to climb back into power by backing Franklin. The king's librarian and another intimate of Louis, the former ambassador to London, risked the ire of their hostess to offer their friendship. The more discreet guests waited until after the soiree to flood Franklin with invitations. He had precisely fit their ideal of the true sage of nature, and word of the party rushed about Paris.[1]

The next night, Franklin visited the Marquis de Mirabeau. The marquis was the leader of France's Physiocrat movement, a collection of economists, bankers, and finance officers that was vital to win over if America was going to get the economic support it needed. Mirabeau, an admirer of Franklin, agreed to intercede with the French finance minister, Jacques Necker, who worried that King Louis would bankrupt France. A military buildup was costly enough, but aiding America seemed particularly risky, especially because a war with Britain could be fatal. Franklin again argued that America could *prevent* France from going to war by winning its own war—with French help. There would be time enough for him to press for deeper French involvement in the Revolution.

IN JANUARY 1777, FRANKLIN LOOKED for a more permanent—and more private—base of operations. Moving about Paris was frustrating because crowds formed everywhere he appeared. He also had to conduct business away from the eyes of spies. As they were closing their first conversation, Vergennes had warned the American commissioners to be particularly wary of David Murray, the Viscount

Stormont. Lord Stormont was the British ambassador in Paris as well as station chief for the most effective spy network in the powerful British secret service. Franklin knew that Stormont had spies in every French port and that agents followed him and Silas Deane everywhere.

In February, Franklin accepted an offer to move out of Paris to a huge estate in Passy, on the edge of the Bois de Boulogne. The Hôtel Valentinois was a huge mansion house with other smaller dwellings, all arranged around a classic garden and park. The grounds led down gentle terraces to the banks of the Seine, and shady walks led to the equally lavish estates of titled neighbors. The owner, Jacques-Donatien Le Ray de Chaumont, was a newly rich tax collector and merchant trader who ardently supported the American cause. He also had contracts from Deane to supply huge amounts of cloth to the Continental Army. Chaumont and Deane shared a vision of America as a future empire equal to those of Britain and Russia—and both wanted a share of this dream. So while Deane rushed about looking for supplies, Chaumont advanced credit and opened his home to Franklin. He turned over one wing of his mansion to the doctor, who moved in with his two grandsons and a French translator-secretary. His host refused to accept rent from his distinguished tenant until later, when John Adams, who would also take rooms there when he supplanted Lee as commissioner, insisted that not to pay for the lodging was an impropriety.

Franklin lived a considerably more lavish life at Passy than he ever had before, and he relished every luxury. Nine servants were devoted to his needs. He leased a coach and pair of horses, with driver, and hired a majordomo (a kind of butler and manager). He allowed another ardent admirer to stock his wine cellar with a mix of Bordeaux reds and whites, champagne, and Spanish sherries; he never had fewer than a thousand bottles at hand. According to the accounts that survive, his food bills alone ran close to 1,500 livres a month—this at a time when his annual salary from Congress was 11,000 livres. That stipend, however, quickly became a fiction between Franklin and the bankers who handled the official American affairs; they advanced him much more money.

Franklin's explanation for such extravagance was that a little luxury often spurred a man on to more energetic work. Since his work in Paris was so important, he needed to pamper himself; he was, after all, not getting any younger. And his old vigor had in fact returned. Every Tuesday he journeyed the fourteen miles to Versailles to seek help from Conrad Alexandre Gérard, Vergennes's secretary, to get stores from the armories or secure a pass for a cargo ship. Several times each week he took the hour's ride to Paris, where he would attend sessions of the French General Assembly, meet with one of the many royal societies devoted to medicine, philosophy, science, and the arts, and go to the salons. The one social institution he avoided was the *levée*, because it tired his feet to slowly promenade about the large room and meet other guests.

Passy became the kind of Franklin outpost that the Craven Street house had been in London. He began to write again, this time to explain America and its desires to the French. He found an immediate outlet in a prestigious periodical, *Affaires de l'Angleterre et de l'Amérique*, which was read throughout Europe, even in Britain. In his first four years in France, Franklin had at least one piece in each of the eighty-two issues of that paper. In one article he argued persuasively that because America was soon to be a much wealthier nation, it was a better credit risk for European lenders than the London capital markets. *Affaires* also reprinted his biting satires, including the *King of Prussia* piece and the *Rules* for reducing Britain's empire, as well as his questioning before the House of Commons.

In the late spring of 1777, word of Washington's surprising victory over the Hessians at Trenton sparked a renewed enthusiasm for the American cause. Franklin seized the moment. As a hoax he published a letter purporting to be from a Hessian count to his commander in America. The count wrote that the British were short-changing him on the money due when his troops were killed in battle; he also urged the commander not to waste too much effort on the wounded, for his fee would be greater if they died. *The Sale of the Hessians*, like most of his satires, was all the more biting because it fit the public conception of how brutal the renting of troops really was.

Lord Stormont, the British ambassador, was not amused. He had tried without success to have Franklin barred from France and then from Paris, and finally he had tried to keep Vergennes from receiving him at Versailles. Each time he would threaten to break off relations and return to London. When the American privateers—led by *Reprisal* captain Lambert Wickes—began to haul British merchant ships into French ports as prizes, he demanded their return, but just one or two were handed back. Periodically he was able to delay French cargo vessels from sailing for the West Indies, but they invariably slipped out to sea before his port watchers could get word to him. While British warships in the English Channel could stop vessels flying the American flag, they could not seize French ships unless they were sure there were war goods on board.

Stormont began a publicity campaign of his own. He made much of the string of defeats suffered by the Continentals, claiming after one battle that the Americans had lost four thousand soldiers and their general. At his next appearance at a salon, Franklin was confronted by the claim. His reply was, *"La verité et le stormont sont deux"* (The truth and the stormont are two different things). Parisian wags quickly turned the ambassador's name into the verb *stormonter*, to lie.

VEXING AS THAT MIGHT BE, LORD STORMONT was playing a more important role as part of Britain's sophisticated global intelligence service. Stormont reported to William Eden, the director, who in turn answered directly to the ultimate consumer of intelligence product, King George III. A large portion of the secret service budget came out of the royal purse, and the king sent direct orders to Eden, to Stormont, and even to agents in place. King George was avidly interested in Franklin, perhaps obsessed. It seemed that Franklin had turned up whenever there was a challenge to his authority. He resolutely believed that America could be reclaimed if only the few malcontent plotters could be bribed, thwarted, or somehow gotten rid of. Franklin symbolized all these plotters in the king's mind, so he ordered the American mission in France flooded with spies, regardless of cost.

Eden and Stormont obeyed, first signing on Paul Wentworth, who had been the agent in London for the New Hampshire colony. Wentworth signed on Edward Bancroft, Franklin's old spy in the corridors of Whitehall. Years earlier, Bancroft had stayed with Wentworth at his plantation in Guyana while he, Bancroft, studied vegetable dyes. The two shared a passion for gambling at cards and trading on inside information on the stock market. Both heavily in debt, they signed on for large yearly stipends (£500 for Wentworth and £200 for Bancroft) and the promise of pensions and jobs after the war.

Bancroft's personal links to the American commissioners made him particularly valuable. He had been at Yale with Silas Deane and was a Royal Society fellow in London along with Franklin. It was not hard for him to get taken on as the commission's chief secretary. Once Franklin was formally inducted into the prestigious Masonic Lodge of the Nine Sisters in Paris, he secured membership for his young friend Bancroft.

The net spread from there. Eden recruited a young cleric in London named Paul Vardill, who hoped to win a high professorship at King's College (now Columbia University) once the war was over. In the meantime, he became a fashionable evangelist among the prostitutes of London. At a brothel favored by sea captains, Vardill met Joseph Hynson, a Marylander who boasted of his contacts with Franklin and his distaste for the colonial cause, and who knew William Carmichael, Deane's personal secretary. Since Carmichael ensured that Hynson carried the American commission's official reports back to Congress, the captain could hand over the reports to British agents. (Although Lambert Wickes was Hynson's half brother, he remained loyal to Franklin and became a potent privateer in the North Sea.) In all, a half dozen of these suspect shipmasters moved into Deane's expanded suite at the Hôtel d'Hambourg.[2] Some of their mistresses moved in as well, and Bancroft helped Deane place the odd investment on the London exchange. It was all one big happy family of espionage and double-dealing.

Vergennes repeatedly warned the Americans that their most private conversations were being read in detail in London within seventy-two hours. In one case, Vergennes showed the three Americans a captured British intelligence report that named the ships sailing with American military cargoes from French ports. It was a verbatim copy of a list Bancroft had prepared for Franklin. Yet the commissioners did not dismiss Bancroft; rather, they sent Carmichael home, mainly because Arthur Lee complained so much about him. (Lee's own personal secretary was reporting to Eden as well.) It is a wonder that Bancroft had any time for the commission's affairs, given how busy he was copying its documents and exchanging messages with Lord Stormont at a "dead drop" in the Tuileries Gardens. At prearranged times, he slipped coded messages into an empty wine bottle and hid it in a hollow tree on the promenade. He also sent Eden letters written in invisible ink. On occasion he met directly with both Eden and Stormont (who referred to him as "Dr. Edwards").[3]

Much has been made of Franklin's laxity about security. Lee wrote volumes about it back to Philadelphia. And there remains a tantalizing question of just how much Franklin knew about Bancroft and the others and why he took no action to plug the security leaks. Lee, and later John Adams, believed that Franklin had gone dotty and was criminally careless. At least two books have suggested that Franklin himself was a British agent.[4] The only evidence offered are extant files of Eden's service that show coded references to the American as "72." But those same files show that Eden's agents used numbers to refer to a host of individuals, places, and even concepts. Deane was "51," and Lee was "115." England itself was "64," and "independency" was a frequently mentioned "107."

In fact, it is more plausible that Franklin was spying *on* the British, not for them. Allen Dulles, the legendary World War II spymaster and director of the Central Intelligence Agency, concluded that Franklin had set up a far better spy network inside the British government.[5] And indeed it was Franklin's boast that within just a few days he had received word of a report General Lord Cornwallis had delivered to Lord North. Though there is no documented proof of either assertion, the American did not need paid agents in place in London. He had friends inside the government—the Pownalls and others in the secretariat, Pitt, Shelburne, Burke, and many more in Parliament. The North ministry leaked like a sieve.

Finally, the important thing about intelligence is not how it is obtained but how it is used. What Franklin got from Britain, he used to prod the French to actions they would have preferred to delay. Wentworth and Bancroft did send a flood of information back to Eden, including the dates weapons shipments would leave for America. Yet even with advance notice, the Royal Navy could not capture many of these ships. What was important from

Franklin's standpoint was that all the reports back to North and his ministers repeated the same message—America must have its independence as a precondition to any peace.

Franklin was winning more important aid from the French, and he wanted King George and Lord North to know about it, for Lord Stormont steadfastly refused to believe it was happening. British officials had refused Franklin's attempts at direct communication, as when he had tried to negotiate better treatment of American prisoners of war. But the British believed their spies, or at least Lord North did.

King George III read everything coming from Paris but refused to believe the Americans were that united. The secret service files contain one of Eden's reports on developments in Paris in the spring of 1778. On the back of the wrapper, the king scrawled a note dismissing all this information:

> April 6th—4 P.M.
>
> I have ever doubted whether any trust could be reposed in Hynson. I am now quite settled in my opinion that he as well as every other spy from N. America is encouraged by Deane and Franklin to give intelligence to deceive. G. R.[6]

Others in London spoke openly about how effective Franklin would be in Paris. Lord Rockingham, who had been prime minister when the Stamp Act was repealed, now led the opposition in the House of Lords since Pitt was ill again. He wrote a friend recalling Franklin's public humiliation at the hands of Alexander Wedderburn:

> The horrid scene at the Privy Council is in my memory, though perhaps not in his. It may not excite his conduct. It certainly deters him not. He boldly ventures to cross the Atlantic

in an American little frigate, and risks the dangers of being taken and being once more before an implacable tribunal. The sight of Banquo's ghost could not more offend the eyes of Macbeth than the knowledge of this old man being at Versailles should affect the minds of those who were principals in that horrid scene. Depend upon it, he will plead forcibly.[7]

Rockingham was not alone. A growing number of parliamentary powers were reaching the same conclusion. Despite optimistic forecasts from British commanders in America, Washington kept his ragged army together and just a step ahead of destruction. And this Franklin, once a nuisance in the corridors of Whitehall, was proving to be a real menace in Paris. Could he really lure France into the war on the American side?

IN THOSE CRUCIAL SPRING AND SUMMER MONTHS of 1777, Franklin was distracted by problems he would have preferred to avoid. His first task was to find something for Arthur Lee to do to keep him out of trouble. Congress, worried about counting so heavily on France, had given Franklin a second commission, to try to win support from Spain, so in February, he sent Lee off to Spain to approach King Charles III. Charles was even less inclined than King Louis to help rebels against a fellow monarch, and, further, he feared American ambitions for a continent-sized nation, since so much of that continent belonged to him. Only one prize could lure the king into risking war with Britain—Gibraltar, the huge fortress gate to the Mediterranean that loomed tantalizingly beyond his grasp.

Unfortunately, Lee was not as successful as Franklin might have hoped. He did secure another one million livres from the king, but he insulted Spanish negotiators and ultimately was forbidden to come to Madrid. In May, Lee volunteered to go to Berlin and Vienna to see what he could win. Franklin disagreed with the policy of "militia diplomacy" that Congress had adopted in late 1776, in which commissioners would try to secure aid and recognition throughout Europe; he thought America should appear aloof and let other nations come to it. Nevertheless, Franklin wanted Lee out of Paris, so he readily consented to the trip. Nothing came of that journey either, except that Lee got his bags broken into by the British ambassador in Berlin. Once back in Paris, Lee fumed because he had nothing to do. Left idle, he began to plot, first against Deane, who had stolen his mission, not to mention his hoped-for profits. Later he turned against Franklin, accusing them both of profiteering in the arms deals.

Despite Lee's complaints, Deane's deals were a boon to the American cause. Chaumont and other merchants were sending enormous quantities of goods to the American armed forces by way of the West Indies. The estimates are that the Hortalez firm had more than 140 merchant ships in transit across the Atlantic to various Caribbean ports. From there, smaller American ships took the cargoes and unloaded them in mainland coves from Savannah to Portsmouth, wherever the Royal Navy was absent. The precious stores of shoes, clothing, and weapons fleshed out the skeleton army that had survived the terrible winter encampment at Valley Forge. Also, cannon and other new weapons were going to Horatio Gates's army, which stood in the path of General John Burgoyne's army in Canada.

During this time Franklin was further distracted by the countless job seekers, ambitious officers, and outright con men who laid siege to Passy. Most he ignored, to others he handed a perfunctory and noncommittal form letter. Two, however, made valuable contributions to the American armed forces. The nineteen-year-old Marquis de Lafayette, who wanted to avenge his father's death in the Seven Years War, had used all the influence he could bring to get Franklin to recommend him to Washington, and the young French noble became the general's most devoted aide-de-camp and later a trusted field commander. Even more valuable was Baron Frederick von Steuben, who had been on Frederick the Great's general staff and had considerable experience and skill. The out-of-work Prussian captain approached Franklin, and the American commissioner recommended the baron to Congress, ultimately earning him the rank of lieutenant general. Steuben went into winter quarters with Washington at Valley Forge, and by the time the army went on the march in June 1777, he had drilled them into a formidable fighting force.

As summer wore on, Franklin became the official admiralty court for the auctions involving British ships that American privateers had seized. These auctions were an important source of money to support the mission, but much of the prize money was disappearing into merchants' coffers. Franklin sent his nephew Jonathan Williams to Nantes to oversee the shipments to America, but Jonathan had little confidence and referred all matters back to his uncle for settling.

Arthur Lee nagged about this and everything else. Franklin had to design the uniforms being assembled for the American soldiers. Lee opposed the design of the buttons; he hated blue as the basic color, considering red the only proper color for battle. Some of the equipment (such as leather goods, gun tools, and leggings) that Americans used did not have a French counterpart, so Franklin had to covertly buy samples in Britain to show contractors what he meant. Lee thought that was improper. Meanwhile, he was writing his brother Richard that Franklin was too old and Deane too corrupt to be kept on. He lied that Congress was being billed for goods that Beaumarchais had donated. In short, America needed a single commissioner, and Arthur Lee felt he was the man.

THE DISMAL WAR IN AMERICA WAS REACHING a turning point. In the north, General Burgoyne's large force inched its way into New York as its supplies dwindled. To the south, General William Howe, instead of marching north to meet Burgoyne or continuing his attacks on Washington in New Jersey, chose to move his army by ship to approach Philadelphia from the south. In September, after Washington failed to block the British at the Battle of Brandywine, Congress fled its capital. The government went first to Lancaster and then to York, Pennsylvania, where it stayed until June 1778.

Although the reports from America made the situation look grim for the Continental Army, Vergennes had not flinched. In June 1777, he had gone to his king and told him that clandestine aid and loans would not be enough. The three-power alliance between France, Spain, and America that Franklin had suggested was the only way to check a certain British success. Louis XVI agreed but said his uncle Charles first had to join in. In September, Franklin and his colleagues prepared a petition for Vergennes asking for formal recognition of the United States and a loan of another fourteen million livres. They were embarrassed to learn that someone on the staff (Bancroft) had taken a draft of the proposal to Lord Stormont, who had formally protested it even before Vergennes had received the original. The document was received without reaction. Franklin knew the minister would act only when it suited him and his king. Good news was now desperately needed.

The news got worse, however. In November, news of the defeat at Brandywine and that the British had taken Philadelphia reached France. Although his family was not harmed, Franklin's house had been vandalized. Howe now held Philadelphia and New York, the two principal cities of the middle of the country. If the Continental Army did not cut off Burgoyne's southern advance, New England would be cut off from the rest of the nation and the end would be a matter of time.

On December 4, a young friend of Franklin's rushed to Passy, having just arrived on a chartered packet from Boston. Franklin, Deane, and the others came outside to learn the news. The first question from Franklin was whether it was true that Philadelphia had fallen. Learning it was so, he turned away in distress. Then, however, the messenger cried out that the British had been defeated at Saratoga. Burgoyne had surrendered his forces to Horatio Gates.

Two days later, Vergennes's secretary, Gérard, came to Passy to offer congratulations and ask Franklin to submit a new proposal for an alliance. Franklin redrafted it, and Temple delivered it on December 8. This time Franklin imposed security. He, Deane, and Lee went to a prearranged spot away from Passy on December 12 and switched to another coach, which took them to a house near Versailles where Vergennes and Gérard waited. The minister told them King Louis had agreed to the alliance but would wait as a courtesy for a messenger to bring his uncle's answer back from Madrid. It had been less than a year since Franklin had arrived in France, and yet it seemed the alliance he sought was becoming reality.

But on December 31, word arrived that Spain would not join the alliance. Would Vergennes change his mind? Would the French stall for more favorable conditions? Franklin turned to his back-channel communications with London to stir things up.

Ever since news of the Saratoga defeat had rocked London, Lord North had desperately tried to stop France and America from signing an alliance. Eden was told to offer Franklin anything. Promises could be reneged later. Wentworth had gone to Paris to lobby Deane, but without success. Bancroft, his best connection, was off in London cleaning up on the stock market. Finally, however, after Vergennes had fallen silent, Franklin agreed to see Wentworth at Passy, after demanding that the British spy use all caution in not being spotted—knowing full well that the French would know of the meeting within the hour.

In a memo to Eden, the spy reported, "I went to call on 72 yesterday and found him very busy with his nephew [Temple], who was directed to leave the room, and we remained together for two hours. . . . I concluded with wishing to be honoured with his opinion of the temper of the Congress, the terms and means he would suggest to induce reconciliation."[8]

Franklin gave Wentworth an earful. He recounted a long list of injuries and barbarities that Britain had visited on its once loyal subjects. He angrily denounced the treatment of American prisoners, most of whom were being kept in prison galleys in terrible conditions. Wentworth was nonplussed, and his report back to Eden showed he was bewildered in the extreme. He did not suspect that Franklin had used him not only to continue his message about independence to London but also to move the French along.

Two days later, Gérard called again. King Louis XVI had given his word to conclude an alliance with the United States. Coming so soon after Saratoga, Franklin's diplomatic victory changed the strategic balance of the war for independence. But he knew the conflict still had a long way to go.

Chapter 19

Dismal Days

he first weeks of 1778 brought Franklin enough sweet triumphs to sustain him through the next five years of disappointment and delay. The American commissioners had secured twin treaties—not only the treaty of amity and commerce they had originally sought but also a treaty of friendship that bound France and the United States into a joint alliance.

It took time for the formal documents to be drafted and engrossed on parchment, but finally, on February 6, the three commissioners arrived at Vergennes's foreign ministry office in Paris to affix their signatures to America's formal welcome into the community of nations. As was his custom, Franklin dressed carefully for the occasion. Both Lee and Deane remarked that their colleague had squeezed himself into an old suit of dark mottled pattern that ɔemed out of fashion. Deane asked him why he had selected that particular suit. Franklin replied, "To give it a little revenge. I wore this coat on the day Wedderburn abused me at Whitehall." He never let abuse distract him, but he never forgot.

The two treaties deserve to be included in any list of America's founding documents. According to the joint alliance, France formally recognized America's independence, and the Americans pledged to fight with France should it be drawn into a war with Britain. The new allies each promised not to negotiate a separate peace, and France pledged that British recognition of American independence was to be a precondition for any settlement.

The commercial treaty was equally important. It welcomed French ships directly into American ports, which implied that the rebuilt French navy would protect the ships, allowing them to break the British blockade. The treaty also meant that American goods would be available in the vast European marketplace. In addition, King Louis had authorized another six-million-livre loan in quarterly installments.

Taken together, the treaties were both a diplomatic triumph for Franklin and tangible evidence for the onlooking world that true independence was moving forward.

RELATIONS AMONG THE COMMISSIONERS WERE TENSE. At the signing ceremony, Deane and Lee snapped at each other when the Virginian wanted to sign his name twice since he was a commissioner to both France and Spain. Lee's accusations about Deane's financial dealings had finally taken effect, for in late 1777 a Congress impatient for action on the treaties with France had summoned Deane home. Congress claimed it wanted a full report of events because dispatches from the commissioners were too often intercepted, but actually he was to account for himself before his accusers. John Adams would be named to take his place, but Adams would not sail until February 13, 1778, a week after the signing of the treaty, and would not arrive in Paris until early April.

Deane returned to Pennsylvania in the autumn of 1777, but he neglected to bring the documents showing he had loaned more of his own money to the American cause than he ever recouped in profits. Congress chose to believe Lee's charge that Beaumarchais and Deane were lining their pockets by billing Congress for goods that had been gifts. Dismissed from public life in America, Deane would return to Europe and try without success to salvage his affairs. He would end up in poverty, accused unfairly of treason, and despised.* In fairness, however, despite his greed and foolishness, he did considerable service for America at an important time.[1]

EVEN THOUGH ADAMS WAS ON HIS WAY TO PARIS, Franklin included Deane when, on March 20, 1778, Louis XVI officially received the American delegation at Versailles. The party included not only the three ministers to France but also William Lee, Arthur's brother, whom Congress had appointed to negotiate with Prussia, and Ralph Izard of South Carolina, who was minister to the Grand Duchy of Tuscany. The last two men were in Paris simply because neither Berlin nor Tuscany was interested in negotiating with the Americans; along with Arthur Lee, they served only to make life difficult for Franklin. Nevertheless, as a gesture of harmony, Franklin had asked that all the ministers be included in the ceremony.

On this occasion, Franklin wore a new suit of modest brown velvet and white hose, but again he went without wig or sword. A tale

---

* After returning to Europe, Deane fruitlessly tried to gather proof of his honesty. By 1781, he had become so depressed that he wrote several indiscreet letters to American friends urging them to work for reconciliation with Britain. Edward Bancroft handed those letters over to the secret service, which had them published in a Loyalist newspaper in New York. Deane died in England in 1789, bankrupt. In 1842, Congress reopened the case at the request of his heirs and found the audit provided by Lee "erroneous, and a gross injustice to Silas Deane." The heirs were voted the sum of $37,000 in partial restitution of the debt owed him.

has it that he had wanted to wear a formal long wig but the one he had ordered was too small. It was a fortunate stroke, for the enthusiastic French took it as proof of Franklin's natural nobility. As a concession to the formality of the occasion, he did tuck a white tricorner hat under his arm. Here, too, the French rhapsodized that the hat was a symbol of the purity of liberty. The French ignored the other four commissioners, who wore the formal dress required by court etiquette. It was the plain, plump old man who drew all eyes that day.

The Americans were escorted from the apartment Vergennes kept at the palace across a courtyard jammed with applauding courtiers to the private apartments of the king. There, in his dressing room (a mark of great intimacy and favor), Louis greeted them with restrained courtesy and said he hoped the new alliance "will be for the good of the two nations." It was clear he still had some doubts. Franklin thanked the king in the name of Congress and assured him America would observe its pledges—that is, no separate peace with Britain. After a celebration dinner given by Vergennes, the Americans rejoined the royal family. Franklin was invited to stand next to Queen Marie Antoinette while she gambled at cards. During lulls in the game she conversed with him cheerfully even though she had grave worries about her husband's fomenting a rebellion against another monarch.

Franklin's promise to Louis was an important one. All Paris knew by this time that the North ministry had been rocked by the news of Saratoga and would be staggered afresh when it learned of the two treaties. Franklin's vow to the French king meant that the rebels would not cave in and seek a quick peace, leaving the French alone to face Britain's might.

WITH THE TREATIES FRESHLY SIGNED, the momentum briefly shifted to the side of the new allies. Despite the determination of King

George III, his prime minister, Lord North, knew he had to stop the American war before the regional conflict became an international one with France, perhaps Spain, and possibly others. It was vital to win at least a truce from the Americans, by any means possible. When the news of the treaties was confirmed in London, prices on the stock exchange plunged to half their value from six months earlier. Upstart opposition leaders in the House of Commons, including Edmund Burke and Charles James Fox, had the temerity to demand hard data from the ministries about casualties and the cost of the war. The ministers refused, but the information leaked to Rockingham and Shelburne.

Lord North moved quickly. Spy Paul Wentworth and others begged Franklin to intercede with Congress for a truce, but attempts to bribe the American failed. At the same time, North rushed a series of conciliatory bills through Parliament to abolish most of the hated taxes against the colonies and to rescind other legal effronteries. He offered home rule for the colonies very much along the lines Franklin had proposed just before leaving London three years earlier.

Now a race to Philadelphia began. North rushed a packet ship to alert Congress to these new measures and inform the Americans that a special peace commission led by Lord Carlisle (and including William Eden) would soon follow. The French were not far behind. In early March, their own ship containing copies of the treaties set off for America, and they later sent their new ambassador to the United States, Gérard (formerly Vergennes's secretary), with firm instructions to stop the British from halting the war. The British ship did arrive first, and for a few weeks the American Congress wavered. But the wavering stopped when copies of the treaties arrived; on May 2, Congress ratified the agreements. In July, the French fleet bringing Gérard arrived at the mouth of the Delaware, and the Carlisle commission was forced to sail for home. Britain and France were now at war, and each nation had recalled its ambassador.

The American commissioners were once again the toasts of Paris, but Franklin was under no illusion of a quick victory. As long as King George controlled his ministers, he would not give up his American colonies until his troops were driven from the land.

FRANKLIN HAD BURDENS BEYOND KING GEORGE'S stubbornness. Not the least of these vexations was Arthur Lee. The Virginian was furious that Silas Deane had been allowed to take crucial trade accounts with him that might have proven fraud against him and, Lee suspected, against Franklin. Lee was in the habit of making charges first and seeking evidence later, but he was convinced that Franklin's refusal to thwart Deane was proof enough of collusion. He also was in a rage because he had not been consulted before Gérard was sent as ambassador in March. In April, Lee wrote to Franklin:

> Had you studied to deceive the most distrusted and dangerous enemy of the public you could not have done it more effectually. I trust, Sir, that you will think with me that I have a right to know your reasons for treating me thus. If you have anything to accuse me of, avow it, and I will answer you. If you have not, why do you act so inconsistently with your duty to the public and injuriously to me?

This brought Franklin's anger to the surface. The next day he vented the last two years of frustration with Lee:

> It is true I have omitted answering some of your letters. I do not like to answer angry letters. I am old, cannot have long to live, have much to do and no time for altercation. If I have often received and borne your magisterial snubbings and

rebukes without reply, ascribe it to the right causes; my concern for the honour and success of our mission which would be hurt by our quarrelling, my love of peace, my respect for your good qualities, and my pity of your sick mind, which is forever tormenting itself with its jealousies, suspicions, and fancies that others mean you ill, wrong you, or fail in respect for you. If you do not cure yourself of this temper it will end in insanity, of which it is a symptomatic forerunner, as I have seen in several instances. God preserve you from so terrible an evil; and for His sake pray suffer me to live in quiet.[2]

John Adams also came to be a burden for Benjamin Franklin. Adams's mandate from Congress had been to secure an alliance with France, but by the time he arrived in Paris in April, the treaties had been signed. Suddenly he had no mission, and unlike the Lee brothers and Ralph Izard, he was ill suited to sitting in Paris and complaining. To his credit, less than a month into his stay in France, he wrote his cousin Sam Adams to argue that the power in the American embassy in France should be concentrated in the hands of one man; he could assume he would not get the job. He showed the letter to Franklin, who encouraged him to send it off.

John Adams certainly was one of the three greatest intellects of the American Revolution, along with Jefferson and Franklin. He had been the fierce voice that rallied wavering support for the Declaration of Independence. He had ruined his health and emptied his purse attending to a thousand details in Philadelphia about the conduct of the war. He held tenaciously to the belief that America already *was* a free and sovereign nation and should be immediately treated so by other governments. He saw no reason why the other European powers should not be eager to come to America's aid, and he could not abide depending on one nation— particularly when that nation was the hated France of bitter New

England memory. In this he differed from Franklin, and as a result Adams grew suspicious of his fellow commissioner as well as of Vergennes, the foreign minister.

The antipathy that developed between Adams and Franklin also lay in personality differences. Adams was a farmer, a lawyer, and had all the moral rigidities of his Puritan heritage. Franklin was a townsman, a craftsman, full of appetites and skepticism. In peacetime they would have been reluctant acquaintances at best. In the harness of a wartime partnership, division was inevitable. Franklin was determined to direct the American campaign in Europe; it was the one great effort that he had been training himself for. Adams was just as determined to lead, for he wanted glory as much as any man, and he firmly believed he was in the right.

Their immediate conflict was over the nature of America and how it should conduct its foreign affairs. Franklin knew America was not yet a truly sovereign state, despite the French alliance. He, more than Adams, realized that without a substantially greater flow of French aid, Britain could bleed America into collapse even if it could not easily establish a serene rule over the colonies. This meant not only more money and guns but now French troops as well. Although General Washington was coming to the same conclusion, the idea of the French actually putting soldiers onto American soil and sending their fleet into American waters was an idea that appalled Adams (and King Louis). Franklin and Vergennes saw no alternative, however; the struggle must intensify if independence was to be a reality.

Adams saw Franklin's frequent and enthusiastic public expressions of gratitude to the French as demeaning. Franklin made no secret about where he stood, either to Adams or in frequent letters to Congress:

It is my intention, while I stay here, to procure what advantages I can for our country by endeavouring to please this court; and I wish I could prevent anything being said by any of our countrymen here that may have a contrary effect and increase an opinion lately showing itself in Paris, that we seek a difference, and with a view of reconciling ourselves to England.[3]

That statement contains the crux of Franklin's strategy. At some point the United States *was* going to have to reconcile with Britain, but at the same time the Americans had to keep the French actively engaged until the final peace and true independence were achieved. Moreover, to insult the French by denying them public thanks certainly would not help Vergennes, who had rivals inside his own government who opposed any new commitments. Also, any visible reserve by America's delegation in Paris might convey to both the British and the French that the United States was not eager to continue the war. As for the Lee-Adams party's call for more ambassadors in Europe, Franklin was adamant:

It seems to me that we have in most Instances, hurt our Credit and Importance, by sending all over Europe, begging Alliances, and soliciting Declarations of our Independence. The Nations perhaps from thence seem to think that our independence is something they have to sell, and that we don't offer enough for it.[4]

Adams saw Franklin's cool game as indolence, and his good-humored serenity as the dotage of a once great mind now corrupted by French luxury and the flattery of radicals. At first, Adams was content to yield to necessity. He accepted Franklin's offer to move into apartments at the Hôtel Valentinois. He put his ten-year-old son, John Quincy Adams, into a nearby school with Benjy Bache. Seeing that the commission's account books were in a muddle, he settled in that summer to set them aright. In his spare time he worked hard to learn French, often taking his boy to the theater so they could learn the Parisian accent. But he never appreciated the French, nor they him. He was ungainly and careless of his dress, suffering by comparison with Franklin's artful simplicity. The public welcomed him warmly at first, but he was affronted to learn that most Frenchmen thought he was the more famous revolutionary Samuel Adams.

All the while Franklin continued his propaganda war against England. He often wrote to his friends in the opposition, sure that the spies around him got copies of the letters to North and his ministers. He hectored the North government about the conditions of American prisoners of war. In London, his friend Benjamin Vaughan published a collection of Franklin's nonscientific writings, including some of the famous satires, and it became a best-seller. At the same time he established a small press at Passy and produced one of his most clever hoaxes, a counterfeit of a Boston Loyalist newspaper with a report that Indian allies of the British had sent King George a collection of scalps—from men, women, children— as tribute. Only a few spotted Franklin's hand in this hoax.

Adams appreciated none of this. To him, the correspondence to England was faintly suspicious; the hoaxes were foolish conceits. Adams saw only confused bookkeeping and Franklin relatives in posts they should not occupy. He was horrified at the amount of money the commissioners were spending, and his Puritan core rebelled at what he saw as Franklin's sinful luxury. Lee, who believed (rightly, in this case) that Bancroft and others who flocked around the commission were spies, easily convinced Adams that he could trust no one in Paris. Most irritating of all, Franklin began to avoid his fellow commissioner, which was hard to do since they lived in the same building. Franklin adopted the pose that he was old and needed rest. In one memoir, Adams recounted:

The Life of Dr. Franklin was a Scene of continual discipation. I could never obtain the favour of his Company in a Morning before Breakfast which would have been the most convenient time to read over the Letters and papers, deliberate on their contents, and decide upon the Substance of the Answers. It was late when he breakfasted, and as soon as Breakfast was over, a crowd of Carriges came to his Levee, or if you like the term better to his Lodgings, with all Sorts of People; some Philosophers, Academicians and Economists; some of his small tribe of humble friends in the literary Way...; but by far the greater part were Women and Children come to have the honour to see the great Franklin.... These Visitors occupied all the time, commonly, till it was time to dress to go to Dinner. He was invited to dine abroad every day and never declined unless We had invited Company to dine with Us.... It was the Custom in France to dine between one and two O'Clock; so when the time came to dress, it was time for the Voiture to be ready to carry him to dinner. Mr. Lee came daily to my Appartment to attend to Business, but we could rarely obtain the Company of Dr. Franklin for a few minutes, and often when I had drawn the Papers and had them fairly copied for Signature, and Mr. Lee and I had signed them I was frequently obliged to wait several days before I could procure the Signature of Dr. Franklin to them. He went according to his invitation to his Dinner and after that went sometimes to the Play, sometimes to the Philosophers, but most commonly to those Ladies who were complaisant enough to depart from the custom of France so far as to procure Setts of Tea Geer, as it is called, and make Tea for him. Ladies I knew as Madam Hellvetius, Madam Brillon, Madam Chaumont, Madam Le Roy etc., and others whom I never knew and never enquired for. After Tea the Evening was spent, in hearing the Ladies sing and play upon their Piano Fortes and other instruments of Musick, and in various games as Cards, Chess, Backgammon &cc; Mr. Franklin, I believe, however never play'd at any Thing but Chess or Chequers. In these Agreeable and important Occupations and Amusements, the Afternoon and Evening was spent, and he came home at all hours from nine to twelve O'Clock at night. This Course of Life contributed to his Pleasure and I believe to his health and Longevity. He was now between Seventy and Eighty and I had so much respect and compassion for his Age, that I could have been happy to have done all the Business or rather all the Drudgery, if I could have been favoured with a few moments in a day to receive his Advise concerning the manner in which it ought to be done. But this condescension was not attainable. All that could be had was his Signature after it was done, and this it is true he very rarely refused though he sometimes delayed.[5]

This ungenerous sarcasm tells more about Adams than he perhaps realized. More recent research points to the probability that Franklin, instead of being indolent, was busier at things he wanted to keep his colleague unaware of. Franklin had little interest in the legalistic approach to affairs or the dogged detail work Adams excelled at. To his mind, not every communication required an immediate response, and sometimes no response was best. Nor was Franklin failing. His gout attacks aside, he was robust enough. Where Adams had Franklin wasting the hours before breakfast, more recent histories show Franklin using those precious early morning hours not only for his own voluminous correspondence but also to run a small navy of privateers in the North Atlantic shipping lanes that was beyond the scope of the other commissioners.[6]

In June 1778, Franklin's little navy assumed a new role. Britain and France were now at war, and war hawks in King Louis's cabinet had forced on Vergennes a risky gamble—a French invasion of England, long the ambition of French kings. Vergennes was dubious about the scheme, but Franklin offered the privateers. These raiders, led by the daring John Paul Jones, had already seized ships and sacked villages on England's western coast. If the invasion did come off, the American privateers could stage a diversionary raid that would draw British troops from their Channel forts. Even if the invasion had little hope of succeeding, for Franklin this was an opportunity to boost the prestige of the American navy and show further gratitude to the French—and of course to bring more booty into the admiralty courts he ran in the French coastal ports.[*]

Like many adventures, this one would end in ultimate disaster. But it confirmed Vergennes in his regard for Franklin. The French minister found Franklin cool and tough-minded, but trustworthy. Vergennes avoided Lee at all costs and disliked Adams for his abrupt manner; the minister also resented that Adams had begun an extensive correspondence with other European governments in an attempt to build alternative relations. So Vergennes and Franklin closed their circle to the other commissioners and plotted anew about how deeply France should plunge into the American war.

Adams resented being pushed aside. He also objected to Franklin's manner, which was so contrary to his own. Adams was brusque and outspoken because he believed that when one possessed the truth it was a virtue to speak out. He wrote of Franklin:

---

[*] Ellen R. Cohn, editor of the Franklin Papers project at Yale, recently discovered a trove of admiralty documents in the French customs offices of these ports, most bearing Franklin's handwriting.

He loves his ease, hates to offend and seldom gives any opinion till obliged to do it.... Although he has as determined a soul as any man, yet it is his constant policy never to say yes or no decidedly but when he cannot avoid it.... His rigid taciturnity was very favourable to this singular felicity. He conversed only with individuals, and freely only with confidential friends. In company he was totally silent.[7]

One reason that Franklin shunned Adams was that the Massachusetts man misread how the American mission's objective had changed dramatically as a result of the two treaties. Formal diplomatic representations to the French were now unnecessary. America was no longer a supplicant but a partner in war. If the war spread to other nations, more aid would come to the Revolution's cause out of the self-interest of the combatants, not through more diplomacy. Indeed, in 1779, a year after Britain had declared war on France, Spain declared war on Britain. But Charles III refused to recognize the former colonies' independence unless Franklin agreed to surrender American claims to the Mississippi River. Franklin, leaving Adams out of the matter, dismissed the notion out of hand. "A Neighbour might as well ask me to sell my Street Door," Franklin sniffed.

ADAMS RECEIVED A FINAL SNUB FROM THE CONGRESS that had sent him to Paris in the first place. Congress finally agreed to what Adams had proposed soon after his arrival in France: that one man assume the role of ambassador to France. But Benjamin Franklin was named minister plenipotentiary. Worse still for Adams, the official dispatch from Congress naming Franklin sole minister did not even mention John Adams; he was in Paris and had no instructions from his government as to what to do. In March 1779, just a few weeks after receiving the communiqué from Congress, Adams gave up and decided to head back for America, though a frustrating series of delays prevented him from sailing until June.

When he finally sailed for America that summer of 1779, Adams remained firmly opposed to Franklin's determination to rely on the French for support. Adams and his allies in Congress were in fact suspicious of Franklin's affinity for France and all things French; where once he had been accused of being too English, he now seemed too much of a Francophile. Back in America, the Lee brothers and Ralph Izard, whom Congress had also called home, were feeding suspicions with their venomous charges against the minister to France. The fact that Temple, the bastard son of a bastard Loyalist traitor, was Franklin's secretary fed the discontent.

Franklin appeared unconcerned at the personal sniping in America, but that was because he seemed unaware that two political parties were developing in Congress. As the pursuing British army drove the legislature from one capital to another,* sometimes fewer than three dozen congressmen could attend. Congress, moreover, could deliver little tangible aid to its armies in the field. It could not tax the states to raise money, but could only print currency and hope French gold would arrive in time to give it value.

Others in Congress shared Franklin's view that France, and only France, could provide the money and arms in time for the Americans to win the war. It was crucial to them that Americans be seen to win their own war. Waiting for other European powers to join in would only make the Revolution a captive of these other nations. Among these pro-French supporters were Thomas Jefferson, John Jay, and merchant bankers such as Robert Morris. France's ambassadors also proved highly skilled advocates in behalf of the alliance.

---

* Congress finally returned to Philadelphia after General Washington recaptured the city in September 1781.

The rival group led by the Lees and the Adamses viewed dependence on France as dangerous. This group still favored the "militia diplomacy" strategy of sending as many ambassadors to as many courts as would receive them. That every commissioner had been turned back merely proved that Franklin and Vergennes had used dirty tricks to keep the American Revolution a strictly French affair. Spain was an obvious target for the Lee-Adams faction. After the British had been defeated, the United States could surely lure Spain, with its holdings stretching to California, to compete with France for America's favor.

Franklin knew not to expect much from Spain because Charles III's ambassador to Paris had told him so. Madrid's only real military contribution was to join its navy with that of the French, resulting in a combined force that in theory rivaled Britain's Royal Navy. Beyond that, however, Charles III was even less inclined to aid rebels than his nephew Louis was. All Charles wanted to do was seize Gibraltar from the British and to protect his holdings in the Caribbean and North America.

Even Spain's contribution of ships turned out badly. In the spring of 1779, John Paul Jones and Franklin's navy of privateers were poised for a raid against Liverpool as a diversion for the grand invasion plan. Two French divisions were encamped at coastal embarkation ports when a combined French-Spanish armada of sixty-four ships with 4,774 guns moved up the English Channel to destroy a British fleet that was half the size. A providential storm, like the one that scattered the Spanish Armada in Elizabethan times, shattered the combined attack, and then smallpox swept through the fleet, killing thousands. That summer, Jones sailed into action in a dowdy surplus warship renamed the *Bonhomme Richard* and captured the British man-of-war *Serapis*. The victory was the only joy brought to Paris that summer.

Chapter 20

The Final Round

$\mathcal{F}$ranklin clung to his partnership with Vergennes as the war in North America moved through the dismal defeats from 1779 through early 1781. Others in King Louis's cabinet began to lose heart for the American cause.

The British during this period not only held New York and Philadelphia but also seized Charleston and Savannah. A royal governor was put back into office in Georgia. General Lord Charles Cornwallis set out in the spring of 1780 to clear the Carolinas of rebel resistance and ultimately to knock the South out of the war altogether by seizing Virginia. With Washington stuck in the north and Congress on the run, the British seemed in control of the war.

Europe's other powers wanted a British triumph even less than American independence. By early 1781, the Dutch, against their will, were at war with Britain, since Admiral George Rodney's fleet had captured St. Eustatius in the Dutch West Indies, seizing £4 million worth of American supplies.* Empress Catherine of Russia floated the idea that the other Continental powers form a League of Armed Neutrality to keep the war from spreading further, in part to prevent a total British triumph over the Bourbon monarchies. After that alliance was formed, Russia and Austria volunteered to arbitrate a peace between Britain and France—a peace that almost certainly would put the colonies back in King George's pocket. Fortunately for Franklin, George refused to mediate. He remained confident that he would win America back on his own terms.

To Franklin's mind, his task was to pull France into America's cause far enough that it could not pull back short of victory. Franklin dropped the role of treaty diplomat and became his country's war minister, treasurer, and quartermaster. He drew a continuing flow of capital out of the French treasury. At each step, however, Congress undercut him by demanding more than he could get and overspending the amounts he did provide.

In 1779, Congress demanded another twelve-million-livre grant and grumbled when Franklin won only three million. Yet King Louis did accede to Franklin's wheedling and during the course of the war handed over a staggering twenty million livres in cash over and above France's materiel aid. Without this subsidy there would not have been an American Revolution. It is too much to say that this sum was a proximate cause of the French Revolution that followed a decade later; the loans, after all, were paid back over time. But France's involvement in the American Revolution certainly did not help matters at home. In a replay of the Seven Years War, France again found itself fighting in India, Africa, the Mediterranean, and

---

* It turned out that London merchants owned much of the supplies; they sued Rodney, creating a new scandal to plague the North ministry.

the West Indies, as well as in the Atlantic. The cost of everything involved in that global war—military operations, the draining subsidies of an inefficient economy, not to mention the lavish expense of the court—was a weight France could not carry.

FRANKLIN'S REPUTATION AT HOME, despite his achievements, was at one of its lowest points. Part of the problem was that almost none of Franklin's reports back to Congress had arrived. The British had penetrated his communication lines, which may have provided good propaganda in London but kept him isolated from the Congress at home. Not hearing from him, many in Congress concluded he was not doing anything. Still, his foes could not muster enough votes on a motion to recall him. In fact, in 1780, when he asked to be relieved of duty because of health problems, Congress greeted the request with stony silence. Instead of approving his return, it formulated a new plan to put more pressure on Franklin and broaden the scope of the mission, against his advice.

Adams was sent back to Paris, this time with a commission to negotiate both a peace treaty and a commerce treaty with Britain. At the same time John Jay of New York, an admirer of Franklin, was sent to wrench formal recognition from the Spanish court and see about getting more money. Henry Laurens, a South Carolinian who was president of Congress, was to do the same in Holland. (Laurens never arrived in Amsterdam; captured by the British navy, he was imprisoned in the Tower of London for two years.) Despite its suspicions of the French foreign minister, Congress blithely instructed the delegates that they should be guided in all matters by Vergennes and must not offend the French. Also, because Congress was nearly bankrupt, the negotiators were to draw their expenses and living allowance from the French treasury, even though that had not been authorized. No one bothered to inform Franklin of this return to militia diplomacy.

Adams arrived in Paris in February 1780, and while he immediately paid his respects at Passy, he did not tell Franklin that he was empowered as the sole negotiator with Britain. Congress had formally instructed him not to make his mission public, which was his pretext for being mysterious with Franklin. Not that Franklin did not guess at once. Within a day or two he wrote to his friend David Hartley in London that someone other than himself might do the peace negotiating. If Congress had decided on someone else, he added, "it is perhaps because they have heard of a very singular opinion of mine, that there hardly ever existed such a thing as a bad peace or a good war; and that I might therefore easily be induced to make improper concessions."[1]

But Adams did have to tell Vergennes of his mission. When he called at Versailles, he had the temerity to lecture the minister on the shortcomings of French naval strategy. The timing was poor, for Franklin had worked hard to convince Vergennes and King Louis to plunge into the American theater of war. In fact, a French fleet was preparing to sail to America along with six thousand troops under France's most able infantry commander, the Comte de Rochambeau.* By committing troops, the French were in the war for good.

Worse, Adams told the foreign minister he intended to make public that he was there to open direct talks with the British. Adams wanted to be off and running; the sooner he secured victory through his diplomacy, the sooner he would be recognized for his contributions to independence. Besides, a quick peace meant that French troops would not be needed. Yet he was bound, as all American envoys were, by strict orders from Congress to be guided

---

* The French troops landed at Newport, Rhode Island, in July 1780. Shortly thereafter, however, the British Navy blockaded the supporting French fleet in Narragansett Bay, keeping the ships there for the better part of a year.

by Vergennes. The French wanted to strengthen their own role in the war theater before any peace talks went on. The minister forbade Adams from contacting the British (knowing full well that Franklin was in almost daily communication with Britain), so the New Englander bitterly kept quiet.

Of course, London knew about Adams's mission almost as soon as he had arrived in France. Later, Vergennes allowed the appointment to be made public but made Adams keep secret a separate commission to negotiate a commercial treaty with Britain. Since there were no peace talks to conduct, Adams once again was a man without a job.

Congress further insulted the French when it ordered yet another devaluation of the Continental dollar—a reduction in value of forty to one. Beaumarchais, Chaumont, and the other merchant traders were horrified, for their credit lines were extended past the breaking point. Arms had been shipped but the prospect for full repayment suddenly vanished. During Adams's next visit to Versailles that summer, Vergennes took him to task for this economic betrayal. Adams hotly retorted that France ought to be grateful for the opportunity to sow liberty for its own sake and that the sovereign U.S. Congress was not in the business of guaranteeing huge profits for French speculators. This sent Vergennes, that cool hand, into a rage. The minister refused to receive Adams thereafter, saying he would deal only with Franklin. He also sent Franklin all the insulting memos Adams had filed and asked him to send them to Congress. Adams was now officially persona non grata, and Franklin was happy enough to oblige the foreign minister. "Mr. Adams has given extreme offense to the court here," Franklin wrote to Congress. Adams never forgave him for it.

Barred from serving in Paris, Adams decamped for Amsterdam in August, firmly convinced that the Dutch would help the Americans in their fight with Britain. A crisis awaited him. The Netherlands was in no mood to endorse independence for America, and the Amsterdam bankers who had extended credit for American war shipments now were trapped—Dutch and French merchants had presented due bills.

This was an insoluble problem for Adams. France was the final guarantor of American credit and now was being dragooned into backing Dutch debt as well. Adams found he could not even borrow enough money to live in Amsterdam. His two sons who accompanied him—John Quincy and Charles—were unhappy in their new school, and they all hated the damp North Sea climate. Adams added to the strain on his health by traveling a great deal. Congress later compounded his gloom by revoking his peace commission for Britain and naming him ambassador to Holland, but the Dutch government was ignoring his entreaties.

In the spring of 1781, worse news came for the proud Adams. This time Congress created a new peace commission to include Franklin; Jay, who was languishing in Spain; Adams himself; Jefferson, who did not come; and Laurens, who was stuck in the Tower of London. Adams was near collapse, and this was final proof that Vergennes (through his ambassador in America, Gérard) and Franklin had conspired against him by denying him control over the talks. It did not occur to him that this new commission was a task in doubt, for at this point the war was going badly everywhere for the allies.

Adams's health gave way in August. It could have been an attack of malaria, but it is more likely from the symptoms he exhibited that he had a return of the extreme hyperthyroidism that had struck him three years earlier in America. He struggled with fevers and headaches, his speech slurred, and his memory failed. His eyes bulged and normal light was unbearably painful to him. He developed a goiter on his neck. Adams became extremely agitated and held a paranoid suspicion that Dutch agents were following him and that he might be assassinated. For six weeks in the late summer of 1781, he drifted in and out of consciousness and later said that he never afterward regained full health.[2]

THE TRAVAILS OF ADAMS AND THE STALEMATE Jay faced in Spain left Franklin on his own in France. While he relished being free of controversy with other Americans, the press of business kept him shuttling between Vergennes and his apartments in Passy. His social and political appearances in Paris began to diminish. He had been a regular member of the Masonic Lodge of the Nine Sisters; indeed, he was its grand master for a time and had presented Voltaire to the lodge for induction. But his Masonic contacts and the scientific societies were time consuming and no longer as useful as they had been when he first arrived. Part of the problem lay in the constant crowds of callers at the Hôtel Valentinois that Adams had described. Military adventurers sought letters of introduction from Franklin, politicians called for the latest news, and mothers brought children to receive his blessing. The American minister turned no one away even though it meant postponing his work for hours. Life became more ritualized and less spontaneous, more confined, more tiring.

There was no time for travel. In his nine years in France he took none of the journeys that he had made from London twenty years before and that revived him so well. He was seventy-four in 1780, and he began to feel his age. Portraits and sketches made at the time show Franklin softening. His hard face began to sag into jowls. Two moles suddenly appeared near his mouth, and his sharp, watchful gaze became weary and complacent. He began to avoid the vigorous exercise that once had been his joy. The sedentary existence (and a diet heavy in salted meat) brought on a form of scurvy that produced rashes on his scalp and back. He also had more frequent episodes of gout; from October to December 1780 he was confined to bed for an agonizing attack that affected all his joints. When he was well, he found his legs had weakened and his feet had become too tender to stand for long. He began to wear soft cloth slippers when he did go out.

From the start of his stay in Passy, Franklin had gone regularly to the famous alkali springs nearby; now he went to bathe his rashes. The man who ran the springs, village mayor Louis-Guillaume Le Veillard, became a friend. It was through Le Veillard that Franklin found something else that revived his spirits. A new love object would make his pleasant apartments in Passy perfect.

JOHN ADAMS HAD BEEN RIGHT: Franklin's passion for women and their attraction to him remained strong despite the passage of time. Madame Chaumont, the wife of his landlord, made him a member of the merchant's large family, and she and the children were in and out of Franklin's apartments with a freedom denied to Adams. But she lacked the intellectual spark that mattered as much to Franklin as youth and beauty. Similarly, he was merely amused by the flattering flirtations of young ladies of the salons. He explained his conduct in a letter to a niece in 1779:

> You mention the kindness of the French ladies to me. I must explain that matter. This is the civilest nation upon earth. Your first acquaintances endeavour to find out what you like, and they tell others. If 'tis understood that you like mutton, dine where you will, you find mutton. Somebody, it seems, gave it out that I loved ladies; and then everybody presented me their ladies (or the ladies presented themselves) to be embraced; that is, have their necks kissed. For as to the kissing of lips or cheeks it is not the mode here; the first is reckoned rude, the other may rub off the paint. The French ladies have, however, a thousand other ways of rendering themselves

agreeable; by their various attentions and civilities and their sensible conversation.[3]

He wanted the kind of deep ties he had with Catharine Ray Greene and Polly Stevenson Hewson. He wanted to be on the edge of danger, but in control as well. His longest-running relationship began soon after his move to Passy when he met Anne-Louise Boiven d'Hardancourt Brillon de Jouy, who lived on a nearby estate. Madame Brillon was a beautiful bisque doll in her early thirties. She had wide celebrity as a player of, and composer for, the harpsichord and the newly popular pianoforte. Boccherini and other famous composers dedicated music to her, and she gathered into her circle an eclectic group of philosophers, poets, and musicians all united in their adoration of her. She was talented and lively when she was happy. Most of the time, however, she was afflicted with bouts of deep spiritual malaise. It was the fashion of that time for European women of the upper classes to be romantically depressed, yet there were real causes for Anne-Louise to be sad.

Her husband was a newly rich tax official twenty-five years older than she, a man whom John Adams described as "a rough kind of Country Squire." Monsieur Brillon kept a mistress, who also served as governess to the Brillons' children. At a dinner, Adams saw that this woman was treated as a family member, and he was shocked to learn of her relationship with Monsieur Brillon. In his diary, Adams recorded his revulsion:

When I afterwards learned both from Dr. Franklin and his Grandson, and from many other persons that this Woman was the Amie of Mr. Brillon and that Madam Brillon consoled herself by the Amitié of Mr. Le Valliant [Le Veillard], I was astonished that these People could live together in such apparent Friendship and indeed without cutting each other's throats.

But I do not know of the World. I soon saw and heard so much of these Things in other Families and among almost all the great People of the Kingdom that I found it was a thing of course. It was universally understood and Nobody lost any reputation by it.[4]

Franklin was enchanted by the mix of sparkle and despair in Anne-Louise. She, in turn, was drawn to the sage idolized by all France. Le Veillard, who had brought Franklin to the Brillon estate, also was devoted to her and cheerfully gave up his claims on her affections once he saw what was going on between the two. For his part, Monsieur Brillon greatly admired Franklin and was delighted to have his wife distracted from his own carrying on.

Claude-Anne Lopez, the Yale scholar on Franklin and his romances, describes the relationship between the two as "more than close friendship and less than love of the flesh—what the French call *amitié amoureuse.*"[5] But while there is strong evidence that Franklin never achieved his fleshly desires, the correspondence between him and Anne-Louise makes clear that it was not for want of trying. He rushed at her with what were called "bagatelles"—amusing poetry, jolly stories, satires, and most of all professions of devotion and desire. He used the small printing press he had set up in Passy to prepare his bagatelles, often employing artistic typefaces and making engravings. While he kept his protestations of love in confidence, he could not resist circulating copies of the more amusing stories. Since everyone knew the object of these exercises, Franklin furthered his reputation as a native wit and as an ardent lover.

Anne-Louise Brillon deeply loved Franklin, and not just on the intellectual plane that Catharine Ray Greene had chosen. She responded equally flirtatiously, writing the most indiscreet confidences and vowing the most perfect love for him. Yet she rationed him with hugs and kisses and no more. In one of their meetings, she looked on from a covered bathtub while Franklin and Le Veillard played chess; Franklin later marveled that he had lost all track of time.

His life with Anne-Louise settled into a pleasant routine. On Tuesdays he usually went into Paris to see Vergennes, but on Wednesdays he never missed dining with the Brillons. Saturdays were also reserved for her, and there were lavish all-day picnics and fêtes where guests competed with poems and songs about her and about that sage Franklin.

As idyllic as his romance must have been, there is something sad and a little suspect about it. The affair looks very much like the father-daughter relationships he had built with dozens of other young women. Anne-Louise for all her flirtation always called him *"mon cher papa."* And for all his obsession with her, Franklin did not behave as a real lover in serious pursuit of his adored one. Everything was in the open and hedged with humor. The couple might slip away from a garden fête for an hour of kisses and confidences, but Monsieur Brillon was always about and well aware of how far things were going.

Whatever stage Franklin's efforts to seduce Anne-Louise Brillon reached, the romance seems to have peaked in 1778, when it is believed she firmly put an end to his hopes while still assuring him of her love. In fact, Franklin worked hard to reconcile the Brillon marriage, and in the summer of 1781 the Brillons left Passy for a long stay in Nice, hoping it would help her regain her emotional health. Although the two remained devoted for the rest of Franklin's life, the intimacy never fully revived and the Brillon family spent more time at their house in Paris.

Was Franklin truly in love with Anne-Louise Brillon? Or was he in love with being in love, or with playing at love? Madame Brillon once joked that Franklin loved a woman only when he could see her face. Another joke went around Passy that when a woman did finally agree to Franklin's begging to spend the night with her, he drew back, saying he would rather wait for winter, "when the nights are longer."

To add to the confusion, Franklin had another true love in the works at the same time. Anne-Catherine Helvétius was in her late fifties, still handsome, and had a bohemian flair that made her irresistible to every man who met her. Recently widowed, she had taken her wealth to a small wild garden estate in a village just beyond Passy that she filled with a menagerie of cats, deer, and three men—two of them priests. The noisy house was filled with debate and laughter. Her late husband, Claude Adrien Helvétius, had been a controversial philosopher and leading light in the Lodge of the Nine Sisters. It was his Masonic apron that Franklin wore when he was inducted, and the Lodge (which the police watched with suspicion) frequently met at the widow's new estate.

Anne-Catherine Helvétius's high-spirited informality drew Franklin to her, yet it was not the fervent romance that he had with Madame Brillon. One of the attractions for Franklin was the salon Anne-Catherine conducted, which drew more prestigious scientists and intellectuals than Anne-Louise's. That is, the affection poured out to him was matched with stimulating conversation. He began to spend more time with the Helvétius community, for he could relax and let himself go among these close friends in a way he never could with people he did not trust.

John Adams liked Madame Helvétius no better than Madame Brillon. Abigail Adams, who came over after the peace was signed, was outraged when her husband and Franklin took her to dinner at the Helvétius estate. She later recorded this bitter portrait of Anne-Catherine:

She entered the room with a careless, jaunty air; upon seeing ladies who were strangers to her, she bawled out, "Ah! mon Dieu, where is Franklin? Why did you not tell me there were ladies here?" You must suppose her speaking all this in French. "How I look!" said she, taking hold of a chemise made of tiffany, which she had on over a blue lutestring [a crinoline], and which looked as much upon the decay as her beauty, for she was once a handsome woman; her hair was frizzled; over it she had a small straw hat, with a dirty gauze, half-handkerchief round it, and a bit of dirtier gauze, than ever my maids wore, was bowed on behind. She had a black gauze scarf thrown over her shoulders. She ran out of the room; when she returned, the Doctor entered at one door, she at the other; upon which she ran forward to him, caught him by the hand, "Helas! Franklin;" then gave him a double kiss, one upon each cheek, and another upon his forehead. When we went into the room to dine, she was placed between the Doctor and Mr. Adams. She carried on the chief of the conversation at dinner, frequently locking her hand into the Doctor's, and sometimes spreading her arms upon the backs of both the gentlemen's chairs, then throwing her arm carelessly upon the Doctor's neck.

I should have been greatly astonished at this conduct, if the good Doctor had not told me that in this lady I should see a genuine Frenchwoman, wholly free from affectation or stiffness of behaviour, and one of the best women in the world. For this I must take the Doctor's word; but I should have set her down for a very bad one, although sixty years of age, and a widow. I own I was highly disgusted, and never wish for an acquaintance with any ladies of this cast. After dinner she threw herself upon a settee, where she showed more than her feet. She had a little lap-dog, who was, next to the Doctor, her favorite. This she kissed, and when he wet the floor she wiped it up with her chemise. This is one of the Doctor's most intimate friends, with whom he dines once every week, and she with him.[6]

Franklin did more than dine and talk with his friend. Early in 1780 he proposed marriage to Anne-Catherine Helvétius, and for the next several months he waged a campaign of humor and insistence that almost overcame her pledge to honor her late husband's memory by remaining single. He bombarded her with bagatelles quite unlike the ethereal confections he dreamed up for Anne-Louise Brillon. To Anne-Catherine he spoke frankly and robustly about the joy of merging their two households and perhaps even moving to America, where he would secure her land for all her animals. In one bagatelle he described a dream in which he met her late husband in Heaven. Helvétius confessed that while he had loved his wife during his time on Earth, now that he was in Paradise he had taken a new wife—Deborah Franklin. The late Mrs. Franklin tartly said to her former spouse, "I have been a good wife to you for forty-nine years and four months, almost half a century; be content with that. I have formed a new connection here, that will last for eternity." Franklin told Anne-Catherine in the bagatelle, "Grieved by this rebuke from my Euridyce, I resolved there and then to abandon those ungrateful shadows, and to come back to this good world, to see the sun again, and you. Here I am! Revenge!"[7]

Anne-Catherine certainly took the proposal seriously. She loved Franklin enough to consider throwing over her carefully arranged life and moving with him to the frightening wilds of America. That summer of 1780 she went to stay with a relative in the country while she wrestled with her composure and her desires. When she returned, she rejected his proposal but still managed to keep his affection. During the remaining years Franklin spent in France, his two rival loves worked out an eminently sensible, classically French compromise—they shared him. He got all the love and affection he required of whatever kind he preferred. When he finally returned to America alone, the two women rebuked each other for not having loved him enough to make him spend the rest of his days with them. Passy may have been the home Franklin loved the best.

FRANKLIN SCARCELY WAS IDLING AWAY HIS DAYS in flowery gardens of love, despite what Adams thought. In May 1781, after being trapped for nearly a year by British forces, the French fleet and Rochambeau's troops broke free from Rhode Island and joined forces with General Washington in New York. As the combined French and American forces wheeled south, Admiral François Joseph Paul de Grasse's French West Indies fleet disembarked three thousand more troops in Virginia. Then the French ships drove away a British squadron sent to relieve General Cornwallis at Yorktown. On October 19, Cornwallis surrendered nearly ten thousand British and German troops to the Americans and French.

Franklin and all of Paris rejoiced when the news arrived a month later, but he knew the war was far from over. While Cornwallis's force was larger than the one General Burgoyne surrendered at Saratoga, it was the weakest of the three divisions the British had in America. The commander in chief, Sir Henry Clinton, was willing to keep fighting from those major ports still in his control. King George III was still determined to carry on the war as well. Only Lord North was undone. When he heard the news, he threw his arms open as if he had been shot, and cried, "Oh, God! It's all over!"

But the war had simply changed form. Franklin knew that the struggle had now shifted to Paris and London. The test would be who would be the more determined—Franklin and Vergennes or King George III.

Franklin being received by King Louis XVI of France.

Chapter 21

The Struggle for Peace

ranklin wrote to John Adams in October 1782:

> I have never known a peace made, even the most advanta-
> geous, that was not censured as inadequate, and the makers
> condemned as injudicious or corrupt. "Blessed are the Peace-
> makers" is, I suppose, to be understood in the other World: for
> in This they are more frequently Cursed.[1]

After Cornwallis's surrender at Yorktown the year before, the
American Revolution entered a perilous phase. The armed conflict
shifted to other areas of the world and a danger arose that the cause
of American independence might be lost in the confused global
struggle.

Franklin determined that the quickest peace was the best—provided that independence was assured. But for the moment he reassured Vergennes that France was America's true and only ally, and he took pains to report every time a British agent called on him privately. There were plenty of contacts to report.

Franklin and the various competing factions in British political life had been carrying on an almost continuous dialogue since his arrival in Paris five years earlier. King George III had a very clear understanding of Franklin's thinking but still chose to believe that some way would be found to bring peace without handing independence to *his* colonies. But by 1781 no one else was confident of this. The king was also certain that Franklin was the man most responsible for the rebellion and for the seduction of France into the conflict. The only good thing Lord North and the king could say about their hated opponent was that he was the only man in Paris who was not enriching himself by trading on inside information on the London stock exchange.

One reason it was so easy for Franklin to convey his intentions to London was that the borders remained remarkably open even after war came between Britain and France. Englishmen came and went across the Channel at will. Agents of the police followed every new arrival closely, but most went unmolested directly to Passy to exchange intelligence with Franklin. The North government used friends of the American's from his London days when it wanted to take official soundings. Benjamin Vaughan, the publisher of Franklin's collected works, and David Hartley, another old friend and pro-American member of Parliament, came often. Franklin used to make Vaughan join him for a soak in the bathhouse so they could converse without being overheard.

At one point Franklin received a strangely worded message that had been shoved through the outer grate of his front door. He came to believe that it was a direct message from King George himself, but the French police spooked the messenger sent for his reply, and nothing came of it. There also was, Franklin firmly believed, an attempt made on his life during this crisis time. Peter Allaire, a Frenchman who had lived in New York, was one of the dozens of men who shuttled between the two capitals, sometimes trying to do legitimate business, other times serving as couriers and spies. Allaire was well known to Franklin and sent him a large bottle of fine Madeira. Franklin fell violently ill after drinking some of it and was quick to believe he had been poisoned. At his request, French authorities rounded up Allaire and kept him in the Bastille for months, where the sight of all the instruments of torture adorning the walls terrified him. When he was finally released, he rushed off to England and never returned.

MEANWHILE, THE TORIES' PARLIAMENTARY MAJORITY began to crumble around Lord North. William Pitt the Elder had died in 1778, but by 1781 his son, known as William Pitt the Younger, was rising in the ranks of Parliament and showing flashes of his father's mastery of debate. This Pitt went beyond his father's calls for conciliation and spoke forcefully for American independence as the price of peace. Day after day men like Jonathan Shipley, the Bishop of St. Asaph, joined with Edmund Burke and Rockingham and Shelburne to decry the cost and casualties of the war. Of the nearly seventy thousand men sent as soldiers and sailors to the American war, nearly thirty thousand were dead, wounded, or prisoners. There were no more Hessians to rent and no more recruits to raise in all of Britain. The African trade was in ruins, the Caribbean sugar colonies were in peril, and the King's exchequer was as barren as the French treasury. Most ominously, the endurance of the Americans raised the prospect of rebellion in Ireland. On March 7, 1782, after losing a test vote on the conduct of the war, Lord North went to his old friend the king and said he could not continue. The long period of the king's dominance of a Tory Parliament was over. The Whigs would have to be brought into the ministries once more.

George III was not completely routed, however. The king had an uncanny ability to use the discord between political rivals to strengthen his own hand. To build a coalition that would have broad support, he had to yield on the choice of prime minister, and Lord Rockingham, whose first term in office had led to the repeal of the Stamp Act, was returned to the top post. Lord Shelburne was made secretary of state for the colonies, and Charles James Fox, a rising Whig voice in the Commons, was made foreign minister. In theory, Shelburne and Fox were to coordinate peace talks between Franklin and Vergennes to get the best deal possible for Britain—hopefully without conceding independence to America or any colonial real estate to France. But George knew they hated each other and would try to cut one another out of the talks; that would produce the stalemate the king was praying for. Delays in the peace talks would offer George hope for a British military victory somewhere.

Rockingham, too, would have preferred to win peace with America without giving it full independence, but first he would have peace. While he sent Hartley, Vaughan, and others to Paris to sound out Franklin, he used his parliamentary majority to quiet Ireland. He repealed a law ordered by George I that gave the British Parliament final say over all legislation for Ireland, then established free trade between the two countries. The Irish responded by raising twenty thousand volunteers for Royal Navy service in America.

Shelburne judged that most of the men carrying messages to and from Franklin were more sympathetic to the American than to the Crown, so he deputized his own man, a blunt Scots merchant named Richard Oswald, to try to pry Franklin away from the French. Fox meanwhile sent his own agent, Thomas Grenville (a son of Franklin's old foe George Grenville), to learn if the French would agree to a deal behind Franklin's back.

Oswald made his first visit to Passy in early April 1782. Franklin by habit said nothing and instead took the emissary directly to Vergennes, who repeated the line that France and America stood loyally by each other. Then, having done his duty by his ally, Franklin took Oswald back to Passy and put a couple of interesting thoughts to the agent. If Lord Shelburne really wanted a quick peace with the United States, he should consider acknowledging independence *and* handing over Canada and Nova Scotia to make Congress enthusiastic about rebuilding relations with Britain. An unadorned peace, he added, might leave America more closely tied to France than was in Britain's interest. It was just a thought in passing, the wily Franklin said, nothing formal. But Oswald might remind Lord Shelburne that giving the United States all that empty land to the north would solve two thorny problems: damage claims against Britain for the destruction of rebel homes and towns, and Loyalist demands for reparations for the lands and property state governments had seized in retaliation. All that new land could either be sold or be deeded to settle both sets of claims, and no one would have to come up with cash. Franklin knew that Shelburne was a friend of both the Penn clan and Lord Baltimore's family and would want to save them from loss; he also knew the state of the British treasury.

Franklin sent an urgent message to John Jay to abandon his quest for Spanish aid and to join him in Paris at once in his new role as peace negotiator. The forces of Charles III were mounting a final, all-out attack on the British garrison at Gibraltar and could not give the Americans anything. Jay came at once but was felled by influenza for several weeks. Talks were also going on to exchange Henry Laurens for Lord Cornwallis, but that commissioner was not yet free. Meanwhile, John Adams remained in Holland, trying without success to win recognition and money. The truth was that Adams had no desire to be put in a subservient role in the Franklin-Vergennes partnership. He might have come if he had realized that the French-American alliance was starting to fray from competing interests.

At this point, Franklin got a break. In June, after just three months in office, Lord Rockingham died, and Lord Shelburne was elevated to prime minister. When Fox resigned in protest, the full range of negotiations came under Shelburne's control. Shelburne knew he had a narrow window of opportunity to win the best peace he could before impatient rivals would combine to topple him; he had a few months at best.

Through Oswald, Franklin signaled that Shelburne could have a peace at once if he first formally acknowledged the independence of the United States. Once that was publicly conceded, Franklin assured the minister, the other issues could quickly be resolved. He also gave Oswald a proposal in which he outlined both nonnegotiable and "advisable" conditions. The nonnegotiable conditions were: the full independence of the United States was to be confirmed and all British troops were to leave; the boundaries of the thirteen states were to be set and the boundary with Canada was to be restored to what it was before the Quebec Act; and American fishermen and whalers were to have complete access to the Newfoundland banks. His so-called advisable conditions were that Americans be repaid for the damage inflicted by the war, that Britain publicly accept blame for causing the war, that free trade between America and Britain be restored, and that Canada and Nova Scotia be ceded to the United States. As for helping the Loyalists, Franklin remained adamant: they should get nothing for their treason.

By July, John Jay had recovered. Having endured insults and frustrations in Madrid, Jay had a deep suspicion of both Spain and France that proved justified. He did not want Spain to have any say at the peace table until Charles III recognized the status of the United States. More to the point, he told Franklin that he suspected France wanted America free, but not too free. He charged that Vergennes was plotting with London to keep the Americans out of the Newfoundland fisheries. The French minister, Jay believed, was stalling for time at the request of Spain so that France could control the Mississippi while Spain took the entire Gulf Coast from Florida to Mexico.

All this was true. Gérard de Rayvenal, the new secretary to Vergennes, had shown Jay a map that staked out the various claims in North America. All the land west of the Appalachians to the Mississippi, north of the Spanish corridor along the Gulf, was supposed to belong to France. Britain had in fact ceded much of that land to the French in the 1763 peace, but France also wanted control of the vital Newfoundland fishing grounds.

While the allies bickered among themselves, the British hand got stronger for a brief moment. In the Caribbean, Admiral George Rodney defeated the same French fleet that had sealed Cornwallis in Yorktown the autumn before; French admiral de Grasse and his flagship were taken. Shelburne slowed the pace of his communications to Franklin in hopes that he could drive a wedge between the allies. And there were other problems. For one, Franklin had not told Vergennes of the peace proposal he had sent via Oswald. Then, just as Jay was fully recovered, Franklin was confined to bed in excruciating pain; his chronic bouts of gout had worsened into urinary bladder stones, from which his brother had suffered thirty years before. Left on his own, Jay continued to demand formal recognition of independence as a precondition for any treaty talks, and he told the British that they need not wait for Spain to come to the table.

In September, Oswald came back to Paris with a commission that specifically stated he was to negotiate peace with "The Thirteen

United States." Franklin recovered and rejoined the talks in early October, and Benjamin Vaughan was sent over to use his friendship to hurry the peace. On October 5, Jay gave Oswald America's first formal proposal for a peace settlement.

Without knowing what Jay had done, Vergennes the next day handed his British negotiator a list of French conditions for peace. He essentially demanded a return of all the land in India, the West Indies, and Africa that France had lost in 1763. He also claimed exclusive control of the Newfoundland fishing banks. In effect, he was trying to slow the pace of the peace talks by crowding the table with claims. The same day, word came that the all-out Spanish assault on Gibraltar had failed and the siege had been lifted. The British once more appeared to be gaining momentum.

This might have been the time for Shelburne to shut down talks. But he dared not because speculation against the pound sterling was drawing traders from all over Europe. False rumors flew from one European financial center to another and then back to London, and the traders made a killing even when news of British victories was confirmed. The bear market was an intolerable burden on the Bank of England, which had to finance the government's staggering debt. The prime minister shut Parliament down until December 5 in order to cool that hot source of rumor making, but he did not have any more time than that. Fox and his allies were building a coalition against him, objecting to the way he was conducting the peace talks.

Shelburne then sent a formal peace commission deliberately constructed to be congenial to Franklin. The group was headed by Henry Strachey, who had been Lord Howe's secretary during the inconclusive meeting with Franklin and Adams at the outbreak of the war. With Strachey came Oswald, Vaughan, and, as secretary, Franklin's dear Craven Street neighbor Caleb Whitefoord.

THE BRITISH NEGOTIATORS ARRIVED IN PARIS in late October. John Adams arrived from Holland within a day or two, bolstered by the fact that he had just won Dutch recognition of America and a one-million-livre loan. He found both Jay and Franklin still suffering the aftereffects of their illnesses and divided on whether to push the peace talks on without consulting Vergennes on the terms.

The first British-American meeting was to be held at Franklin's apartment at Passy on October 27; the evening before, Adams and Jay pressed Franklin to negotiate without the supervision of the French. To do this would be to disobey Congress's strict orders and to betray Vergennes, who had been Franklin's friend through the whole war. Until now he had dealt fairly and openly with the French minister, with the exception of the first peace feelers he had sent through Oswald. Yet going behind his old colleague's back now might be permissible diplomatic self-interest, since he knew what the French were likely to demand as their share of the peace. But that night, Franklin, in his usual way, said nothing.

Just before the meeting the next day, Franklin told Jay he had agreed to act with him and Adams. When the negotiations began, the Americans pressed the same points that Franklin had outlined to Oswald earlier in the year. Jay argued the case for a United States boundary on the east bank of the Mississippi and free navigation of the river for both America and Britain. Adams wore the British down over fishing rights. The financial questions were finessed: all the Loyalists got was a promise that Congress would refer all claims to the states—which meant no action. Jay and Adams were in their element arguing the legal details and Franklin gave them free rein, except on the matter of paying the Loyalists. William Franklin had become the president of the Loyalist association in Britain, and Franklin was determined to deny him a penny. He and Jay both had suffered vandalism of their properties at the hands of the British; Franklin's library and laboratory in

Philadelphia had been destroyed, and his son's betrayal could not be forgiven.

The talks dragged on through November, and the American position got stronger as Shelburne's deadline approached. Tactically, Strachey, Oswald, and Vaughan were at a disadvantage, for they were merely messengers for the prime minister, whereas the three Americans were fully empowered to act on their own. So many draft versions were sent back by courier to Shelburne that French agents could not have missed reading many of them. Vergennes had to know what was going on, but he claimed to be surprised and miffed when, on November 30, the preliminary treaty of peace between the United States and Britain was signed and sealed.

Not surprisingly, the burden of facing the French minister fell to Franklin. On the next Tuesday, he presented himself at Versailles with copies of the treaty details, which Vergennes had already obtained. Nothing was said at the time, but later, when Franklin pressed him to commit to yet another loan that had been in the works, Vergennes gave him a gently worded letter of reproach. How could he assure his king that America and France were still allies? he asked artfully.

Franklin's equally cagey reply conceded that the complaint was "apparently just; that in not consulting you before they were signed we have been guilty of neglecting a point of *bienséance* [propriety]." He warned that the British might think they had separated the two friendly nations, but, he assured the minister, "this little misunderstanding will therefore be kept a secret and that they [Britain] will find themselves totally mistaken." In addition to charming Vergennes out of his temper, the letter served notice on Britain that America still clung to France despite the new treaty. A copy of the letter, obtained by Edward Bancroft, has been discovered in Shelburne's papers. Within a week, Franklin was able to inform Robert Morris that the first six hundred thousand livres of a six-million-livre loan had been received, with the balance to come in quarterly installments.

THE PACE OF EVENTS BECAME LESS HECTIC AFTER THAT. The final formal treaty with Britain was not signed until September 1783. In the meantime, France and Spain hurried through their own settlements. In 1784, Congress named Franklin, Adams, and Jefferson as commissioners to seek treaties with the rest of Europe. This was boilerplate diplomacy, and Franklin left the details to his lawyer colleagues. His recurring attacks of gravel in his urinary tract made him wonder if he would ever return to America alive. Numbers of French ladies—Anne-Louise Brillon and Anne-Catherine Helvétius chief among them—cheerfully offered him their homes for his retirement.

At the ceremonial treaty signings at Versailles, Franklin was singled out for honor, and at the lavish demonstrations that Paris organized to celebrate French victory over the hated English, he had crowns of laurel pressed upon his brow. Jay and Adams were honored too, but not so well. While Franklin clearly reveled in all the fêtes, in the eulogies, poems, and paintings that portrayed him as the man "who stole lightning from the skies and the scepter from tyrants," it came at a cost. He should have sensed the gathering strength of his critics in America. He had made urgent pleas to Congress to find some official position for his grandson Temple, who had served so faithfully as his secretary. But Adams communicated back to Philadelphia that he suspected Franklin of trying to win Temple the post of ambassador to France and thus enable the grandfather to retire there among his lady friends in luxury and position. Congress ignored Franklin's requests with the same brusqueness it had used earlier when Richard Bache, Franklin's son-in-law, was removed from the job he had held as postmaster general.

If Franklin appeared disengaged from events in Philadelphia now that the peace was won, it perhaps was because he occasionally toyed with staying in France for good, particularly as he began looking beyond politics. King Louis named him to a committee of scientists to investigate (and debunk) Anton Mesmer, whose hypnosis techniques had become a great fad in Paris for those who sought cures for disease. He was also inducted into more royal academies in Europe, and his old science colleagues resumed writing to him about the latest experiments.

While he did not have the energy to take up new electrical studies, he was fascinated by the first attempts at balloon flight by the Montgolfier brothers and other French experimenters. He attended several ascensions in Paris and wrote so enthusiastically about them to Joseph Banks of the Royal Society in London that in short order a British doctor managed to cross the English Channel in a balloon of his own devising. He carried with him a letter for Franklin—the first air mail. Franklin was so charmed that he published an epigram that had a skeptic asking him what was the use of these new balloons. "What use is a new-born baby?" he replied, and all Paris nodded at the wisdom.

Moreover, his circle of friends had widened once more to give him free access to his old comrades in the English Enlightenment. After Joseph Banks wrote a note of apology for the way Franklin had been treated during the war, the Royal Society through Lord Howe (and with the king's permission) sent him a copy of Captain James Cook's report on his second voyage to the Pacific. (During the hostilities, Franklin had ordered American vessels not to interfere with Cook.) Britain's establishment was quick to patch things up with Franklin, and he responded just as cordially. He secured for Joseph Priestley one of the scarce foreign memberships in the French Academy of Science. Prominent English political leaders made pilgrimages to Passy to see this hero of the Revolution, among them Pitt the Younger and William Wilberforce, who led the fight in England to stamp out the global slave trade.

As much as he loved France, however, Franklin also felt the pull of America. Adams had calmed down considerably since the treaties were rolling in from other nations, and especially since his wife, Abigail, had finally joined him. Soon he went off to London to be the first American ambassador to the Court of St. James, where George III received him with stiff formality. Jefferson arrived in 1784 to succeed John Jay and soon would succeed Franklin as ambassador to France. The Virginian openly admired the older man and never resented the effusive praise heaped on Franklin. The Articles of Confederation had been formally adopted in 1781, but Jefferson informed him that this new form of government was not working out the way Franklin and others had intended. Franklin had no doubt the government could be improved, and he was now eager to return.

There was a further lure about America. Polly Stevenson Hewson came to stay at Passy during Franklin's final winter there. Margaret Stevenson had died recently and Polly now had children that needed education and a better future than they could find in England. She could not be persuaded to stay long in France, but Franklin encouraged her to come and live with him in Phila-delphia. If he had to move again, he would set up yet another con-genial and affectionate family.

Finally, in May 1785, he received the long-awaited permission from Congress to come home. But Franklin was still very weak from his attacks of the gout and stones, and it was uncertain that he could stand the jolting carriage ride to the port of Havre, where his ship waited. Marie Antoinette sent one of her own litters—a carriage slung between two gentle Spanish mules—which could carry the still stone-ridden American in gentle rocking comfort. (King Louis sent a miniature of himself set with 408 diamonds.)

Sent ahead on government barges were 128 boxes of Franklin's papers and memorabilia. Franklin did not take everything; he gave his writing table, his chair, and even his magic hollow cane as souvenirs to friends, and they became instant holy relics.

When the time came to leave on July 12, Anne-Louise and Anne-Catherine wept together, and Jefferson reported, "When he left Passy it seemed as if the village had lost its patriarch." Franklin was now in his seventy-ninth year.

As it had so often, Franklin's health improved during the next ten days as towns along the way to the coast turned out to celebrate his arrival. On July 24, Franklin landed at Southampton, England, to change ships for the trip across the Atlantic, his eighth and last. Bishop Shipley and his family rushed for a reunion, and Jonathan Williams, his nephew, arrived to accompany his uncle home. Franklin waited, hoping that Polly Hewson would come on the voyage to Philadelphia. She hesitated a while longer, however.

There was one bit of sad business left. His son, William, had written to him in Passy to patch things up. William was fifty and still led the effort to win relief for the Loyalists who had been ruined, many of whom had fled to England. Franklin had sent Temple to visit his father for two months and fretted when the young man stayed on in London. If William had been trying to win his father's influence to the reparations cause, Franklin would have no part of it. Before leaving France he had bluntly stated his resentment in a reply to his son:

> I ... am glad to find that you desire to revive that affectionate intercourse that formerly existed between us. It will be very agreeable to me; indeed nothing has ever hurt me so much and affected me with such keen sensations as to find myself deserted in my old age by my only son and not only deserted, but to find him taking up arms against me in a cause wherein

my good fame, fortune, and life were all at stake. You conceived, you say, that your duty to your king and regard for your country required this. I ought not to blame you for differing in sentiment with me in public affairs. We are men, all subject to errors. Our opinions are not in our power; they are formed and governed much by circumstances that are often as inexplicable as they are irresistible. Your situation was such that few men would have censured your remaining neuter, though there are natural duties which precede political ones and cannot be extinguished by them. This is a disagreeable subject. I drop it.[2]

When they did meet in Southampton, the chill remained. William Franklin needed money and his father gave him some. In return, William had to give Temple his deeds to land in New Jersey and New York. William also was empowered to seek what money was owed Franklin in claims from the British government (which meant nothing), and the father deeded over his claims to land he had optioned years before in Nova Scotia (which also meant nothing). The rest was silence between them; they were too much alike to admit error or ask forgiveness.

WHEN THE PACKET FOR AMERICA FINALLY LEFT ENGLAND at the end of July, the remarkable Franklin resilience rebounded once more. In his view, he had been forcibly retired from public life and could now resume his scientific investigations. Once more he made the captain's life a plague of questions about the new ways of rigging sails. He wrote letters to scientific friends on everything from watertight compartments that would keep ships from sinking to paddlewheels that could augment sails. He dangled Jonathan Williams over the side, as he had both William and Temple, to take temperature readings of the Gulf Stream. It was the old encyclopedic Franklin. He even wrote a letter to his old fellow experimenter

Jan Ingenhousz in Vienna on some improvements he had devised for his old stove design.

On September 14, 1785, Franklin came ashore one last time at the Market Street dock and was carried amid a cheering throng to his house.

"Found my family well. God be praised and thanked for all His mercies," he wrote.

Franklin's great adventure was over.

Chapter 22

Home at Last

hen Franklin arrived home in September 1785, he found much had changed beyond recognition—his home city, his new nation, and his own political reputation.

Philadelphia rushed to honor its preeminent son. It still was the richest and largest city in America, but it had not been the seat of government (except for intermittent visits) since Congress had fled from British troops in December 1776. The lawmakers had been driven up and down the seaboard from Princeton to Annapolis, and as far west as York. In two months Congress was to begin its first session after independence in New York in another temporary home. This wandering was part of the problem Congress had conducting the war in anything resembling an efficient manner. The other part of the problem was the government Benjamin Franklin had helped design.

The Articles of Confederation were adopted in 1777, and ratified in 1781, but they provided no way for Congress to carry out its laws. Franklin by experience feared a strong central government, for he had seen in London how it could be corrupted by the rich and powerful. He favored the broadest possible franchise for the largest number of voters; he feared lawyers and the bureaucracy they create. Yet the system provided neither an executive nor a court system. Congress could do little more than adopt laws and then rely on the thirteen state governments to provide the material for the war effort. And now that peace had come, the shortcomings of the Articles had become even more apparent.

While America was still mostly rural (four to five people per square mile), the coming urban and industrial change could transform the country into the united empire Franklin had dreamed of, or tear it apart. Population was booming, because of the birth rate as well as immigration from a Europe faced with revolutionary upheaval of its own. From 1780 to 1790, America would gain one million new citizens, and by the end of the decade the total population would be 3.9 million. Franklin saw the settlement of his country push past the Appalachians and west to Cincinnati and Louisville. Inventors tinkered with steamboats on both the Delaware and Chesapeake. A year before Franklin died, English carpenter Samuel Slater memorized the plans for an English cotton mill and smuggled himself at great risk to Pawtucket, Rhode Island, where Quaker investors erected the first factory in America. American merchant ships were starting to trade as far away as China.

Franklin did not immediately involve himself in the debate over how to reorder the constitutional compact of these new, not-so-united states. He was seventy-nine, for one thing, and was plagued by his painful ailments. He stopped drinking wine and tried to resume exercising with dumbbells, but when the episodes became even more severe he turned to opium, which relieved the pain but left him weak and enervated. His home state of Pennsylvania snatched up what time he had. Within a month of his arrival he was elected to a three-year term on the state's three-man Executive Council and then to a one-year term as president (governor) of Pennsylvania; that term would be extended for two more years, until his formal retirement from office in the autumn of 1788.

Franklin's role in Pennsylvania's government was that of an avuncular adviser. He faithfully attended the Council meetings, which were held in the old State House room where the Declaration of Independence had been drafted nine years earlier. He was carried to the building in a chair and helped up the stairs by trusties from the city's prison. There he held forth with long reminiscences that illustrated whatever point he wanted to make. The Council members listened with affectionate tolerance until noon. Then Franklin would have himself hoisted homeward for his dinner, and the meeting would get down to business.

There was much business to do. Pennsylvania now pushed to the edges of Lake Erie and encompassed the headwaters of the Ohio River. The state had made parcels of land in the far west available (for a modest price) to those who had served in the Revolution. The land rush that followed had produced demands for new roads and dams, and for a greater say in political affairs for these westerners.

While Franklin was not actively involved in these policy discussions, he did take advantage of the government's land offer and acquired a tract northwest of Pittsburgh big enough to hold eleven large farms. He playfully offered to deed a thousand acres of the tract to Anne-Catherine Helvétius for an animal sanctuary if she would join him. He left this and other landholdings as part of his estate to Richard and Sally Bache. For Benjamin Franklin Bache (no longer little Benjy), the grandfather set up a printing business.

Franklin later published pamphlets so effusive in praise of France and things French that his enemies pointed to them as final proof that he had been wickedly seduced while in Paris.

THE SAD TRUTH WAS THAT WHILE THE PUBLIC venerated Franklin, many of his brothers-in-arms in the Revolution wanted nothing more than that he sit down and shut up. Younger men such as Alexander Hamilton had their own reputations to build and definite ideas about what kind of government this new experiment in democracy merited. George Washington treated him with cool affection that stopped short of true generosity. Washington's reserve toward Franklin was understandable. He had borne the battle under the most arduous conditions, not only fighting the British, the Hessians, and the Loyalists but also coping with a nearly paralyzed Congress and the plots of his own officers to replace him. He had won the battles and now would not hear of Franklin being congratulated for winning the war. Washington had enough rivals in politics; he would have none in honor. He was fair enough to recognize the older man's specific contributions, but there was something about the way foreigners fawned over Franklin that put him off. Even when installed as our first president, Washington ignored Franklin's pleas to restore Richard Bache to the post office and to find a job for Temple Franklin. Temple had taken possession of his father's farm in New Jersey but disliked the life and took to hanging about his grandfather's home. And while Congress heaped honors and thanks on others like Jay and Adams, it never voted any recognition of Franklin's nine years of service to the Revolution. In later years an audit of Franklin's Paris accounts showed that Congress owed him more than seven thousand livres, but Vice President John Adams and Senator Richard Henry Lee blocked any move to pay him.[1]

For the first time in his public life, Franklin no longer was the essential ingredient in the affairs of the moment. There were many questions at the core of the reorganization that Franklin had never considered during his nearly thirty years in America's service. The most immediate issue was what to do about the new country's staggering burden of debt. The cost of the American Revolution is estimated at $170 million, two-thirds of which was spent by the Continental Congress. Most of that outlay had come from debt certificates issued by the government.[2]

Led by Alexander Hamilton, the men who later would be known as Federalists favored turning the public debt into a monetized credit system like the one the British had with their Bank of England. Those from smaller and southern states feared a central bank that would take the first slice of import duties, which were the core of all government income in those days. That might leave the states without adequate funds for their own needs.[3] A large segment of the population (merchants, planters, and factory owners) feared paper money in general because it could lose value more quickly than precious metal. Franklin knew little of such matters. He favored a national bank because a state-chartered bank for Pennsylvania had worked well, and he believed that the more money in circulation, the more an economy would grow. If he thought about fiscal matters at all, he favored income taxes to keep too much wealth from the hands of the few.

Beyond the pressing points of the moment was a broader division of opinion on how government was to be designed. Many of the younger men like Madison, Hamilton, and James Monroe had studied Franklin's old Scots friend David Hume. It was Hume who taught that government should have delicate checks and balances against public men, whose self-interest so often turned to tyranny. Franklin knew full well that self-interest drove mankind both in public and private, but his solution was primitive—from the start, deny public officeholders the power that they could use to entrench themselves. Officeholders should not be paid, and their terms should be limited, their powers restricted. Yet the new national government must have more power to be effective.

After an early attempt to meet in Annapolis in 1786 fell apart, Congress finally called a special convention for the limited purpose of improving the Articles of Confederation. The delegates would convene in Philadelphia in May 1787 and would work outside the purview of Congress. Whatever was decided would have to be ratified by the state legislatures. Hamilton carefully worded the call so as not to alarm the states, which were wary of any attempt to give the national government more control. Patrick Henry of Virginia, among many others, "smelled a rat" and refused to be a delegate; later he would be an outspoken foe of the Constitution. Others saw the meeting as a talking shop where nothing could be accomplished.

Many of the original signers of the Declaration of Independence would not attend. Some were dead, others too old; Jefferson was in Paris; Adams in London. When the fifty-five delegates from twelve states* finally assembled in May, none of them envisioned that they would sweat for four months during a summer along the Delaware as hot and contentious as when the Declaration of Independence was drafted eleven years earlier.

IT ALL BEGAN PLEASANTLY ENOUGH. Once enough delegates trickled into town, Franklin hosted them to a lavish dinner in the new addition to his Market Street house. He had found the home Deborah had built too crowded with the Baches and six grandchildren, so he built a second structure that was connected by a cov-

---

* Rhode Island suspected a conspiracy against the smaller states and refused to send delegates.

ered walkway through his large and pleasant garden. In this second house he had two bedrooms, a dining room capable of hosting two dozen guests, and a huge library for his collection of three thousand books from around the world, the largest in America at the time. There he displayed his most recent inventions—a writing chair with a foot-operated fan, a mechanical arm to retrieve books from the top shelves, a press to copy letters, and the bifocal glasses he had invented in Passy. The mantels and shelves were adorned with busts of his famous European friends; there were also two portraits of himself, and an artist had put his likeness on the face of his hall clock.

Soon after the Constitutional Convention began deliberations on May 25, Franklin found his role reduced to that of conciliator between the strong- and weak-government factions. He had argued for a unicameral legislature and a plural executive branch; he had also stated that government officeholders should not be paid (his prescription against political abuse). But all of his ideas were voted down. He could not even get Temple Franklin chosen as secretary of the convention. He did, however, argue successfully to give Congress the power to override a presidential veto and to provide a mechanism for presidential impeachment through trial.

At the base of it, Franklin fit neither in the camp that favored the sovereignty of the states nor with those who wanted an overriding national government. He believed, because he thought it worked well in Pennsylvania, in a government that was broadly responsive to popular will while remaining strongly united. But he quickly saw that almost no one shared his view, so he set out to work for the necessary compromises.

The main sticking point from the start had been the question of representation in the new Congress: strict proportional representation gave dominant advantage to populous states like Virginia, Pennsylvania, and Massachusetts, but the current system of giving each state a single vote offered less populous states an equally unfair weight. Franklin did not favor the creation of a Senate because he saw it as a House of Lords for Americans bent on privilege, but he recognized the need to break the impasse. During a recess for the Fourth of July holiday, meeting with a small committee, Franklin proposed a compromise: a Senate in which all states would have equal representation, plus a House of Representatives apportioned by population. The House would have the sole right to draft money bills; the Senate could either pass or reject such bills—but not change them.

Although modified later by Roger Sherman and others, this was Benjamin Franklin's great contribution to the Constitution, even though it went against his beliefs. He argued before the full convention:

> When a broad table is to be made, and the edges of planks do not fit, the artist takes a little from both and makes a good joint. In like manner here both sides must part with some of their demands in order that they may join in some accommodating proposition.[4]

IN LATE JULY, FRANKLIN WAS OUT OF THE DEBATE altogether with urinary tract stones. When he returned to the fray in August, he had no better luck influencing the shape of the new government. He failed with a motion to limit the presidency to one term. He spoke out against a rule that would require officeholders to be property owners, and against a fourteen-year residency requirement for foreigners to become citizens, but still the wrangling went on. Tempers grew short. Some of Delaware's delegation at one point threatened to secede from the United States and seek alliance with a foreign power if its rights were trampled. No one was happy with the document that was taking shape. Those who had wanted a Bill of

Rights put in a prominent place in the Constitution sulked when they were overruled.

Moreover, the slavery question hung over the entire Constitutional Convention. It was intertwined with the questions of representation and of what kind of money system the nation would have. Slaves were both a form of money that could settle debts and also a source of labor necessary for cultivating the crops of the Deep South. By the time of the convention, all of the New England and Mid-Atlantic states, including Maryland and Virginia, had laws prohibiting the further importation of slaves. Massachusetts in its new constitution had effectively outlawed slavery altogether. Yet it was impossible to close the entire United States to the slave trade, let alone to emancipate the 740,000 slaves already here, because both Georgia and the two Carolinas were determined to drop out of the nation rather than allow their economies to be ruined by abolition. If they went, Virginia and Maryland might bolt too. In fairness, there was ambivalence throughout the thirteen states on the question. Many shipping families in New England still shipped slaves into the South even though they piously owned none themselves. Others felt the matter would resolve itself soon enough, believing that slavery was becoming uneconomical and would wither on its own.

The convention finessed this issue with an unsatisfactory agreement that made slaves equal to three-fifths of a free man for the purposes of setting a state's representation in the House (as well as for purposes of direct taxation). This reduced the power of the populous southern states in the House. In turn, the convention agreed to place a twenty-year moratorium on any effort to put a national ban on slave importation. States might do what they wanted in the meantime. In securing twenty years of peace on the subject, the framers of the Constitution brought no relief to those in bondage. Even after Congress outlawed the importation of

Africans in 1808, another 250,000 slaves were brought in illegally in the years up to 1860.

It is interesting to muse what the solution would have been if both Adams and Jefferson had been there with Franklin when the debate began. The question of slavery's legality might have turned out differently since both Adams and Franklin were fervent abolitionists. Jefferson in 1784 had sponsored a bill in Congress to ban the slave trade, but it failed by a narrow margin.

After the Revolution, the abolition movement in America had reorganized itself into the Society for Promoting the Abolition of the Slave Trade, and upon his return Franklin became its president and most vocal spokesman. The evolution of Franklin's attitude about black Americans had been slow, but it was a sincere transformation. He had owned slaves and traded in them, but later he saw captive labor as bad economics. For Franklin—and for most people of that time—the concept of race was far different from what it is for people today. In the eighteenth century, race referred to nationality, to the traits of other Western people. One spoke of the Irish race or the Spanish race as if the cultural differences were genetic. Non-European people, those of the Middle East, Asia, and Africa, were not considered races at all—barbarians, basically. Yet the Bray School in London, and the schools he helped start in America, gave Franklin his first insight into this flawed conception of race; he was amazed and stirred by the abundant talents shown by the young orphans. Still, only when he arrived in France did he come to recognize slavery's savagery. Leaders of the French Enlightenment considered the enslavement of Africans in its sugar colonies to be a human abomination because it contradicted their deep belief in the natural nobility of mankind. The Marquis de Condorcet, who was the secretary of the French Royal Academy of Science, had been among the founders of the *Société des Amis des Noirs* and spoke against slavery at every opportunity. Condorcet was one of the insiders in Franklin's intellectual circle at Passy and soon converted him to the view that the American Revolution's premise of all men being born equal was a sham if the slaves were not free.[5]

But despite his deep feelings on the subject, the Constitutional Convention's most eloquent denunciation of slavery came not from Franklin but from Virginia's George Mason. Franklin believed the convention's task was to push the new Constitution through to completion or risk the new nation's unraveling. On the matter of slavery, Franklin kept silent in the debate, and the majority gave way on the issue.

But even that concession was not enough to ensure that all the delegates would embrace the new Constitution. Some prominent men were outraged that the document offered too much democracy, while others thought there was not enough. Virginians George Mason and Edmund Randolph (who had proposed the first draft) and Elbridge Gerry of Massachusetts vowed never to sign the finished product, each for vastly different reasons.

September 17 was the day the delegates were to approve and sign the Constitution. Although it seemed a majority of the delegates favored the document, would all twelve states be represented? If a delegation hesitated or refused, the political momentum could be lost. Washington, who was the presiding officer, recognized Franklin to propose adopting the Constitution. Franklin was too weak to stand to deliver his remarks, so his old Philadelphia ally James Wilson read the speech for him. For Franklin, who did not excel in public speaking, it proved the most effective speech of his life. James Madison, who was the self-appointed stenographer of the debates, recorded Franklin's plea:

> I confess that there are several parts of this Constitution which I do not at present approve, but I am not sure I shall never

approve them; for, having lived long, I have experienced many instances of being obliged by better information or fuller consideration to change opinions, even on important subjects, which I once thought right but found to be otherwise. Most men, indeed, as well as most sects in religion think themselves in possession of all truth. . . . But though many private persons think almost as highly of their infallibility as that of their sect, few express it so naturally as a certain French lady who in dispute with her sister said: "I don't know how it happens, sister, but I meet with nobody but myself that's always in the right."

In these sentiments, Sir, I agree to this Constitution with all its faults, if they are such; because I think a general government necessary for us, and there is no form of government but what may be a blessing to the people if well administered; and believe farther that this is likely to be well administered for a course of years and can only end in despotism, as other forms have done before it, when the people shall become so corrupt as to need despotic government, being incapable of any other. I doubt too whether any other Convention we can obtain may be able to make a better Constitution. For when you assemble a number of men to have the advantage of their joint wisdom, you inevitably assemble with those men all their prejudices, their passions, their errors of opinion, their local interests, and their selfish views. From such an assembly can a perfect production be expected? It therefore astonishes me, Sir, to find this system approaching so near to perfection as it does. . . . Thus I consent, Sir, to this Constitution because I expect no better, and because I am not sure that it is not the best. The opinions I have had of its errors I sacrifice to the public good. I have never whispered a syllable of them abroad. Within these walls they were born, and here they shall die. . . .

On the whole, Sir, I cannot help expressing a wish that every member of the Convention who may still have objections to it would, with me, on this occasion doubt a little of his infallibility, and to make manifest our unanimity, put his name to this instrument.[6]

Of the forty-two men present in the room, only three refused to sign. James Madison reported that, while the signatures were being affixed, Franklin quietly observed to those members sitting near him that he had often looked at the sun painted on the back of the chair from which Washington had presided. He had not been able to tell whether it was a rising or a setting sun, he remarked. "But now at length I have the happiness to know that it is a rising and not a setting sun."[7]

IN THE NARROW TERMS OF HIS OWN POLITICAL STANDING, the new United States Constitution was a disaster for Franklin. The document reflected none of his major beliefs about government. He worried greatly that the Constitution would lead to the tyranny of larger states. And because he had compromised and led others to compromise, he found himself derided by old political allies. Worse, the young men whose cause he had helped dismissed his contribution.

It took eighteen months of violent demonstrations and intense pamphleteering before the Constitution was formally ratified by the required nine states. Franklin was uncharacteristically silent about politics. He took no part in the Pennsylvania convention that endorsed the new government. During the debate he wrote just one newspaper essay endorsing the series of essays penned by Madison, Hamilton, and Jay—known today as the Federalist Papers. No one asked him to take a seat in either the new House or the new Senate for the state he had served for sixty years.

He became more devoted to his ease, to his home, to his books and correspondence. He found that in his nine-year absence his real estate holdings had made him comfortably wealthy, and he allowed himself to enjoy his life without any remnant of Puritan restraint. Polly Hewson and her three children had finally followed him to Philadelphia in 1786 and settled near the Market Street house. He had the last of his little families about him. Sally Bache saw to his creature comforts, while Polly kept him company. His Bache grandchildren played cribbage with him, and Temple Franklin and Benjamin Bache were on call to undertake business errands.

In January 1788, Franklin tripped in his garden and fell heavily, spraining his wrist and arm. He confined himself more and more to Market Street, and the Executive Council obliged him by holding meetings in his dining room. There they revised the state's penal code, ending the penalties of whipping, branding, and hanging for scores of offenses.

Even as his health failed, he found humor in the descent. He frequently recalled a traditional drinking song in which an old man wishes for "a warm house in a country Town, an easy Horse, some good old authors, ingenious and cheerful Companions, a Pudding on Sundays, with stout Ale, and a Bottle of Burgundy, etc." The chorus goes, "May I govern my Passions with an absolute sway / Grow wiser and better as my Strength wears away, / Without Gout or Stone, by a gentle Decay."

He wrote self-mockingly to a friend:

> But what signifies our Wishing? Things happen, after all, as they will happen. I have sung that wishing Song a thousand times, when I was young, and now find, at Fourscore, that the three Contraries have befallen me, being subject to the Gout and the Stone, and not being yet Master of all my Passions. Like the proud Girl in my Country, who wished and resolv'd

not to marry a Parson, nor a Presbyterian, nor an Irishman; and at length found herself married to an Irish Presbyterian Parson.[8]

Now out of public life, Franklin continued to speak out on the issue that had been left unanswered in the Constitution—slavery. When the first U.S. Congress under the new Constitution convened in New York in February 1790, the Abolition Society presented a petition urging that it outlaw slavery at once. The demand provoked a firestorm of reaction among southerners, who charged that it broke the pledge to leave the issue alone for twenty years. If Congress took up the slavery question, let alone put it to a vote, the Constitution would collapse. Not surprisingly, Congress refused to deal with the petition. A Georgia congressman named James Jackson was particularly virulent in his accusations against Franklin.

Franklin was failing. Since the autumn of 1789 the effects of his opium dosages had ruined his appetite, and he lost an alarming amount of weight. Yet he had strength for one last hoax. On March 23, he published *Observations on the Slave Trade*, which dryly called Congressman Jackson's attention to the similarities of his remarks with those the Divan of Algiers supposedly made in 1687 in response to a petition from a religious sect to end his piracy and enslavement of Christian captives. In 1790, attacks by the Barbary Coast pirates threatened the merchant ships of the new republic, and Americans were outraged that their countrymen were made slaves when captured. In Franklin's hoax, the Algerian chief mimicked each of the congressman's arguments about slavery, including that Christians were happier and lived longer in the care of the Muslim masters and that the economy of Algiers would be devastated if the slaves were freed. The Franklin wit refused to die.

He was cheerful enough in these final weeks. Sally Bache had presented him with a new granddaughter, and he doted on her as he had on all his offspring. Jefferson came to the house on his way to New York to become President Washington's secretary of state. He received an affectionate welcome and was touched to be given a copy of Franklin's *Autobiography*. Others, the old allies who still survived and not a few curiosity seekers, dropped by for a last contact; he saw them all. When the pain was bad, Polly Hewson read to him. When he revived, as he did often, he would take up his pen again and finish just one more letter to some distant friend. Alarmed by the violent course the French Revolution was taking, he wrote letters of concern and encouragement to his dear friends in France. To Ezra Stiles, the president of Yale, he sent his testament of personal belief:

Here is my creed. I believe in one God, Creator of the universe. That he governs it by His providence. That He ought to be worshipped. That the most acceptable service we render Him is doing good to His other children. That the soul of man is immortal, and will be treated with justice in another life respecting its conduct in this. These I take to be the fundamental principles of all sound religion, and I regard them as you do in whatever sect I meet with them.

As to Jesus of Nazareth, my opinion of whom you particularly desire, I think the system of morals and his religion, as he left them to us, the best the world ever saw or is likely to see; but I apprehend it has received various corrupt changes, and I have, with most of the present Dissenters in England, some doubts about his divinity though it is a question I do not dogmatize upon, having never studied it, and think it needless to busy myself with it now, when I expect soon an opportunity of knowing the truth with less trouble....

I shall only add, respecting myself, that, having experienced the goodness of that Being in conducting me prosperously through a long life, I have no doubt of its continuance in the next, without the smallest conceit of meriting it. . . . I have ever let others enjoy their religious sentiments, without reflecting on them for those that appeared to me unsupportable and even absurd. All sects here, and we have a great variety, have experienced my good will in assisting them with subscriptions for building their new places of worship; and, as I never opposed any of their doctrines, I hope to go out of the world in peace with them all.[9]

It is a serene and tolerant creed, and so it should have been. Franklin was now eighty-four, but he had long ago become the man he wanted to be. While he continued to express concern about his many and varied "passions," the dominant feature of his personality was the iron control he had fashioned to govern himself. Indeed, it was this self-imposed discipline that irritated Franklin's enemies the most. They saw it as insincerity, whereas he saw their irascible tempers and plots as the ultimate in destructive indulgence. He had lived as long as his father and accomplished more than any man of his time. The only wish he voiced to friends was to live another fifty years to see the outcome of so many things he had set in motion.

On April 10, 1790, Franklin suffered a chest cold, which quickly turned into the pleurisy that had attacked the lining of his lungs fifty years before. There was a brief day of respite when he could breathe comfortably, and he rose from his bed to ask Sally to change the linen so, he said, he could die decently. When his daughter replied she was sure he would live many years longer, he quietly replied, "I hope not." When the infection filled his lungs again and he was urged to roll over on his side to make his breathing easier, he observed, "A dying man can do nothing easy."

Sally and Polly took turns keeping watch by the bedside as he finally slid into a coma. Temple and Benjamin stood by as well. At about eleven at night on April 17, Benjamin Franklin died.

Franklin would have found much laughter in the public observance and mourning that followed his passing. The funeral procession that carried his coffin to the plot in Christ Church's cemetery where Deborah and little Frankie lay included every member of every government body, a minister from every religious congregation, and members of every guild and fraternity from the Masons to the Philosophical Society. The cortège was a substantial fraction of the population of Philadelphia; the rest of the city looked on. In a supreme irony, his most passionate enemy, the ingrate parson William Smith, delivered the graveside eulogy. In New York, the House of Representatives voted unanimously, on James Madison's recommendation, to wear mourning for a month. But the Senate, where the Adams-Lee clique still reigned, refused to do the same, and Jefferson would later recall that President Washington coldly turned down his request that the executive department wear mourning.[10] In Paris, even though Franklin had warned against the excesses of the violence there, the Revolutionary Convention unanimously declared mourning for the American who was the friend of all France.

He rests in that quiet churchyard burial ground at Fifth and Arch Streets in downtown Philadelphia. His legacy touches all mankind.

Epilogue

hat then to make of this man, Benjamin Franklin?

Carl Van Doren, still after sixty years the preeminent Franklin biographer, called him "a harmonious human multitude."[1] A "multitude" he certainly was; any Franklin biographer must try to fit all the fragmentary—yet vitally significant—parts of his life into a single, coherent narrative. He often seems to have lived the life of more than one man.

But was this man "harmonious"? One has to doubt. The internal conflicts of Benjamin Franklin were what drove him to the heights he reached. He was born into a rigorous Puritan heritage but rejected it and ended up fashioning his own (equally demanding) code. He had a wide tolerance of other people's foibles, other faiths, and other political doctrines, and yet he could be coldly

unforgiving and Machiavellian. For good reason his critics suspected the bland exterior he adopted; his hot temper bubbled just
beneath the surface. He was generous but could be indifferent.
Throughout his life he thought of himself as the humble tradesman
he had been as a young man, and yet he reveled in the luxuries his
prominent status afforded him. His most famous literary character,
Poor Richard Saunders, issued rules and advice that he did not
much follow himself. He was a man of passion who stopped short,
often just short, of seeking true fulfillment and intimacy with any
of the many women whose love he coaxed.

The number of persons throughout the world who were deeply
and personally devoted to Franklin must be counted in the thousands, but his friendship could be costly. Although Congress finally
repaid the French government's loans in the decade after independence, the French merchants whose credit aided the Revolution in
its earliest moments suffered huge losses with only partial repayment. The excitable Beaumarchais and Franklin's landlord
Chaumont were bankrupted, and the Hôtel Valentinois had to be
sold. Franklin tried to get the resentful Congress to acknowledge
America's obligation to his old friends, but in these final years he
was far more committed to the antislavery campaign.

Franklin had other, more personal flaws. He was not much of a
husband to Deborah in the last decade of her life. Nor was he a wise
father. Sally and William Franklin, as well as grandsons Temple
Franklin and Benjamin Bache, were treated with material generosity, but Franklin's love for them was conditioned on their perform-
ing the tasks he demanded. All were raised to a state in life that
they were not prepared to sustain once he was gone. William died
in poverty in London, still clinging to the hope that a forgetful king
would redeem the Loyalist claims. Temple drifted most of his life
and also ended in London, where he published a poor edition of his
grandfather's papers. Benjamin Bache had drunk too deeply at the

wells of the violently egalitarian French Revolution and had a troubled career publishing tracts that reviled the growing power of the American merchant elite; he died at age twenty-nine during a fever epidemic. Sally and Richard Bache continued to live their days as improvident heirs of a celebrated name. Congress, after first balking in envy, finally allowed Sally to keep the miniature that Louis XVI had given Franklin. The Baches pried loose the 408 diamonds to finance a grand tour of Europe, then returned home to obscurity.

In part because of his flaws, Franklin had critics all his life. Some of his fellow Founding Fathers did not much mourn his passing,* though it must be noted that Jefferson and Madison always gave him credit for his achievements. To be sure, Franklin has more modern critics, ranging from Mark Twain, who found Poor Richard's injunctions restrictive, to D. H. Lawrence, who considered Franklin a sexual monster, to Cambridge historian J. H. Plumb, who judged Franklin's scientific accomplishments not to amount to much.[2] But one suspects that Twain was being humorously provocative; Lawrence was ill advised to denounce anyone's sexual habits; and Plumb presumably wrote his article without the aid of an electric light over his desk. To his credit, Franklin endured far worse calumny during his lifetime and laughed off all of it.

The question remains, however: How do we take the measure of Benjamin Franklin? After all, despite his critics, he was celebrated all over the Western world. When he was born in 1706, Franklin's world was still firmly rooted in the just-ended seventeenth century. At his death, America was on the march into a new century, the

---

* John Adams, for example, did not think to honor Franklin. Instead, he fretted that Franklin would forever overshadow the other Founders (not least Adams himself). Writing to Benjamin Rush, Adams said that the history of "our revolution" would be all lies. "The essence of the whole," he wrote, "will be that Dr. Franklin's electrical rod smote the earth and out sprung General Washington. That Franklin electrified him with his rod and thence forward these two conducted all the policy, negotiation, legislation, and war."

nineteenth. In his eighty-four-year life, he had a hand in much of that substantial progress.

Franklin remains an influence over American lives even as we approach the three-hundredth anniversary of his birth. The man and his work still touch our lives directly—be it through bifocals or stoves, learned societies or prestigious universities, firehouses, lending libraries, or post offices. But ingenious devices and civic improvements alone cannot account for his enduring legacy.

An easy descriptive word is "first." Benjamin Franklin accomplished so many firsts that he overloads imagination. He was America's first master of the communications technology that shaped the time, establishing himself as a literary genius famous throughout the colonies. He was also America's first world-class scientific wizard. More than twenty years before the American colonies declared independence, he was the first to put forward a plan to unite those colonies. He played a key role in developing this nation's first constitution, the Articles of Confederation, and he was one of only six men to sign both the Declaration of Independence and the Constitution. Late in his life, he became one of the first prominent spokesmen for the abolition movement.

But to concentrate on the firsts in his life is to get lost in the thicket of Franklin's accomplishments. It is also to miss the point. Although he took the lead in many important endeavors, one must not lose sight of the fact that there were other inventors in America before him, others who speculated and wondered. Others thought of liberty and unity as well. Indeed, America bubbled over with questing minds and political revolutionaries.

One also misses the point by going further and calling Franklin the archetype for the American people—the "first American," as a recent biographer has it. Franklin was not the first person to reflect the characteristics that we assign to ourselves as American. And while no one doubts his identification with his native land, it also must be noted that Franklin was a citizen of the world.³ He lived nearly one-third of his life—twenty-six years—abroad. One of the most traveled men of his day, he journeyed the length of the British Isles and visited France, Germany, and Holland—forty-two thousand miles in total. By one count, he spent five of his eighty-four years either on primitive roads or on transatlantic voyages.⁴

Although Franklin was ever an American by inclination, he built homes for himself both in England and France. Usually he was loath to leave those homes and come back across the ocean to where his responsibilities lay. He loved the potential of America but despised many of its character traits. He hated the pressure for conformity—in religion, custom, and thought. Instead of a mass standard of correct morality imposed from the top down, Franklin believed that one served God best by serving other people, in individual acts of goodness ("the most acceptable service we render Him is doing good to His other children"). In fact, it is in this image of Franklin going about his life, seeing ways to help others, that we find a key to each of the numerous contributions he made to mankind: each invention or discovery was an act of grace.

What is important about Benjamin Franklin is not that he was the first in any one field or other. Rather, it was that he was so critical a catalyst in setting ideas in motion; he usually was the essential ingredient that made change happen. Although in many cases he took the lead, often he was just as valuable working behind the scenes, sharing what he knew and urging others to join the cause. In an age of ornate oratory, Franklin generally kept quiet in debate. His two best skills were to plot strategy in private and to write documents for public purposes.

And the change Franklin effected often was dramatic. His twenty-year battle with the Penn family not only won important concessions for his home colony, it also showed colonial Americans that they could, successfully, challenge London's power elite. His struggle with King George and his grasping ministers gave Americans a sense of common identity separate from their English ties; he convinced his countrymen that theirs was a just cause. Franklin's diplomatic triumphs in Paris rescued the desperate Revolutionary War from likely defeat and set a vastly expanded new nation firmly on its own feet. True, we likely would have had a revolution even without Franklin—some sort of estrangement from Britain was inevitable—but his accomplishments hastened the break from the Mother Country and supplied the raw ingredients of the Revolution's success. He also gave the newborn United States a character (his character) that the rest of the world applauded. At each critical turning point in those early days of America's creation, Franklin could be found, pointing the way, urging, making things happen. He was the essential Founding Father.

Of course, the measure of Franklin's life can be found not just in what he accomplished but also in what he stood for. He counseled open dealing and fair bargains in public affairs. He did not put his faith in rigid doctrines. He believed in democracy, but at the same time he distrusted mobs and recognized that the young American nation needed leadership. He urged peaceful solutions wherever possible but was not afraid to fight. And once the fight was on, victory was the only outcome. Just as he believed there never was a good war, he was quick to make a generous peace once victory was secure. He was proud of his American birth but loved other cultures and nations.

While Benjamin Franklin might not be the marble model of what an American is, he serves well as a guide for what we hope to become.

Notes

Prologue

1   Carl Van Doren, *Benjamin Franklin* (New York: Penguin Books, 1991), 180–81. The first edition of this Pulitzer Prize–winning biography was by Viking Press in 1938. It remains the standard complete biography of Franklin to this day.

2   It is impossible to be certain about the purchasing power of money then against today's values. Food, clothing, and shelter took up vastly different portions of personal income; wages for tasks are correspondingly elusive; and the exchange rate between the currencies of major nations such as Britain, France, and Holland against sums available in the colonies vary wildly.

  Still, readers might find it convenient to use the estimate published in 2000 by the research service of Britain's House of Commons that a penny in 1760 had a similar purchasing power to a pound today. Since there were 240 old-style pennies in a pound and currency rates in the fall of 2001 put the U.S. dollar at 1.50 for each British pound, one can do the two calculations and get a rough idea of the sums cited in the narrative. So a typical colonial agent in London in those days would have approximately $72,000 in today's terms, except that such a sum would have purchased far more of the basic necessities and there were fewer luxuries. One suspects that at least part of the lavish funds provided Franklin for his mission were to be used to bribe government officials, although there is no record of such. Another note: during the years leading up to the Revolutionary War, colonial pounds, such as those issued by Pennsylvania, usually were valued at half a British pound sterling in America and at less than that in London.

Chapter 1: Traits and Prospects

1 Samuel Sewall, *Diary: Collections of the Massachusetts Historical Society*, 5th series, Vol. 6, 73. See also Sewall's *Letter Book* in the same collection.

2 J. A. Leo Lemay and P. M. Zall, eds., *The Autobiography of Benjamin Franklin* (New York: W. W. Norton Critical Editions, 1986), 7–8. Hereafter, *ABF*.

3 Ibid., 8.

4 Ibid., 11.

5 Lawrence C. Wroth, *The Colonial Printer* (Charlottesville, VA: The University of Virginia, Dominion Books, 1964), 12–15.

   The first press set up in the American colonies was in Cambridge, Massachusetts, in 1639, but its main purpose was the production of Bibles in Indian languages and other evangelistic literature. In 1690, six years before the first English provincial newspaper began, the *Boston Public Occurances Foreign and Domestick* was printed without a license and quickly suppressed. *The Boston News Letter* began regular publishing in 1704 and kept in business until 1776. Within five years, there were regularly circulating weekly newspapers in Massachusetts, Connecticut, New York, Pennsylvania, and Maryland. By the time Franklin sailed for London in 1757, presses were in operation from Portsmouth, New Hampshire, to Charleston, South Carolina.

6 Ibid., 155–62.

7 *ABF*, 10–11.

8 Ibid., 13–14.

9 Van Doren, *Benjamin Franklin*, 7–33. Also, Ronald W. Clark, *Benjamin Franklin: A Biography* (New York: Random House, 1983), 3–25; Esmond Wright, *Franklin of Philadelphia* (Cambridge: Belknap Press of Harvard University Press, 1986), 14–29.

10 Leonard Labaree, Barbara Oberg, Ellen Cohn, et al., eds., *The Papers of Benjamin Franklin* (New Haven: Yale University Press, 1959), Vol. 8, 46. Hereafter, *Papers.*

11 *ABF*, 23–28.

12 J. A. Leo Lemay, *Benjamin Franklin Website* (University of Delaware, 1999) www.english.udel.edu/lemay/franklin (a wonderful work in progress). Hereafter, *Website.*

13 *ABF*, 32.

Chapter 2: Hope and Glory

1 Stephen Inwood, *A History of London* (London: Macmillan Publishers, 1998), 293–96.

2 Ibid., 315–57. Also, Liza Picard, *Restoration London* (New York: Avon Books, 1997), 3–16; Liza Picard, *Dr. Johnson's London* (London: Weidenfeld & Nicolson, 2000), 1–18.

3 *ABF*, 33.

4 Ibid., 33.

5 Ibid., 36.

6 Ibid., 34. Also, Van Doren, *Benjamin Franklin*, 48–51; Clark, *Benjamin Franklin*, 27–29.

7 *Papers*, Vol. 3, 54.

8 Van Doren, *Benjamin Franklin*, 90–91. "Franklin was not all mind and will. There was also his warm, indocile flesh.... Strongly built, rounded like a swimmer or a wrestler, not angular like a runner, he was five feet nine or ten inches tall, with a large head and square, deft hands. His hair was blond or light brown, his eyes grey, full, and steady, his mouth wide and humorous with a pointed upper lip.... Though he and others say he was hesitant in speech, he was prompt in action."

9 Albert Henry Smyth, ed., *The Writings of Benjamin Franklin* (New York: Macmillan, 1905–7), Vol. 2, 53–86. Hereafter, *Writings*. Also, *Papers*, Vol. 1, 72–79.

10 Jared Sparks, ed., *The Works of Benjamin Franklin* (Boston: Tappan & Whittemore, 1836–40), Vol. 1, 104–5. Also, *Papers*, Vol. 1, 72–79.

Chapter 3: The Pursuit of Virtue

1 *ABF*, 41. Also, *Website*, 1726, 1.

2 Samuel Eliot Morison, *Builders of the Bay Colony* (Boston: Houghton Mifflin, 1958), 37. "The simplest way to describe the populating of

colonial Pennsylvania is to picture a stake driven into the ground at the waterfront of Philadelphia. A 25-mile radius from this peg would encompass the area of Pennsylvania settled mainly by English immigrants between 1680 and 1710. Extend the radius to the length of 75 miles, and the outer 50 miles of the circle would correspond roughly to the 'Dutch' country.... Here, from 1710 to 1750, the German-speaking immigrants to colonial Pennsylvania made their homes. Again extend the radius to 150 miles, and in the outermost circumference, corresponding roughly to the arc of the Allegheny Mountains and valleys, the Scotch-Irish settled from 1717 to the Revolutionary War."

3   Carl and Jessica Bridenbaugh, *Rebels and Gentlemen: Philadelphia in the Age of Franklin* (New York: Reynal and Hitchcock, 1942), 10.

4   E. Digby Baltzell, *Puritan Boston and Quaker Philadelphia* (New York: The Free Press, 1979), 166.

5   *ABF*, 41.

6   Ibid., 45.

7   Ibid., 43–44. Also, Wroth, *The Colonial Printer*, 97; Wroth credits Franklin with making the first type in America.

8   *Papers*, Vol. 3, 101. Also, Van Doren, *Benjamin Franklin*, 80–83.

9   *ABF*, 66.

10 Kerry S. Walters, *Benjamin Franklin and His Gods* (Urbana: University of Illinois Press, 1999), 76.

11 *Papers*, Vol. 1, 101.

12 *ABF*, 71.

13 Ibid., 56.

Chapter 4: Rising Citizen

1   *Website*, 1736, 1.

2   Francis Jennings, *Benjamin Franklin, Politician* (New York: W. W. Norton, 1996), 32.

3   *Website*, 1737, 3.

4   Ibid., 1731, 4.

5   Jennings, *Benjamin Franklin, Politician*, 49–58.

Chapter 5: The Eminent Mr. Franklin

1   *Website*, 1744, 1.

2   Edward M. Hallowell and John J. Ratey, *Driven to Distraction* (New York: Pantheon Books, 1994), 192.

3   *ABF*, 130–31.

4   *Writings*, Vol. 2, 324–25. Franklin wrote, "Were I a Roman Catholic, perhaps I should on this occasion vow to build a chapel to some saint; but as I am not, if I were to vow at all, it should be to build a lighthouse."

5   Ibid., Vol. 3, 118–19.

6   Van Doren, *Benjamin Franklin*, 156–57. Also, I. Bernard Cohen, *Benjamin Franklin's Science* (Cambridge: Harvard University Press, 1990), 51–60; I. Bernard Cohen, *Science and the Founding Fathers* (New York: W. W. Norton & Co., 1995), 110–17.

7   Cohen, *Benjamin Franklin's Science*, 26–27.

8   Ibid., 26–27.

9   Van Doren, *Benjamin Franklin*, 161–62.

10 I. Bernard Cohen, *The Two Hundredth Anniversary of Benjamin Franklin's Two Lightning Experiments and the Introduction of the Lightning Rod* (Philadelphia: Proceedings of the American Philosophical Society, June 1952), Vol. 96, No. 3, 331–66.

11 Ibid., 336. Also, Van Doren, *Benjamin Franklin*, 164.

12 Van Doren, *Benjamin Franklin*, 138.

13 *Writings*, Vol. 3, 336–53. Also, *Papers*, Vol. 3, 184–204.

Chapter 6: Join or Die

1   *Writings*, Vol. 3, 63–73. Also, *Papers*, Vol. 4, 225–34.

2   Jon Butler, *Becoming America* (Cambridge: Harvard University Press, 2000), 9–11, 30–36.

3   *Writings*, Vol. 3, 72–73. Also, *Papers*, Vol. 4, 225–34.

4   *Website*, 1738, 21. On June 15, the *Pennsylvania Gazette* advertised, "To be SOLD for her Passage, A LIKELY young Woman, well cloathed, can sew and do Houshold Work. Term as Time as you can agree with her. N.B. Her Passage is 8 pounds. Also a Breeding Negro Woman about 20 Years of Age, can do any Houshold Work. Enquire of the Printer hereof."

5   Van Doren, *Benjamin Franklin*, 128–29.

6   *Website*, 1754, 1.

7   Van Doren, *Benjamin Franklin*, 222.

8   See "Plan for Settling Two Western Colonies in North America," *Writings*, Vol. 3, 358–66. Also, *Papers*, Vol. 5, 345, 367.

9   Leonard W. Labaree and Whitfield J. Bell Jr., "Franklin and the 'Wagon Affair,' 1755," *Proceedings of the American Philosophical Society*, December 1957, Vol. 101, No. 6, 551–58.

10 Jennings, *Benjamin Franklin, Politician*, 98.

Chapter 7: First Blood

1   ABF, 142–43.
2   Papers, Vol. 7, 243.
3   Ibid., 294. Lemay, in his footnote on page 142 of his edition of the Autobiography, notes that "BF seems actually to have stayed with Peter Collinson his first night (July 26) in London, then at the Bear Inn for three nights (July 27–29), and beginning on July 30, with Mrs. Margaret Stevenson at No. 7 Craven Street."
4   Ibid., 296.
5   ABF, 143–44. Emphasis added.
6   Papers, Vol. 7, 247–52.
7   Ibid., Vol. 8, 100.
8   Ibid., Vol. 7, 110–11.
9   Ibid., Vol. 5, 255–63.
10 Sparks, Works, Vol. 3, 529–30. Also, Van Doren, Benjamin Franklin, 286.
11 Van Doren, Benjamin Franklin, 274. Also, Papers, Vol. 8, 129.
12 Van Doren, Benjamin Franklin, 285.
13 Ibid., 285. Also, Writings, Vol. 4, 195.
14 Papers, Vol. 5, 278.
15 Ibid., 286. Also, Bernard Fay, Franklin: The Apostle of Modern Times (Boston: Little, Brown & Co., 1929), 289, 528.

Chapter 8: A New Nemesis

1   Writings, Vol. 3, 265. Also, Papers, Vol. 6, 86.
2   Writings, Vol. 3, 278. Also, Papers, Vol. 6, 171.
3   Papers, Vol. 3, 479.
4   Writings, Vol. 4, 376.
5   Dictionary of National Biography (Oxford: Oxford University Press, 1997).
6   "The Interests of Great Britain Considered with Regard to Her Colonies and the Acquisitions of Canada and Guadeloupe," Papers, Vol. 9, 47–110. Also, David T. Morgan, The Devious Dr. Franklin, Colonial Agent: Benjamin Franklin's Years in London (Macon: Mercer University Press, 1996), 48–50.
7   Papers, Vol. 9, 47–110.

Chapter 9: Degrees and Separation

1   D. G. C. Allan, *"Dear and Serviceable to Each Other": Benjamin Franklin and the Royal Society of Arts* (Philadelphia: Proceedings of the American Philosophical Society, September 2000), Vol. 144, No. 3, 244–50.

2   *Papers*, Vol. 5, 372–402. Also, Morgan, *The Devious Dr. Franklin, Colonial Agent*, 60–63.

3   James Hutson, *Pennsylvania Politics, 1746–1770* (Princeton: Princeton University Press, 1972), 144–47.

Chapter 10: Rejection and Return

1   *Papers*, Vol. 10, 160–61. Also, Van Doren, *Benjamin Franklin*, 301.

2   *Papers*, Vol. 10, 400–401. Also, Morgan, *The Devious Dr. Franklin, Colonial Agent*, 77.

3   *Papers*, Vol. 11, 72, 77, 103–104.

4   Ibid., 103–104.

5   Ibid., 153–73. Also, Historical Society of Pennsylvania, Penn Papers, May 5, 1764.

6   *Papers*, Vol. 11, 380–84. Also, Robert Middlekauff, *Benjamin Franklin and His Enemies* (Berkeley: University of California Press, 1996), 97.

7   James Trager, *The People's Chronology* (New York: Henry Holt, 1994).

8   Ibid.

9   *Papers*, Vol. 11, 180–83.

10   Ibid., 145–47.

Chapter 11: Back to London

1   *Papers*, Vol. 7, 295–98.

2   For Franklin's correspondence with Catherine Ray Greene, see *Papers*, Vol. 5, 502–4, 535–37; Vol. 6, 225. For articles on Franklin and women of the eighteenth century, see Larry E. Tise, ed., *Benjamin Franklin and Women* (University Park, PA: Pennsylvania State University Press, 2000). For more about Franklin's relationships with women, see Claude-Anne Lopez and Eugenia W. Herbert, *The Private Franklin: The Man and His Family* (New York: W. W. Norton, 1975), 78–80; Claude-Anne Lopez, *My Life with Benjamin Franklin* (New Haven: Yale University Press, 2000); and Claude-Anne Lopez, *Mon Cher Papa: Franklin and the Ladies of Paris* (New Haven: Yale University Press, 1990).

3   Van Doren, *Benjamin Franklin*, 235–36.

4   Claude-Anne Lopez, "Three Women, Three Styles," in Tise, *Benjamin Franklin and Women*, 53.

5   Van Doren, *Benjamin Franklin*, 242.

Chapter 12: Countdown to Revolution

1   *Papers*, Vol. 10, 371–72. Also, Morgan, *The Devious Dr. Franklin, Colonial Agent*, 96.

2   Samuel Fallows, *Samuel Adams* (Milwaukee: H. G. Campbell, 1903), 43.

3   Van Doren, *Benjamin Franklin*, 332.

4   "Pitt's Speech on the Stamp Act," *The American Revolution—an HTML Project* (University of Groningen (Netherlands), 1999) http://odur.let.rug.nl/ ~ usa/LIT/Franklin.htm. A good new website of basic source documents.

5   Van Doren, *Benjamin Franklin*, 336–52. Also, Verner W. Crane, *Benjamin Franklin and a Rising People* (Boston: Little, Brown & Co., 1954), 118–21.

6   Van Doren, *Benjamin Franklin*, 354–55.

7   *Website*, 1766–69.

8   Van Doren, 381. See also, *Writings*, Vol. 5, 133.

Chapter 13: The Death of a Dream

1   Crane, *Benjamin Franklin and a Rising People*, 155.

2   Wroth, *The Colonial Printer*, 233.

3   *Papers*, Vol. 18, 120–27. Also, Van Doren, *Benjamin Franklin*, 387–88.

4   Van Doren, *Benjamin Franklin*, 387. The emphasis is Franklin's.

5   Ibid.

6   Ibid., 390.

7   Ibid., 418.

8   *Website*, 1772.

9   Fay, *Franklin*, 342–44.

10   *Papers*, Vol. 20, 120–34.

11   Sir Francis Dashwood, *The Dashwoods of West Wycombe* (London: Arum Press, 1987). Also, Geoffrey Ashe, *The Hell-Fire Clubs* (Phoenix Mill: Sutton Publishing, 2000). Also, Ronald Fuller, *Hell-Fire Francis* (London: Chatto & Windus, 1939).

12   Whitfield J. Bell, *Benjamin Franklin at West Wycombe Park,* a paper before the American Philosophical Society, 1977.

13   *Papers*, Vol. 20, 388–90.
14   Ibid., 414–18.
15   Ibid., 436–39.

Chapter 14: To the Brink of War

1   B. D. Bargar, *Lord Dartmouth and the American Revolution* (Columbia: University of South Carolina Press, 1965).
2   Bernard Bailyn, *The Ordeal of Thomas Hutchinson* (Cambridge: Harvard University Press, 1974).
3   To Thomas Cushing, June 10, 1771. From a collection of Franklin letters on file at the Public Records Office, Kew, England, Colonial Office File 5, Volume 118, No. 29.
4   Ibid.
5   Fay, *Franklin*, 359–72. Also, Van Doren, *Benjamin Franklin*, 458–61. In 1781, Temple wrote to Franklin claiming to have been the source of the letters and asking for an acknowledgment to take to America as a reference. Franklin never responded.
6   Fay, *Franklin*, 363.
7   *Papers*, Vol. 21, 37–70. Also, Fay, *Franklin*, 366, and Van Doren, *Benjamin Franklin*, 470.
8   *Papers*, Vol. 21, 37–70.
9   Van Doren, *Benjamin Franklin*, 474.
10   Henri Doniol, *Histoire de la Participation de la France à l'Etablissement des Etats-Unis d'Amérique*, 5 Volumes (Paris: Imprimerie Nationale, 1886–92).
11   Helen Augur, *The Secret War of Independence* (New York: Duell, Sloan & Pearce, 1955).

Chapter 15: Revolution

1   Robin May and Gerry Embleton, *The British Army in North America 1775–1783* (London: Osprey, 1997), 5.
2   Mark M. Boatner III, ed., *Encyclopedia of the American Revolution* (Mechanicsburg, PA: Stackpole Books, 1994), 929–30.
3   Albert E. Bergh, ed., *The Writings of Thomas Jefferson* (Washington, D.C.: Thomas Jefferson Memorial Association of the United States, 1905), Vol. 1, 84.
4   *Papers*, Vol. 22, 91–93. Also, *Writings*, Vol. 6, 409.
5   *Papers*, Vol. 22, 217–18.

6   Thomas Jefferson, *The Jefferson Bible* (Boston: Beacon Press, 1989).

7   Boatner, *Encyclopedia of the American Revolution*, 245. The first price paid to the Duke of Brunswick per man was seven pounds four shillings and four and a half pence for the first year of service and an additional seventeen and a half shillings each year thereafter. Other provinces held out for more money and the total cost exceeded £4,584,450 for the eight years of the war. Of the nearly 30,000 troops finally leased, 7,754 died in America and another 5,000 deserted—a loss rate of more than 40 percent. The Hessians won no major contests with American Continental regulars.

8   Philip S. Foner, ed., *The Complete Writings of Thomas Paine* (New York: The Citadel Press, 1945), 45.

Chapter 16: Declaring for Liberty

1   Boatner, *Encyclopedia of the American Revolution*, 173–75.

2   Pauline Maier, *American Scripture: Making the Declaration of Independence* (New York: Knopf, 1997), 143–48.

3   Ibid. Also, Pauline Maier, *From Resistance to Revolution: Colonial Radicals and the Development of American Opposition to Britain, 1765–1776* (New York: Knopf, 1972), Chapters 7–8.

4   Maier, *American Scripture*, 104.

5   Ibid., 143–50.

6   Van Doren, *Benjamin Franklin*, 555–56.

7   Ibid.

Chapter 17: The Diplomacy of War

1   Augur, *The Secret War of Independence*, 118–19.

2   David Schoenbrun, *Triumph in Paris* (New York: Harper & Row, 1976), 64–65.

3   Ibid., 72.

4   Doniol, *Histoire de la Participation de la France à l'Etablissement des Etats-Unis d'Amérique*, Vol. 2, 114–15. Also, Gerald Stourzh, *Benjamin Franklin and Foreign Policy* (Chicago: University of Chicago Press, 1954), 136–37. Also, Schoenbrun, *Triumph in Paris*, 78–79.

5   Ibid.

6   Ibid., 81.

Chapter 18: Winning Recognition

1 Schoenbrun, *Triumph in Paris*, 78–80.

2 B. F. Stevens, *Facsimiles of Manuscripts in European Archives Relating to America, 1773–1783*, 25 Vols. (London: 1889–98). A letter in the handwriting of Paul Vardill to Eden detailing the relationships of the various residents of the Hôtel d'Hambourg and assessments of their character and politics, Vol. 5, No. 242.

3 Ibid., Vol. 2, No. 235. A Paul Wentworth letter, dated December 1776, described "Dr. Edwards" as a spy and detailed what Eden wanted to know about Franklin and Deane's activities in Europe: "the progress of the Treaty with France...the Assistance expected...the same with Spain...their agents...their correspondence with the Congress... ships commissioned to carry war materials and dates of sailing."

4 Cecil B. Currey, *Code Number 72: Ben Franklin, Patriot or Spy?* (Englewood Cliffs, NJ: Prentice-Hall, 1972). Also, Richard Deacon, *A History of the British Secret Service* (New York: Taplinger, 1969). Note: Deacon is the pen name of British intelligence writer Donald McCormick, who is the author, in his own name, of *The Hell-Fire Club* (London: Jerrold's, 1958). As part of his proof that Franklin was recruited, Deacon in *History* asserts that the Dashwood "monks" were part of the secret service. But as McCormick he does not claim that Franklin was a British agent, nor do any other of the books on West Wycombe.

5 Allen W. Dulles, *The Craft of Intelligence* (New York: Harper & Row, 1963), 34–36. Also, George J. K. O'Toole, "Benjamin Franklin: American Spymaster or British Mole?" *International Journal of Intelligence and Counterintelligence*, Spring 1989, Vol. 3, No. 1, 45–54. O'Toole judges the "mole" charges to be "absurd." Also, Louise Atherton, *A Brief History of British Intelligence Gathering and Its Organization* (Kew: British Public Records Office, 2001), 5–11.

6 Stevens, *Facsimiles of Manuscripts in European Archives Relating to America, 1773–1783*, Vol. 5, No. 249.

7 Van Doren, *Benjamin Franklin*, 572–73.

8 Wentworth to Eden. British Public Records Office, Kew, Colonial Office file 280. Also, *Papers*, Vol. 25, 435–40.

Chapter 19: Dismal Days

1 Allen Johnson, ed., *Dictionary of American Biography* (New York: Chas. Scribners Sons, 1929), 173–74. Deane's papers have been published by the New York Historical Society.

2   *Papers*, Vol. 26, 222–23. Also, Van Doren, *Benjamin Franklin*, 598.

3   Stourzh, *Benjamin Franklin and Foreign Policy*, 157.

4   Ibid., 161. Also, *Papers*, Vol. 33, 357.

5   Wright, *Franklin of Philadelphia*, 268–69.

6   Schoenbrun, *Triumph in Paris*, 219–30, 287–88. Also, Samuel Flagg Bemis, *The Diplomacy of the American Revolution* (Bloomington: Indiana University Press, 1957), 239–64. In addition, I am particularly indebted to Dr. Ellen Cohn of Yale for her guidance on this topic.

7   John Adams, *The Works of John Adams* (Boston: Little, Brown & Co., 1850–56), Vol. 2 (of 10), 73–77. Also, Page Smith, *John Adams* (Garden City: Doubleday & Co., 1962), 382.

Chapter 20: The Final Round

1   Van Doren, *Benjamin Franklin*, 621.

2   John Ferling, *Setting the World Ablaze* (New York: Oxford University Press, 2000), 239–40.

3   Van Doren, *Benjamin Franklin*, 639–40.

4   L. H. Butterfield, ed., *The Diary and Autobiography of John Adams* (Cambridge: Harvard University Press, 1961), Vol. 4, 46.

5   Lopez, *Mon Cher Papa*, 32.

6   Charles Francis Adams, *Letters of Mrs. Adams, the Wife of John Adams* (Boston: Charles C. Little and James Brown, 1841), 3rd edition, Vol. 2, 55–56.

7   Lopez, *Mon Cher Papa*, 266–67.

Chapter 21: The Struggle for Peace

1   *Papers*, Vol. 35, lxiv.

2   Van Doren, *Benjamin Franklin*, 718.

Chapter 22: Home at Last

1   Van Doren, *Benjamin Franklin*, 764–65.

2   Boatner, *Encyclopedia of the American Revolution*, 366.

3   Forrest McDonald, *Novus Ordo Seclorum* (Lawrence: University of Kansas Press, 1985), 187–90.

4   Carl Van Doren, *The Great Rehearsal* (New York: Viking Press, 1948), 103–4. Also, Van Doren, *Benjamin Franklin*, 748–50; Fred Rodell, *55 Men:*

The Story of the Constitution (Harrisburg, PA: Stackpole Books, 1983), 87–107.

5   Lopez, *My Life with Benjamin Franklin*, 196–205.

6   Van Doren, *Benjamin Franklin*, 753–54.

7   Rodell, *55 Men*, 194.

8   Wright, *Franklin of Philadelphia*, 345–46.

9   Van Doren, *Benjamin Franklin*, 777–78.

10 Ibid., 764–65.

Epilogue

1   Van Doren, *Franklin*, 782.

2   Mark Twain, *The Writings of Mark Twain* (Hartford: American Publishing Co., 1899–1907), Vol. 19, 211–15. Also, D. H. Lawrence, *Studies in Classical American Literature* (New York: T. Seltzer, 1923), 13–31. "Middle-sized, sturdy, snuff-colored Doctor Franklin, one of the soundest citizens that every tried or used venery." Also, J. H. Plumb, "Ravaged by Common Sense," *New York Review of Books*, Vol. XX, No. 6, April 19, 1973, 4–8. "[Franklin] changed neither politics nor science in any fundamental sense."

3   J. A. Leo Lemay, ed., *The Oldest Revolutionary: Essays on Benjamin Franklin* (Philadelphia: University of Pennsylvania Press, 1976), ix–x.

4   Percy G. Adams, "Benjamin Franklin and the Travel-Writing Tradition," in Lemay, *The Oldest Revolutionary*, 33–50.

Bibliography

$\mathcal{B}$enjamin Franklin died on April 17, 1790, and within two weeks the first serialization of a biography of his life began to appear in a monthly periodical, *The Universal Asylum and Columbian Magazine.* A rival, *The American Museum,* entered the fray a month later, and the flood of Franklin history has continued unchecked ever since. So the problem for anyone who wants to learn about Franklin is to avoid being overwhelmed by the mass of material that overhangs the topic and the man.

Undaunted readers who want to pursue their own study of the man and his times should first turn to Carl Van Doren's biography, *Benjamin Franklin,* which won the Pulitzer Prize in 1938 and which remains the most complete cradle-to-the-grave chronology of his life.

Of all the versions of Franklin's *Autobiography,* the best is a Norton Critical Edition paperback issued in 1986 and edited by the current dean of Franklin scholars, J. A. Leo Lemay. It contains a wealth of background information and criticism by other leading scholars. Other books the author found useful are listed in the bibliography below.

Archival Sources

Those interested in more specific study should turn to *The Papers of Benjamin Franklin*, an ongoing collection and annotation of Franklin's private and public correspondence being done by Yale University. The project began in 1959 and has reached Volume 35—the middle of the 1780s—as of this writing.

The Library of Congress has its own large collection of Franklin papers, and of course it is a repository of writings about, and pictures of, him. Similar archival work on other Founding Fathers that cross-references with Franklin can be found at many universities. Most notably, George Washington's papers are at the University of Virginia, John Adams's papers are at Harvard University, Thomas Jefferson's papers are at Princeton University, and Alexander Hamilton's papers are at Columbia University. The American Philosophical Society in Philadelphia has a trove of documents and memorabilia devoted to its founder. So, too, do the Franklin Institute and the Friends of Franklin, both in Philadelphia. The latter is a membership group of those fascinated with Franklin's life, and its newsletter contains articles by leading historians. The staffs of these organizations are cordial and helpful to anyone who seeks them out.

Foreign Sources

The new British Library in London contains all of the manuscripts and books that once were housed at the British Museum, as well as its own vast holdings—thirty-two million volumes in all. Most notably one can find two collections that are indispensable: *Facsimiles of Manuscripts in European Archives Relating to America, 1773–1783*, 25 Volumes, 1889–1898; and *Introduction to the Catalogue Index of Manuscripts in the Archives of England, France, Holland, and Spain Relating to America, 1763 to 1783*, London, 1902. Both were compiled by B. F. Stevens. Some U.S. libraries have sadly incomplete collections of these remarkable reproductions of original material. The Public Record Office at Kew has files from both the Foreign and Colonial offices of the time. The London Library is a subscription library that houses a fine collection of history books on a range of topics, including many older American volumes no longer available at home.

In France, a range of original documents can be found in the *Archives du Ministère des Affaires Etrangères*, the *Bibliothèque du Ministère de la Marine*, the *Bibliothèque Nationale*, and the *Archive Nationale*. A reader should refer first to the various B. F. Stevens reproductions for guidance to official sources and private collections in both countries.

Published Sources

Two dated, but nonetheless useful, resources are worth examining. Albert Henry Smyth's *The Writings of Benjamin Franklin,* in ten volumes, 1905–7, predates the compilation undertaken by Yale but is complete through 1790. It has a good summary biography and time line.

Henri Doniol's *Histoire de la Participation de la France à l'Etablissement des Etats-Unis d'Amérique,* in five volumes, 1886–92, is an excellent chronology of Franklin's time in Paris and a guide to the main characters of that episode.

Anderson, Fred. *Crucible of War.* New York: Alfred A. Knopf, 2000.

Anderson, Troyer Steele. *The Command of the Howe Brothers.* New York: Octagon Books, 1972.

Augur, Helen. *The Secret War of Independence.* New York: Duell, Sloan & Pearce, 1955.

Bailyn, Bernard. *Faces of Revolution.* New York: Random House, 1992.

———. *The Ideological Origins of the American Revolution.* Cambridge: Harvard University Press, 1967.

———. *The Ordeal of Thomas Hutchinson.* Cambridge: Harvard University Press, 1974.

Becker, Carl L. *The Declaration of Independence.* New York: Vintage Books, 1970.

Bemis, Samuel Flagg. *The Diplomacy of the American Revolution.* Bloomington: Indiana University Press, 1957.

Bober, Natalie S. *Abigail Adams.* New York: Aladdin Books, 1995.

———. *Thomas Jefferson.* New York: Aladdin Books, 1997.

Butterfield, Herbert. *George III and the Historians.* New York: Macmillan Co., 1959.

Cappon, Lester J. *The Adams-Jefferson Letters.* Chapel Hill: University of North Carolina Press, 1959.

Cohen, I. Bernard. *Benjamin Franklin's Science.* Cambridge: Harvard University Press, 1990.

———. *Science and the Founding Fathers.* New York: W. W. Norton, 1995.

Crane, Verner W. *Benjamin Franklin and a Rising People.* Boston: Little, Brown & Co., 1954.

Currey, Cecil B. *Code Number 72: Ben Franklin, Patriot or Spy?* Englewood Cliffs, NJ: Prentice-Hall, 1972.

———. *Road to Revolution.* Garden City, NY: Anchor Books, 1968.

Ellis, Joseph J. *Founding Brothers.* New York: Alfred A. Knopf, 2000.

———. *Passionate Sage.* New York: W. W. Norton, 1994.

Fallows, Samuel. *Samuel Adams*. Milwaukee: H. G. Campbell, 1903.

Fay, Bernard. *Franklin: The Apostle of Modern Times*. Boston: Little, Brown & Co., 1929.

———. *The Two Franklins*. Boston: Little, Brown & Co., 1933.

Greenway, John. *The Inevitable Americans*. New York: Alfred A. Knopf, 1964.

Gruber, Ira D. *The Howe Brothers*. Chapel Hill: University of North Carolina, 1972.

Hallowell, Edward M., and John J. Ratey. *Driven to Distraction*. New York: Pantheon Books, 1994.

Hutson, James H. *Pennsylvania Politics, 1746–1770*. Princeton: Princeton University Press, 1972.

Jefferson, Thomas. *The Jefferson Bible*. Boston: Beacon Press, 1989.

Jennings, Francis. *Benjamin Franklin, Politician*. New York: W. W. Norton, 1996.

Labaree, Leonard W., and Whitfield J. Bell Jr., eds. *Mr. Franklin: A Selection from His Personal Letters*. New Haven: Yale University Press, 1956.

Labourdette, J. F. *Vergennes, Ministre Principal de Louis XVI* (in French). Paris: DesJonquières, 1990.

Lemay, J. A. Leo, ed. *Benjamin Franklin: Writings*. New York: Library of America, 1987.

———, ed. *The Canon of Benjamin Franklin*. Newark: University of Delaware Press, 1986.

———, ed. *The Oldest Revolutionary: Essays on Benjamin Franklin*. Philadelphia: University of Pennsylvania Press, 1976.

———, ed. *Reappraising Benjamin Franklin*. Newark: University of Delaware Press, 1993.

de Lomenie, Louis. *Beaumarchaisand: His Times* (in French from unpublished documents). 2 Volumes. Geneva: Slatkin Reprints, 1970.

Long, J. C. *Lord Jeffery Amherst*. New York: Macmillan and Co., 1933.

Lopez, Claude-Anne. *Mon Cher Papa: Franklin and the Ladies of Paris*. New Haven: Yale University Press, 1990.

———. *My Life with Benjamin Franklin*. New Haven: Yale University Press, 2000.

——— and Eugenia W. Herbert. *The Private Franklin: The Man and His Family*. New York: W. W. Norton, 1975.

Maier, Pauline. *American Scripture: Making the Declaration of Independence*. New York: Knopf, 1997.

———. *From Resistance to Revolution: Colonial Radicals and the Development of American Opposition to Britain, 1765–1776*. New York: Knopf, 1972.

Malone, Dumas. *Jefferson and the Ordeal of Liberty.* New York: Little, Brown & Co., 1962.

———. *Jefferson and the Rights of Man.* New York: Little, Brown & Co., 1951.

de Maurepas, Arnaud, and Florent Brayard, eds. *The French Through Their Own Eyes* (in French). Paris: Robert Lafont, 1966.

Middlekauff, Robert. *Benjamin Franklin and His Enemies.* Berkeley: University of California Press, 1999.

Morgan, David T. *The Devious Dr. Franklin, Colonial Agent: Benjamin Franklin's Years in London.* Macon: Mercer University Press, 1996.

Morris, Richard B., ed. *John Jay—Unpublished Papers.* New York: Harper & Row, 1980.

Morton, Brian N., and Donald C. Spinelli, eds. *Correspondence of Pierre Augustin Caron de Beaumarchais* (in French). 4 Volumes. Paris: Nizet, 1969.

Nolan, J. Bennett. *Benjamin Franklin in Scotland and Ireland.* Philadelphia: University of Pennsylvania Press, 1938.

Onuf, Peter S. *Jefferson's Empire.* Charlottesville: University of Virginia Press, 2000.

Randall, Willard. *A Little Revenge: Benjamin Franklin and His Son.* Boston: Little, Brown & Co., 1984.

Russell, Phillips. *Benjamin Franklin, The First Civilized American.* New York: Brentanos, 1926.

Schoenbrun, David. *Triumph in Paris.* New York: Harper & Row, 1976.

Skemp, Sheila L. *William Franklin.* New York: Oxford University Press, 1990.

Smith, Page, ed. *John Adams.* Garden City: Doubleday & Co., 1962.

Sparks, Jared, ed. *The Works of Benjamin Franklin.* 10 Volumes. Boston: Tappan & Whittemore, 1836–40.

Stearns, Raymond Phineas. *Science in the British Colonies of America.* Chicago: University of Illinois Press, 1970.

Stourzh, Gerald. *Benjamin Franklin and American Foreign Policy.* Chicago: University of Chicago Press, 1954.

Thompson, C. Bradley. *John Adams and the Spirit of Liberty.* Lawrence: University of Kansas Press, 1998.

Tise, Larry E., ed. *Benjamin Franklin and Women.* University Park, PA: Pennsylvania State University Press, 2000.

Van Doren, Carl. *Benjamin Franklin.* New York: Penguin Books, 1991 (first edition, 1938).

———. *The Great Rehearsal.* New York: Viking Press, 1948.

———, ed. *The Letters of Benjamin Franklin and Jane Mecom.* Princeton: Princeton University Press, 1950.

Van Doren, Carl. *Secret History of the American Revolution*. New York: Viking Press, 1941.

Wallace, Anthony F. C. *Jefferson and the Indians*. Cambridge: Harvard University Press, 1999.

Walters, Kerry S. *Benjamin Franklin and His Gods*. Urbana: University of Illinois Press, 1999.

Webb, Stephen Saunders. *Lord Churchill's Coup*. New York: Alfred A. Knopf, 1995.

Wilson, P. W. *William Pitt, the Younger*. Garden City: Doubleday, Doran & Co., 1930.

Wood, Gordon S. *The Creation of the American Republic*. Chapel Hill: University of North Carolina Press, 1998.

————. *The Radicalism of the American Revolution*. New York: Alfred A. Knopf, 1992.

Wright, Esmond, ed. *Benjamin Franklin: His Life as He Wrote It*. Cambridge: Harvard University Press, 1990.

————. *Franklin of Philadelphia*. Cambridge: Belknap Press of Harvard University Press, 1986.

Background Reference Works

Allen, Theodore W. *The Invention of the White Race*. London: Verso, 1997.

Baltzell, E. Digby. *Puritan Boston and Quaker Philadelphia*. New York: The Free Press, 1979.

Barnes, Ian, ed. *The Historical Atlas of the American Revolution*. New York: Routledge, 2000.

Boatner, Mark M., III, ed. *Encyclopedia of the American Revolution*. Mechanicsburg, PA: Stackpole Books, 1994.

Buruma, Ian. *Anglomania*. New York: Random House, 1998.

Butler, John. *Becoming America*. Cambridge: Harvard University Press, 2000.

Durant, Will and Ariel. *The Story of Civilization*. Volumes 9–10. New York: Simon & Schuster, 1965.

Inwood, Stephen. *A History of London*. London: Macmillan, 1998.

Kennedy, Roger C. *Burr, Hamilton, and Jefferson*. New York: Oxford University Press, 2000.

Klepper, Michael, and Robert Gunther. *The Wealthy 100*. Secaucus, NJ: Citadel Press, 1996.

Kupperman, Karen Ordahl. *Indians and English*. Ithaca: Cornell University Press, 2000.

Picard, Liza. *Dr. Johnson's London.* London: Weidenfeld & Nicolson, 2000.

———. *Restoration London.* New York: Avon Books, 1997

Porter, Roy. *English Society in the Eighteenth Century.* London: Penguin Books, 1982.

Tilly, Charles. *The Contentious French.* Cambridge: Harvard University Press, 1986.

Webb, Stephen Saunders. *1676—The End of American Independence.* New York: Alfred A. Knopf, 1984.

Wright, Esmond, ed. *The Fire of Liberty.* New York: St. Martin's Press, 1983.

Acknowledgments

No one ever writes a book alone, and this is no exception. I owe a debt to so many.

Among the first owed thanks are some of editors who labor in that vast archeological site known as the Papers of the Founding Fathers. We met at a seminar organized by the Pew Charitable Trust in Philadelphia in June 2000 on "National Visions of the Founders." Barbara Oberg, editor of the Papers of Thomas Jefferson at Princeton, Philander Chase, editor of the Papers of George Washington at the University of Virginia, and Professor Pauline Maier, of the Massachusetts Institute of Technology, were generous in their guidance and advice. I owe a special debt to Ellen R. Cohn, editor of the Papers of Benjamin Franklin at Yale, who went beyond the call in answering questions and offering cheer.

I also thank the dedicated staffs of the Library of Congress in Washington, D.C., the American Philosophical Society library in Philadelphia, and the British Library, the London Library, and the Public Record Office in Britain. They were amazingly cooperative in helping me find my way.

My way would have been far harder if it had not been for the research assistance in London of Charles Bell, my friend, and of Sara Abraham, who both surveyed and translated documents in the archives of Paris. Dr. Sandy Read provided invaluable guidance on Franklin's many health problems. Sincere thanks also to Jed Donahue of Regnery Publishing for his editing skill and good counsel in shepherding the book into final form, and to Patricia Bozell for her meticulous copyediting.

Much gratitude goes to those who made possible the happiest months of my life. Alfred Regnery, publisher, patron, and friend, has backed the project from the start. The Thomas Skelton Harrison Foundation of Philadelphia generously ensured that I would have the full resources to bring the book to completion. Finally, let me thank the finest manuscript editor and best wife a man could have, Cecile Srodes.

Index

Page numbers in italics refer to illustrations

as are contained in this MAP.

in Philadelphia.

Printed & Published according to Act of Parliament for J. Almon in Piccadilly, London.

March 25th 1776.

English Miles

0 10 20 30 40 50 60 70 80 90 100 110 120 130 140 150

E. The Lakes Cataraqui

The Confederates, July 19, 1701, at Albany, surrendered
their Beaver-Hunting Country to the English, to be defended
them, for the said Confederates, their Heirs and Successors
forever. And the same was confirmed Sept. 14, 1726; when
the Senecas, Cayugas and Onondagas surrendered their Habita-
tions from Cayahoga to Oswego, and Sixty Miles inland, to
the same, for the same Use.

LAKE ONTARIO

Oxniagara Falls

Long Pt

LAKE ERIE

The Confederates, formerly of 5, now of 7, Nations, called by the French Iroquois, consist of 1 Cantingaes or Mo-
hocks, 2 Oneyuts, 3 Onondagaes, 4 Cayugaes, 5 Chenandoanes
or Senecas, 6 Tuscaroras, 7 Sississogaes.

SENECAS

Ohio or Allegeny R. or la Belle R.
and Palava Thepiki by the Shawanese

The Allegeny, or Endless, or Red Ridge of Mountains

Level rich Land intermix'd
with Swamp & Pond. Salt Springs

for the WIANDOTS.

Pittsburg
F. du Quesne

West
moreland
Co.

Bedford Co.

Ohio R.

O H I O

Shawane T.

Kanhawa R. Falls

S C I O T O   M O U N T A I N S

Mountains about
is not yet there

right across
40 Miles in these Parts
Walker's occupied Path in these Parts

The Blue Ridge

The Great Ridge

TUSCA

The Parts in Virginia as published in 1755
were taken from Fry and Jefferson's Map.

V I R G I N I A